MW00717575

START TO FINISH GUIDE TO

Distributing Software with *Systems Management Server 2003*

PUBLISHED BY

Agility Press - An imprint of the Mann Publishing Group
710 Main Street, 6th Floor
PO Box 580
Rollinsford, NH 03869, USA
www.agilitypress.com
www.mannpublishing.com
+1 (603) 601-0325

Copyright © 2006 by Mann Publishing Group.

All rights reserved. No part of the contents of this book may be reproduced in any form or by any means without the written permission of the publisher. For questions about rights and permissions, send e-mail to permissions@mannpublishing.com.

ISBN: 1-932577-23-8
Library of Congress Control Number (LCCN): 2006931419
Printed and bound in the United States of America.

10 9 8 7 6 5 4 3 2 1

Trademarks

Mann Publishing, Mann Publishing Group, Agility Press, Rational Press, Inc.Press, NetImpress, Farmhouse Press, BookMann Press, The Rational Guide To, Rational Guides, ExecuGuide, AdminExpert, From the Source, the Mann Publishing Group logo, the Agility Press logo, the Rational Press logo, the Inc.Press logo, Timely Business Books, Rational Guides for a Fast-Paced World, and Custom Corporate Publications are all trademarks or registered trademarks of Mann Publishing Incorporated.

All brand names, product names, and technologies presented in this book are trademarks or registered trademarks of their respective holders.

Disclaimer of Warranty

While the publisher and author(s) have taken care to ensure accuracy of the contents of this book, they make no representation or warranties with respect to the accuracy or completeness of the contents of this book and specifically disclaim any implied warranties or merchantability or fitness for a specific purpose. The advice, strategies, or steps contained herein may not be suitable for your situation. You should consult with a professional where appropriate before utilizing the advice, strategies, or steps contained herein. Neither the publisher nor author(s) shall be liable for any loss of profit or any other commercial damages, including but not limited to special, incidental, consequential, or other damages.

Credits

Author:	Dana Daugherty
Technical Editor:	Paul Thomsen
Editorial Director:	Jeff Edman
Book Layout:	Molly French
Index:	Christine Frank
Production Assistants:	Scott Gardenhire, Kim Turner
Series Concept:	Anthony T. Mann
Cover Concept:	Marcelo Paiva

All Mann Publishing Group books may be purchased at bulk discounts.

START TO FINISH GUIDE TO

Distributing Software with Systems Management Server 2003

Dana Daugherty

Dedication

This book is dedicated to my lovely wife Patty, who has been patient and understanding throughout this project, and to my sons Zachary, Solomon, and Sawyer.

About the Author

Dana Daugherty has been working with Microsoft Systems Management Server for more than eight years. He has developed and applied his skills in SMS systems engineering, administration, and project roles with mid-sized and large companies in the US and abroad. In 1999, Dana found a lack of SMS documentation for administrators in the field. To fill this void, he began writing articles for Swynk.com, an online community of systems administrators, to help others with administering SMS. He continued this effort with myITforum.com, where he also serves on the myITforum Advisory Committee. MyITforum.com is the largest online community for systems management professionals. In 2002, Dana relocated to Dhahran, Saudi Arabia with his family to work for an oil company there. He is a member of a systems management team where he provides SMS 2003 administration services. Dana's professional accomplishments include speaking at the Microsoft Management Summit in 2002 and 2004 and publishing the original version of this book, called *The Start to Finish Guide to SMS Software Delivery*. He currently holds Microsoft MCSE and Cisco CCNA certifications.

Acknowledgements

This book is the product of many hours work from a team of dedicated professionals. I appreciate the efforts of everyone who helped to make it available. My agent Neil Salkind of StudioB helped to negotiate a contract. Anthony Mann of Mann Publishing saw the value of the original version of this book, which was written for SMS 2.0 in ebook form. He asked me to update the book to make it applicable for administrators of SMS 2003. Jeff Edman, also from Mann Publishing, provided me plenty of encouragement as he guided this project to completion. He and the editing staff provided the copy editing expertise that helped to smooth out the rough spots in my writing. Paul Thomsen of the internal SMS administration team at Microsoft provided the technical editing required to ensure this book is accurate. He also offered many suggestions to make this book as useful as possible to its readers. Finally, the layout staff at Mann Publishing assembled all the pieces and put this book together.

Who Should Read This Book

A wide range of IT professionals will find the topics in this book useful to them. IT planners and implementers will find Chapters 1 through 3 helpful for learning about various SMS 2003 subjects such as software distribution features, sizing, system requirements, return on investment, and security planning. SMS administrators and desktop technicians who support the SMS Advanced Client can find a wealth of information about all areas of SMS software distribution. The entire software distribution process is covered in detail, including troubleshooting. There is additional value added through chapter topics such as Windows Installer architecture, software distribution add-ons, software distribution examples, and software distribution public relations.

Conventions Used In This Book

The following conventions are used throughout this book:

- *Italics* — First introduction of a term.

- **Bold** — Exact name of an item or object that appears on the computer screen, such as menus, buttons, dropdown lists, or links.

- `Mono-spaced text` — Used to show a Web URL address, computer language code, or expressions as you must exactly type them.

- **Menu1** ⇨ **Menu2** — Hierarchial Windows menus in the order you must select them.

 BONUS

This box lists free additional materials or content available on the Web after you register your book at `www.agilitypress.com`.

 NOTE

This box gives you additional information to keep in mind as you read.

 CAUTION

This box alerts you to special considerations or additional advice.

 TIP

This box gives you additional technical advice about the option, procedure, or step being explained in the chapter.

Contents

Chapter 4: Configuring and Optimizing Software Distribution 95

Chapter 7: Creating Advertisements and Targeting Clients 179

Part I

Planning and Preparation

Software Distribution Overview

Microsoft Systems Management Server 2003 (SMS) is an enterprise-level, client-server application that offers multiple features. SMS is designed to provide customers with change and configuration management of Windows workstations and server systems. Of all the features included with SMS, software distribution can provide the quickest increase in *Return On Investment (ROI)*. This is the amount of profit or cost savings that is realized over a certain length of time (typically 2 years) as a result of purchasing and implementing a certain technology. In the world of information technology, financial investments are typically made by purchasing and implementing technology. In the case of SMS, an organization must invest in hardware, software, and man-hours for implementation. Unfortunately, software distribution may be one of the most misunderstood features within SMS. It doesn't have to be though. In this chapter, you will learn about the specifics of software distribution, become familiar with software distribution terminology, walk through the software distribution process in detail, and discover how to increase the ROI for your SMS implementation.

Assumptions

This book assumes that you have implemented the SMS 2003 infrastructure, including SMS Advanced Security mode, SMS Advanced Clients, Active Directory (AD) integration, and Active Directory (AD) schema extensions. It is also assumed that the SMS infrastructure is operating properly. These are the most popular installation and configuration options chosen by the vast majority of administrators.

Advanced Security uses the SMS server's domain computer account to access other network resources and uses the Local System security context to run services. AD integration allows for utilizing AD topologies and Organizational Units for site boundaries, reporting, and software distributions. AD schema extensions allow for Advanced Client global roaming and secure key exchange between SMS sites. While the book has been written with these assumptions mind, a description of the other available installation and configuration options has also been included.

Terminology

In this section, you will learn about Systems Management Server terminology. This will help you to better understand the rest of the book.

- **SMS PACKAGE** — This is the SMS package object that will appear in the SMS Administration Console, the core component of a software distribution. An SMS package is required for every distribution. When creating a package, administrators can configure SMS to pull source files from a location of their choosing. Then the files will be placed on a distribution point (DP), also specified by the Administrator. The source files include the executable and any files necessary to complete a distribution.

- **SOFTWARE DISTRIBUTION PACKAGE** — These are the source files that contain many other files necessary to install a program. The software distribution package uses some type of installation technology, such as Windows Installer, to extract the files and perform the installation.

- **DISTRIBUTION POINT (DP)** — SMS packages are stored on a server that has been designated the role of distribution point for the SMS site server. The SMS client will access the installation files from a distribution point. By default, SMS places distribution points on the site server drive with the most space. Distribution points are usually hidden from users. The default UNC path for a distribution point on the D: drive of a site server would look like this: \\site_server\smspkgd$. The server that is chosen to be the distribution point should have plenty of disk space and disk throughput capacity.

- **DISTRIBUTION POINT GROUP** — A distribution point can be located on an SMS site server or another server. An SMS site can have multiple distribution points, which can be managed as a *distribution point group*. Distribution point groups allow administrators to more easily select multiple DPs during the SMS package creation process.

- **PROTECTED DISTRIBUTION POINT** — Access to this type of distribution point is restricted by configuring site or roaming boundaries properties based on IP subnet, IP address range, or Active Directory Site. Advanced Clients outside the boundaries cannot download software. This protects the distribution point from excessive traffic. This configuration option is quite useful for scenarios where a branch office is connected to the main office over a low-speed WAN link.

- **SMS PROGRAM** — In SMS, software installations are driven by SMS programs. SMS programs hold configuration information that will be performed by the SMS client. The location of executables and batch files that start an installation will be specified here. Among other options, administrators can restrict programs to run only on specific platforms, under certain accounts, and other programs can be configured to run first.

- **ADVERTISEMENT** — SMS notifies machines and users of available programs using advertisements. They are used to target machines or users with SMS programs, based on a specific schedule. Advertisements also have many configuration options including, but not limited to: target collections, programs to advertise, scheduler, and optional and mandatory advertised programs.

- **COLLECTION** — Machines or users can be grouped together in collections. They can be based on hardware or software attributes, causing them to be *dynamic*. In this case, the collection membership will change automaticlly. Collections can also be *static*, or based on specific computer, user or user group names. SMS programs are advertised to a target collection.

- **ADVERTISED PROGRAMS CLIENT AGENT** — The SMS client is comprised of several agents that carry out tasks specified at a particular site server. This book focuses on the Advertised Programs Client Agent. This agent is responsible to check for programs that may be advertised to the computer where it resides or to the current user. It interacts with the user based on the settings that have been configured at the site server.

- **MANAGEMENT POINT (MP)** — The point of contact for communications between an SMS Site Server and Advanced Clients. Information about client configuration, available advertised programs, software metering rules, and hardware inventory customization is passed down to the Advanced Client in the form of policies. Inventory, status message, and discovery data records are passed up to the site server through the management point.

- **ADVANCED CLIENT POLICY** — Specific configuration details for the Advanced Client. They are retrieved from the client's assigned management point.

Increasing ROI by Implementing Software Distribution

Return on Investment is an important topic to the folks that hold the purse strings of your organization. ROI is computed by adding the net benefit over a time period and dividing it by the implementation and operating cost over the same period. While ROI is not typically used in conversations among the technical staff, understanding the term will defiantly help your cause. You will do a much better job of selling upper management on something that you want if you can use the ROI angle. If you properly evaluate the product, and it actually works as you expect, it will be a bonus for your organization and for you. The next time you come to the boss with a "sell," he or she will be more likely to trust your instincts. You never know, you may reap some additional benefits in terms of a raise or promotion. The SMS software distribution feature alone has the ability to bring a higher ROI for the SMS implementation. By using the information and examples in this book, you will be in a better position to get the most out of the software distribution feature in your SMS implementation.

Properly implemented, centralized management of software distribution can save your organization a substantial amount of time, and we all know that "time is money." SMS acts as the delivery vehicle for virtually any installation or configuration change that can be developed.

Here's a simplified example of how the software distribution feature can cause SMS to increase your company's ROI. Company XYZ has 2000 end-users at 10 locations. Seven of these locations have full-time IT staff. They decide to implement a mixture of SMS primary and secondary servers, one at each site. Hardware and software for 10 SMS servers costs $60,000. It takes two full-time technicians six months to complete the implementation, which costs the company another $80,000, for a total of $140,000. For our example, the on-going yearly cost of maintenance, backups, and networking for our SMS infrastructure is $20,000.

The company needs to install a large application to all of its users. If the IT staff were to distribute the application the old way (by walking to each workstation), one staff member could only do about three installs per hour. Some staff members would also have to travel to the three sites that have no IT staff. Installation time alone would take about 667 man-hours (2000 computers / 3 installs per hour). The support staff makes $40,000 a year. ((40,000 / 52 weeks) / 40 hrs per week = $20 per hr. $20 per hour * 667 = $13,340). Over a two year period, the company needs 20 large packages distributed, which totals $266,800. It also requires 30 smaller applications that can be completed in about 400 man-hours, totaling $240,000. SMS is also utilized to distribute 24 monthly software updates from Microsoft, which requires 300 man-hours, totaling $144,000. Over the two year period, the grand total for manual software installation is $650,800.

Using SMS software distribution, it would be quite possible for one staff member to distribute the large application in three days. At $20 an hour, it would only cost $480 using SMS software distribution. Smaller applications can be completed in two days at $320 and software updates can be delivered in a day at a cost of $160. For the same two year scenario described previously, the installation cost is substantially less than if you did not use SMS distribution. Large software packages cost $9600. Small packages cost $9600, and software updates cost $3840. The grand total for software installation with SMS over the two year period is $23,040.

The value that SMS software distribution brought to company XYZ over the two year period is $627,760. Because there was an initial investment and on-going cost totaling $160,000 for the SMS implementation over the two year period, we need to divide that into the value to compute the ROI. The ROI for our scenario is 400%. Quite impressive!

The company will also realize some additional savings that could be directly added to the ROI provided by SMS 2003. It will not be necessary to send IT staff members to the three remote sites. The IT staff can take advantage of bandwidth-conserving features like SMS secondary sites, protected distribution points, and the SMS Advanced Client. Secondary site servers don't require as much in the way of maintenance as primary servers, but they provide software distribution and other SMS features while offering the lowest WAN bandwidth cost for all types of SMS communications. All communications between SMS Primary Site Servers and SMS Secondary Site Servers is compressed before it is sent over WAN links. Site servers can be configured to throttle (use a percentage) bandwidth and can be configured to schedule communications to be sent during off-hours. Some remote locations can simply have protected distribution points installed so SMS clients don't have to pull software installations over the WAN. SMS site servers are not required in this scenario if the available WAN bandwidth is acceptable to sustain sending the software package files without being compressed. Protected distribution points can be configured to restrict access to Advanced Clients on specific IP subnets, IP address range, or Active Directory Site name. The SMS Advanced Client has been designed to use lightweight communication protocols when sending or receiving messages. In one case, a remote office with a low number of clients didn't need an SMS Site Server or a protected distribution point. The features offered by the Advanced Client provided enough bandwidth savings to allow the company to forego the added expense of additional server components.

There are several less tangible advantages as well. Users will avoid the loss of productivity that comes from being interrupted during the workday, because advertised programs can be scheduled to run during off-hours. The company will also benefit from having the latest software features available to them sooner, rather than waiting for the IT staff to get it deployed.

Productivity within IT will remain constant, because daily responsibilities will be completed throughout the distribution. Typically, rolling out an application requires a limited timeframe from the beginning of a distribution until the final workstation receives the installation. Sometimes rollouts have requirements of minutes or hours. Without a remote software distribution system, IT staff must place all other activities on hold in order to roll out software packages with such requirements.

If company XYZ finds it necessary to reclaim licenses from machines that no longer need to use a particular program, they can utilize SMS software distribution as well. This can be done by sending an uninstall program to targeted users. The Software Metering feature can be utilized in this situation to track application usage. The usage information can be used to create a target collection for an uninstall program.

Defining Software Distribution

Software distribution is the process of automating various types of software installations and configurations from a central point. The main goal of software distribution is to take the footwork out of installing and configuring software. SMS accomplishes this through its client-server architecture. The client-server architecture is designed to separate the processing load required to install a particular application. Client-Server applications place the processing burden wherever it is appropriate. Some processing occurs on the client and some occurs on the server. Where the processing occurs and the level of processing burden required depends on what is happening at the moment.

The scope of a software distribution can range anywhere from an entire operating system upgrade to a simple file copy. Software distribution can occur on servers, desktops, laptops, and mobile devices running Windows CE 3.0 or later. The additional features provided with SMS 2003 have allowed software distribution to be much more effective over VPN, WAN, and dialup connections. Obviously, bandwidth must be considered for distributions that include large packages.

Using SMS for software distribution offers flexibility and still allows an administrator to have control over the distribution. Distributions can be scheduled, targeted to specific machines or users, and can be optional or mandatory.

How a Distribution Works

This section is an overview of the server and client processes necessary to distribute software to an SMS client. This information is intended to provide a general overview of creating and distributing a package. SMS client and server processes that occur during each step of package creation will be described as well. Detailed instruction for configuring a package and troubleshooting client and server processes are included later in this book.

Preliminary Work

Before beginning the distribution process, there are a few preliminary items that should be completed:

- Develop and test the software package that will be distributed.

- The source files should be moved to a standard source location, sometimes called a *master software repository* (MSR). Generally, there are a limited number of users provided with security access to the MSR.

- Advertised Programs Client Agents and distribution points must be configured. (See Chapter 3 for more information on this topic).

After completing the preliminary distribution tasks, the various components of the distribution must be built. Software distribution is initiated at an SMS primary server. In order to distribute software, an SMS administrator must create a package, a program, a target collection, and an advertisement. He or she must also assign distribution points to the newly created package. This configuration occurs within the SMS Administrator Console (which is an MMC (Microsoft Management Console) application).

Creating a Package: The Administrator's view

A package has three components to configure: the package, the distribution point, and the program. Let's review the process in a general way, with the specifics of each step to be discussed later in this book. You would start the process of creating a new package by right-clicking on the **Package** tree, selecting **New** and then **Package**. The **Package Properties** window will appear. As shown in Figure 1.1, all text boxes will be empty.

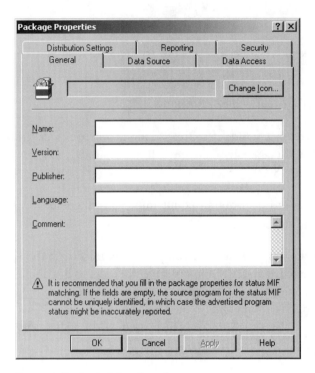

Figure 1.1: Viewing the Package Properties.

1. Add information, within **Package Properties**, to the following tabs: **General**, **Data Source**, **Data Access**, **Distribution Settings**, **Reporting**, and **Security**. After clicking the **OK** button, the new package appears under the Package tree.

2. Expand the new package in the tree to see its contents. Right-click **Distribution Points**, and select the **New⇨ Distribution Points** menu item. A wizard appears, as shown in Figure 1.2. Use the wizard to select the distribution points where you want your package to be distributed from.

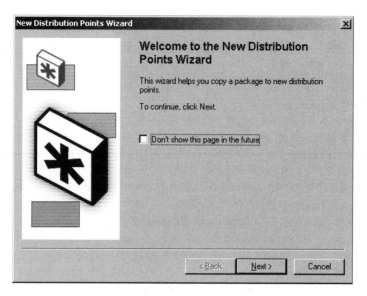

Figure 1.2: New Distribution Points Wizard.

3. In the SMS Administrator Console, right-click **Programs** and select **New**. The **Programs Properties** window appears, as shown in Figure 1.3. Next, you would complete the necessary information on the **General**, **Requirements**, **Environment**, and **Advanced** tabs.

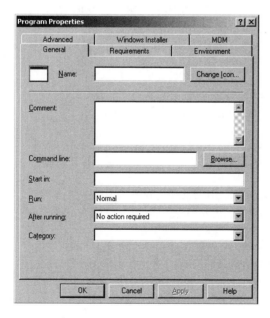

Figure 1.3: Create a New Program.

Creating a Package: Behind the Scenes

These SMS server processes work together to create a package:

1. **SMS Provider** writes package information to the site database, which causes a SQL Trigger (Package_Notification_Ins) to execute.

2. **SMS SQL Monitor** writes the package notification to \\<ServerName>\SMS_<SiteCode>\Inboxes\Distmgr.box\<PackageID>.pkn.

3. **Distribution Manager** begins to process the notification.

   a. If the package is configured to compress the source files, or if there are child site distribution points selected for the package, these additional steps occur first:

      (1) Distribution Manager compresses the package source directory into a temporary directory: \\<Servername>\<sms_install drive _root>_s_m<Randomstring>.tmp.

      (2) Distribution Manager places the source files in \\<ServerName>\>\<sms_install drive _root>\SMSpkg\<PackageID>.pck.

   b. If the package is not configured to compress source files, and if there are no child site distribution points selected for the package, Distribution Manager begins here:

      (1) Distribution Manager copies the package source directory to the specified distribution point: \\<ServerName>\SMSpkg<DriveLetter>$\<PackageID> or the custom share name.

      (2) Distribution Manager creates the package in \\<ServerName>\SMS\Inboxes\Pkginfo.box\<PackageID>.pkg.

      (3) Distribution Manager creates a distribution point list in \\<ServerName>\SMS\Inboxes\Pkginfo.box\<PackageID>.nal.

      (4) Distribution Manager creates icon files in \\<ServerName>\SMS\Inboxes\Pkginfo.box\<PackageID>.ico\<SequentialNumeric>.ico.

4. **Inbox Manager** copies the following package property files to the client access point (CAP):

```
\\<ServerName>\CAP_<SiteCode>\Pkginfo.box\<PackageID>.pkg
\\<ServerName>\CAP_<SiteCode>\Pkginfo.box\<PackageID>.nal
\\<ServerName>\CAP_<SiteCode>\Pkginfo.box\<PackageID>.ico\
<SequentialNumeric>\.ico.
```

If there is a child site for replication, the following will also occur:

1. **Distribution Manager:**

   a. Creates the package replication file in \\<ServerName>\SMS\Inboxes\ Replmgr.box\Outbound\Normal\<ObjectID>.rpt.

   b. If a compressed copy of the source files already exists, Distribution Manager sends it to the child site.

   c. If a compressed copy does not exist, Distribution Manager creates it and stores it in \\<ServerName>\SmSpkg\<PackageID>.pck.

2. **Replication Manager** creates a mini-job for the sender in \\<ServerName>\SMS\ Inboxes\Schedule.box\<SequentialNumeric>.job.

3. **Scheduler:**

   a. Packages objects for transfer in \\<ServerName>\SMS\Inboxes\Schedule. boxTosend\<RandomString>.p<RandomString>.

   b. Creates the sender request in \\<ServerName>\SMS\Inboxes\Schedule.box\ Outboxes\<SenderName>\<RandomString>.srq.

4. **Sender:**

   a. Renames *.srq files to *.srs files.

   b. Sends package files and instructions to \\<ServerName>\SMS_<SiteCode>\ Inboxes\Despooler.box\Receive\<RandomString>.p<RandomString> on the child site.

5. **Despooler:**

   a. Decompresses the replication objects to \\<ServerName>\SMS\Inboxes\ Replmgr.box\Incoming\<RandomString>.rpt.

    b.   Stores the package in \\<ServerName>\SMSpkg\<PackageID>.pck.

6. **Distribution Manager** sends the package to the distribution point(s): \\<ServerName>\ SMSpkg<DriveLetter>$\<PackageID> or a custom share name.

7. **Replication Manager** moves the replicated objects to proper inboxes: \\<ServerName>\ SMS\Inboxes\Offerinf.box\<OfferID>.ofr and \\<ServerName>\SMS\Inboxes\Distmgr. box\<PackageID>.pkg.

8. **Distribution Manager** moves the replicated objects to these inboxes: \\<ServerName>\ SMS\Inboxes\PackageInfo.box.\<PackageID>.nal.

Creating a Target Collection: The Administrator's View

A *target collection* is a group of machines or users that will receive an SMS distribution. To create a collection, right-click on the **Collections** tree and select the **New⇨ Collection** menu item. The **Collection Properties** dialog box appears, as shown in Figure 1.4. Supply the necessary property information on the **General** and **Membership Rules** tabs.

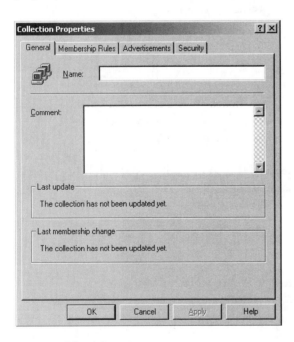

Figure 1.4: Collection Properties.

Creating a Collection: Behind the Scenes

These SMS processes occur when a collection is created:

1. A file is created in \\<SiteServer>\SMS\Inboxes\Colleval.box with an extension of .adc.

2. **Collection Evaluator** creates a result table in the SMS site database.

If there is a child site for replication, the following will also occur:

1. **Collection Evaluator** writes the collection rules in a .psd file.

2. **Replication Manager**, **Scheduler**, and **Sender** work together to replicate the collection file. **Despooler** (on the child site) receives the package, decompresses it, and places it in the proper inbox.

3. **Collection Evaluator** reads the .psd file and writes it to the database if it is a primary server. Otherwise, it is written to disk under the \\<SiteServer>\SMS\Inboxes\Colleval. box folder with an extension of .clf.

Creating an Advertisement: The Administrator's View

To begin the process of creating an advertisement, you would right-click on the **Advertisement** tree and choose the **New**⇨ **Advertisement** menu item. The **Advertisement** properties appear. Provide the necessary information on the **General**, **Schedule** and **Advanced Client** tabs (see Figure 1.5).

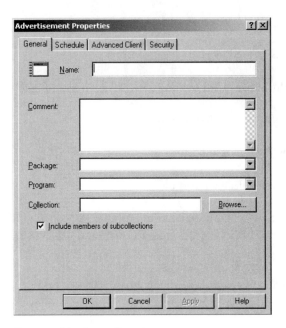

Figure 1.5: Advertisement Properties.

Creating an Advertisement: Behind the Scenes

These SMS processes occur when an advertisement is created:

1. **SMS Provider** writes information to the SMS database. When this occurs, a SQL trigger (Offer_Notification_Ins) executes.

2. **Offer Manager** starts processing:

    a. If the package is not ready, a SQL trigger is set—waiting for the package to be ready.

    b. If the package is ready:

        (1) Offer Manager creates an advertisement file in
            \\<SiteServer>\SMS\Inboxes\Offerinf.box\<OfferID>.ofr.

        (2) Offer Manager evaluates the selected collection membership.

(3) Offer Manager creates advertisement files and installs them to:
\\<SiteServer>\SMS\Inboxes\Offerinf.box\system.lkp
\\<SiteServer>\SMS\Inboxes\Offerinf.box\user.lkp
\\<SiteServer>\SMS\Inboxes\Offerinf.box\usrgrp.lkp
\\<SiteServer>\SMS\Inboxes\Offerinf.box\<RandomString>.ins.

(4) SMS Policy Provider creates a policy and a policy assignment based on the package, program, advertisement, and target collection. The policy is made available to the assigned Advanced Clients on the MP.

If there is a child site for replication:

1. **Offer Manager** creates an advertisement file in \\<SiteServer>\SMS_<SiteCode>\ inboxes\ReplMgr.box\Outbound\<ObjectID>.rpt.

2. As in the package creation process, **Replication Manager**, **Scheduler**, and **Sender** work together to replicate the advertisement file across the WAN. **Despooler** (on the child site) receives the package, decompresses it, and places it in the proper inbox.

3. From there, the advertisement is made available on the CAPs and MPs.

Client Processes

To complete the distribution, SMS Advanced Clients must first contact the Management Point (MP). The MP is the SMS component where all SMS Advanced Clients exchange data with the site server. Here, the Advanced Clients retrieve *policies*, which are specific configuration details. Policies can contain advertised programs notifications, which are details about programs that are available for a system or a user to run. Next, the Advanced Client begins the program execution phase, which includes downloading distribution points, downloading source files (if necessary), and starting the program. Finally, the Advanced Client tracks the program activity locally and sends advertised program installation status messages to the site server via the MP. By tracking program execution, clients won't repeatedly run the same program. Status messages can be monitored with the SMS Administrator Console, SMS Web Reports, or any other reporting mechanism that connects to the SMS database.

The software distribution processes that occur on the Advanced Client should be viewed as two separate functions: *program execution* and *content access*. Content access is concerned with locating source files on a distribution point and downloading that content when the Advanced Client is configured to do so. The remaining information in this section depicts these functions.

Program Execution

The following steps occur during program execution.

1. **POLICY AGENT** — Sends a policy request to the MP of its assigned site and, if authorized, downloads new policies. One policy contains the advertisement notification.

2. **POLICY AGENT PROVIDER** — Sends new advertised program notification to Execution Manager containing the properties of the advertised program. Records the program's properties and activity in WMI.

3. **SCHEDULER** — Notifies Execution Manager when it is time to run the program.

4. **EXECUTION MANAGER**

    a. Sends informational status message ID 1002 to the MP after it receives the notification from Policy Agent Provider.

    b. Creates an *Execution Request* for the new program (could be mandatory or optional).

        (1) If the start time is set for the future, then go to Step 4d later in this section and then return to this step and wait for the start time to arrive.

        (2) Otherwise, go to step 4c.

    c. If the program is configured as *Optional*, the **Run Advertised Program** icon is displayed in the System Tray and may make the program available in the **Add or Remove Programs** icon. Nothing further happens until the user chooses to run the program.

    d. Requests content location and the package source version from the **Content Access Service (CAS)** for the package (see "Content Access" later in this section).

    e. Receives communication from CAS, including package information and content access status notifications.

    f. Sends content access-related status messages to the MP, when necessary, with information or error text:

        (1) Message ID 10035 indicates the program will be run after the content is downloaded.

        (2) Message ID 10051 indicates a content download problem.

(3) Message ID 10053 indicates a content download problem.

(4) Message ID 10058 indicates a content download problem.

(5) Message ID 10060 indicates a content download problem.

(6) Message ID 10061 indicates a content download problem.

(7) Message ID 10062 indicates a content download problem.

(8) Message ID 10065 indicates a content download problem.

g. Verifies that the program is in the location identified by CAS.

h. Displays the **Advertised program is about to run** icon if the program is configured to do so.

i. Runs the program after all package and advertisement configuration criteria have been met. These criteria are configured on the program property tabs and the advertisement property tabs. An informational status message ID 1005 is sent to the MP.

j. Monitors installation status MIFs at program completion. MIFs are Management Information Format files that use a standard format to store data. SMS uses MIFs to store the status of program installations as they occur on a client. The file is then sent to the site server by way of the management point. If there is no MIF file specified on the SMS Package **Reporting** tab, then Execution Manager returns the program exit code.

k. Sends installation status messages to the MP with one of the following messages:

(1) Message ID 10009 for status MIFs with a value of Success.

(2) Message ID 10007 for status MIFs with a value of Failed.

(3) If a status MIF cannot be found, Message ID 10008 indicates that the installation succeeded.

(4) If a status MIF cannot be found, Message ID 10006 indicates that the installation failed.

Content Access

The following steps occur during the content access stage of the distribution.

1. **CONTENT ACCESS SERVICE**

   a. Checks the cache to see if the source files have been downloaded.

      (1) If so, it returns the package source version to Execution Manager.

      (2) If not, it creates a folder in the %Windows%\system32\CCM\Cache folder, based on the package ID, version, and context. It makes a request to **Content Transfer Manager (CTM)**, including the package ID, version, and destination folder name (in the Cache folder).

2. **CONTENT TRANSFER MANAGER (CTM)** — Requests a list of DPs from **Location Services**.

3. **LOCATION SERVICES** — Queries the management point (MP) for a list of DPs.

   a. The MP returns the path of the content on each available DP to Location Services, using the following metrics:

      (1) If the client is included in protected distribution point boundary(s), the MP will verify that the content is available at the protected DP(s). If the content is available, only the protected DP(s) will be provided to the client.

      (2) If the client is not included in a protected distribution point boundary, then the MP will attempt to provide a local DP—first on the same subnet, next within the AD Site, then any DP local to the client and finally, a remote DP within the SMS site.

      (3) If the Advanced Client cannot contact a DP in its resident site, it will contact the MP again with the same request. The MP will then return a list of all assigned MPs. The client then chooses a DP from the list at random.

   b. Returns the list of DPs to CTM.

   c. If the MP doesn't reply, Location Services makes multiple attempts until it eventually fails.

4. **CTM** — Stores the DP locations in WMI and calls Data Transfer Service (DTS) to download package content from the first DP in the list.

5. **DTS**

   a.   Retrieves the list of files and folders from the MP.

   b.   Creates the sub-folder structure under the existing top-level source folder in the local Cache directory.

   c.   Attempts to contact a DP, starting from the top of the list. After a connection is made, it begins the download process.

   d.   If the DP is BITS-enabled, the client will begin a BITS session, under a **SvcHost** process. Otherwise, a FileCopy operation will be performed.

   e.   If a download error or timeout occurs, a connection with the next DP on the list will be attempted.

   f.   Notifies Execution Manager upon successful completion or failure of the download.

   g.   Return to Step 4F in the "Program Execution" section.

Summary

Of all the SMS features, software distribution provides quickest increase in ROI. Software can be distributed much more efficiently than utilizing support technicians to visit each desktop, as illustrated in the chapter's sample scenario. One person can distribute a software package with SMS in three days that would require 667 man-hours using the manual method. Even when considering the cost of installation and on-going maintenance, SMS software distribution provides a huge increase in ROI.

This chapter gave a high-level overview of the steps necessary to create and distribute SMS software packages. It also offered details on the SMS software distribution components and processes. It described how the SMS administrator creates a new package, including a new program. SMS Provider, SQL Monitor, and Distribution Manager work together to create the package with the source files placed on the distribution point(s) and package information files placed in the proper inbox. If an SMS Child Site will be used for distribution, Replication Manager, Sender, and Scheduler will also be utilized to copy the source files to the proper location on the child site. Following the transfer of files, Despooler, Distribution Manager, and Inbox Manager at the child site will also get involved.

Once the package is created, the administrator must create a collection of users that will receive the advertised program (or a target collection). After creating the target collection, an advertisement must be created for the new program. SMS Provider, Offer Manager, and Inbox Manager work together to place advertisement files in the proper inbox and CAP locations. SMS Policy Provider places the policy and policy assignment on the MP.

On the Advanced Client, Policy Agent downloads new policies from the MP, notifies Execution Manager about any new available advertised programs, and tracks the advertised program's activity. Scheduler notifies Execution Manager when it is time to run the program. Execution Manager makes a request to CAS manager to locate the package source files and return package properties and location. CTM, Location Services, and DTS work together to gather package property information, find DPs that contain the source, and to download source content when advertised programs are configured to do so. Execution Manager runs the program from either the Cache folder or the DP, depending on the advertised program configuration. It also monitors the program status and reports the result to Policy Provider, which in turns forwards it to the MP.

Preparing to Implement Software Distribution

When preparing to implement the SMS software distribution feature, there are many factors to consider. Even with the improvements included in SMS 2003, accurately selecting and optimizing server and network hardware is crucial. Depending on the features implemented and the number of SMS 2003 Advanced Clients at a site, SMS can be very resource-intensive. Site systems will require additional disk I/O and network bandwidth after enabling software distribution. Additional resources are needed, mainly because program source files must be compressed, decompressed, and copied to distribution points (DPs). As Advanced Clients download software from distribution points, additional disk resources from the distribution point server and network bandwidth resources are required. As the numbers of clients accessing the DP increase, the server disk and network resources also rise accordingly.

Adequate testing will help to ensure the success of your implementation. Implementing new technologies should always follow plenty of testing. Adequate testing is more likely to occur if a test plan is used and a lab is available. After properly testing the steps for implementing software distribution, you will know what to expect in your production environment. Testing helps to reduce the number of surprises that may occur during implementation. Also, in the lab you can test the additional stress on server and network hardware caused by distributing applications.

Proper training will help SMS software distribution team members to be ready to create and distribute software packages. Software distribution is a powerful and somewhat complicated feature. Team members need to be trained in the techniques of software repackaging, SMS package creation and distribution, and the software distribution guidelines in place at his or her organization. The way to receive a higher Return on Investment for an SMS implementation is to have team members prepared to distribute software as the implementation is completed.

There are many variables that should be considered when preparing to implement software distribution. You will need to consider:

- The software distribution usage plans for your organization. This could include items such as package size, installation complexity, target users or computers, time of the day when distributions will occur, and type of software—such as software updates or office productivity suites.

- The computing environment of your organization

- Necessary disk space on SMS site servers and servers that will perform the role of distribution points

- Server disk subsystem specifications

- Performance Tool objects and counters

- Existing SMS server optimizations

- Microsoft's recommendations for your environment

- Local Area Network (LAN) Optimization

- WAN links

- Testing and Training

This chapter will help you to determine your organization's hardware needs by providing details on these considerations. Two groups of administrators will benefit from this information: those who have not implemented SMS, and those who have implemented SMS 2003 but have not implemented software distribution.

Determine the Usage Plans for Software Distribution

What are your plans for software distribution? The answer to this question will have a major impact on all of the other issues detailed in this chapter. While SMS can distribute nearly any application, you need to find out how your organization plans to use it. Do they plan to primarily use SMS to apply software updates to Windows operating systems? Will they use it to deploy images with the SMS 2003 Operating System Deployment Feature Pack (SMS 2003 OSDFP)? Do they only want to distribute to remote offices and have IT staff manually perform the installs at the home office? Will you be using SMS to distribute everything you possibly can? Will you configure advertisements to have the Advanced Client download source files locally or leave them on the distribution point? As you see, there are quite a few options to consider. But the most important consideration is what the IT decision makers want SMS software distribution to do. Organizations that use SMS to distribute all applications will need to consider the impact on network performance, the distribution points' disk space, and the number of distribution points. Organizations that intend to distribute large applications (or all applications), and leave the package source files available for future use, will need to plan accordingly for the extra resources that are required. At these sites, increased usage of disk I/O, disk space, and network bandwidth utilization will be apparent. Read through the other sections in this chapter to properly prepare for these issues.

Become Familiar with the Current Computing Environment

Environment is a major consideration with any technology implementation. Knowing your computing environment will help you to properly size new hardware components and to be successful with your software distributions. Communicating with the proper systems support teams and viewing any available systems support documentation at your organization is the best way to understand your environment. When considering your computing environment, research the following points: network infrastructure design, number of servers, load on existing servers, disk sub-systems of existing servers, number of workstations, workstation software, and operating systems.

You should become familiar with your organization's network infrastructure design. Understanding the limits of your network can keep you from over-utilizing it. Some packages that you may want to distribute could be quite large, possibly 700 MB or larger. All SMS packages need three times their space available, so a 700-MB package would need 2100 MB free on all targeted distribution points. The SMS 2003 OSDFP can deliver an image with a maximum size of 1.5 GB. By knowing the limits of your network, you can properly stage distributions to occur at different intervals in order to keep the network from becoming saturated. The limits of your network will also affect the number of distribution points that you choose to create. If there are multiple bottlenecks, for example, you will want to provide a distribution point on each side of the bottleneck. In addition, as you plan to distribute software, you will want to base target collections on Organizational Units (OUs), network addresses, or some other property. This can help to give you more control over the distribution process. Look at the "Optimize the Local Area Network" section in this chapter for help with optimizing your local area network.

Remember to include the human aspects of the computing environment. These aspects are largely affected by the business culture and can include the technical ability of the employees, work hours, regional culture, risk tolerance, and the control users have over their computing environment. Users with higher technical ability may be capable of performing some role in the software distribution process, such as initiating an installation or selecting options during an installation. Users with low technical ability generally require all aspects of software distribution to be automated. If a company utilizes shift work, there will be little opportunity for software distribution team members to install software without disrupting employees. The regional culture affects many aspects of the computing environment of an office, such as length of the work day, types of applications, and language support. Companies with low risk tolerance require more precise planning to avoid unexpected down time. In organizations where users have more control over their computers, there may be an expectation for the software distribution team to provide a more flexible experience to its customers.

Server Infrastructure

If you plan to select an existing server as a distribution point, it is a good idea to become familiar with the servers in your organization. Gather information such as server load, disk sub-system, and operating system. This section provides details about gathering this information.

Server load is defined as information requests. Typically, the information requests originate from client machines. It is possible though, for a server to make information requests to another server. For example, a SQL server could have a job configured to import a database from another SQL server. This would be a server-to-server information request. Server load includes usage of any server resources. The type of request will determine the resources that are taxed the most. Simply copying a large amount of data from a server would result in heavy disk I/O load. Running complex queries on large databases will tax processors and disk I/O.

Most likely, you will want to create SMS distribution points on servers other than the SMS site server. It is possible to use the SMS site server as a distribution point, but the capacity of the server must be able to support the load. Capacity and load are quite variable, depending on the hardware components, number of clients, and which of the SMS site server roles and features will be utilized. Use the SMS 2003 Capacity Planner for detailed server requirements based on your specific scenario. This tool is located at `http://www.microsoft.com/smserver/techinfo/productdoc/default.mspx`.

Other options to consider for reliable high-speed storage include *Network Attached Storage (NAS)* and *Storage Area Networks (SAN)*. Network-attached storage is hard disk storage that is set up with a unique network address rather than being attached directly to a server. NAS consists of hard disk storage, including multi-disk RAID systems, and software for configuring and mapping file locations to NAS devices. A NAS device could be utilized as an SMS DP to offload processor and disk I/O resources from the site server, offering faster storage access to SMS clients. A SAN is a high-speed, special-purpose network that interconnects different kinds of data storage devices with associated data servers. SANs allow for centralizing data storage and then allocating portions of that storage for specific server access via a SAN storage interface card and, typically, fiber optic cables.

NOTE

SAN storage is supported by Microsoft for use as an SMS DP, but NAS devices may not be supported.

If the site server is the only distribution point, the site would need to have less than 400 workstations and the LAN should support 100-MBPS full duplex from the SMS server to the workstations. "Full duplex" describes the ability of a network device to simultaneously send and receive data.

To be a candidate for a standalone SMS Site Server Distribution Point role, a server needs to have plenty of free disk space, a fast disk sub-system, and its existing load should be light. The amount of space and server load required is determined by your planned usage. On average, I would recommend selecting a server with at least 50 GB of free space that can be allocated to software packages, with the ability to expand. The server also requires a RAID controller and 15,000 rpm hard disks. Select a server that is not used heavily for other purposes. It would be best not to select an Active Directory Domain Controller, because these servers have the responsibility of authenticating domain login users and tend to have high disk utilization, as does the SMS site server. This will cause contention for hard drive access. Also, avoid using database servers, because they experience heavy processor and disk usage. This is where the knowledge of the organization's Systems Administrators comes in handy. Server load is probably not the type of thing that gets documented, but the local systems administrators should be able to point you to servers that are under the lightest load. You can take it from there and perform some System Monitor or Performance Monitor testing. See the "Disk Subsystem" and "Assess and Baseline Existing SMS Servers" sections later in this chapter for more details on these topics.

Software Distribution to Server Clients

It helps to become familiar with the server infrastructure when planning to distribute software to the servers in your organization. Accomplishing this is a definite possibility, but it is much trickier than distributing to workstations. Many times, reboots are only acceptable at night or on the weekends, so scheduling becomes very important. If server operations problems are caused by an SMS distribution, you could receive some "heat" from your coworkers and managers. Before distributing software to servers at your organization, you will want to be up to speed regarding standard software builds for your servers. By knowing all you can about the software that resides on these servers, you can properly test distributions in a lab environment. You can also gather information from online SMS support sites before you distribute software to your production servers (see the end of this chapter for some links). Find a time that will be acceptable for distributing software to your servers and keep in mind that reboots may be necessary. Take this task very seriously. You can damage relations with your coworkers for a long time with careless software distribution. Workstations can be repaired easily if they become corrupted, and in the worst case this would mean re-imaging them. However, server downtime can cost an organization a premium. Rebuilding a server can take much longer and there is always the possibility of lost data.

Workstation Infrastructure

Having an in-depth knowledge of the workstations in your environment will improve the performance and success of your distributions. The number of workstations at a particular site should have a considerable effect on the number of distribution points that you choose to install. As a rough estimate, install one local distribution point for every 1500-2000 Advanced Clients at any given site where large packages will be deployed. Up to 4,000 might work where only small software updates programs (2-3 MB) are deployed. If your organization doesn't meet this criteria, another option is to use a *phased distribution*. Phased distributions target various groups within an organization at different times. This avoids over-utilization of server resources or network resources. Also become familiar with the standard software that exists at your organization. Hopefully, there is *image version control* for your workstations. Image version control means assigning versions to standard workstation images. This will allow you to know what software exists on a specific workstation. Image version control will allow you to better test a distribution with all images that may be available at a certain company. In the end, you will have more successful distributions in such an environment.

Distribution Point Disk Space

Be sure to plan for a sufficient amount of free disk space on distribution points. Running out of free space will stop the distribution process. In general, I recommend starting with about 10 GB of free space. There is, however, a way to calculate the amount of disk space that your organization will need. If the site server (where the package is created) is also the distribution point, you need to plan for at least three times the amount of space as the source files. There will be a copy of the source files on the distribution point and a compressed copy of the source files for replication to parent or child sites. Additional temporary space is also required for compressing and decompressing the source files. A server that is designated only as a site server software distribution point will only need enough space for the package source files. On the other hand, if the site server (where the package is created) is *not* the distribution point, you need to plan for 1.5 times the amount of space as the source files. This space will be needed for a compressed copy of the source files.

Based on your organization's planned usage of software distribution and the results from the previous guidelines, you should be able to estimate the amount of disk space that you will need. For example, if you expect to distribute an application that requires 300 MB of disk space for installation on a client, you will need at least 900 MB of free space on the distribution point. This is true if the distribution point is located on the same site server where the package has been created. However, if the distribution point is on a server other than the server where you created the package, you need to plan for 300 MB. By adding up all the space required by all the applications you plan to distribute in the next year, you should be able to develop some planning guidelines. Keep in mind that you will probably want to keep the package source files on the server and distribution point until you are ready to distribute a new version of software. At that point, you will probably want to remove the source files.

Disk Subsystem

The disk subsystem includes hard disks and disk controllers. It is always preferable to have disk controllers that support Redundant Array of Inexpensive Disks (RAID), NAS, or SAN storage over standard disk controllers without support for RAID. RAID is a fault tolerance technology that allows for recovery and continued operation in the case of hard disk failure. If a disk containing the SMS distribution point is configured as a mirrored disk (RAID 1) or a disk array (RAID 5), or a combination of the two (which is a striped array of mirrored sets (RAID 10)), SMS clients will still be able to access the distribution point if one of the disks fails.

In addition to fault tolerance, disk mirrors (RAID 1) offer faster disk reads than do disk arrays (RAID 5). RAID 10 offers better fault tolerance than RAID 1 (with the same overhead as RAID 1) but provides the recovery performance of RAID 5. In some scenarios, RAID 10 can withstand the simultaneous loss of multiple hard disks without data loss. The negative aspect is a higher cost, due to an increased number of hard disks. Windows Server software RAID should only be used if hardware RAID is not an option, because it is slower and less reliable than hardware RAID. If it is not possible to place the distribution point on a disk in a RAID mirror or RAID array, be sure to create multiple distribution points for that site. This will also provide fault tolerance. As long as there is one distribution point left, the packages for a site will not be lost if a distribution point fails. If a disk fails, a new distribution point can be created when the new disk is installed. Unless protected distribution points are enabled, Advanced Clients are not restricted from using other DPs. If one distribution point fails, they will use the remaining ones at the assigned site or the site they're visiting (in a roaming scenario), given that the package is configured to be copied to the other DPs.

Disk drives should be 10,000 rpm or higher. In a typical scenario, hundreds of clients are accessing this disk in order to read hundreds of megabytes of data for an installation. In order to distribute the software as quickly and smoothly as possible, you need high-speed disks. Beyond these minimums, there is a range of configuration options based on your needs. Let's look at these now.

You will want to base your disk hardware configuration on the total number of SMS clients at a given site. A quad-channel RAID controller is required to keep up with the amount of I/O requests at mid-sized to large sites. At least ten local drives are required to provide an adequate amount of fault tolerance. As you can see, it costs considerably more in terms of hardware costs to implement an SMS server to mid-size to large sites. The "real" cost is in the server chassis required to support the ten or more drives. One alternative is SAN or NAS. These technologies allow for large amounts of disk storage to be housed centrally and shared among multiple servers. The data is treated as though it were local to the server.

Use the guide in Table 2.1 when performing quad channel configuration for primary site servers at sites with more than 6,000 clients. These are minimum requirements.

Channel	Container Type	Disk Size	SMS Components
0	Mirror	9.1 GB or 18.1 GB	OS and Pagefile
1	Mirror	36 GB	SQL Server logs and SMS logs
2	RAID 5	72 GB	SQL installation and databases
3	RAID 5	32+ GB	SMS installation

Table 2.1: Local Disk Configuration for Mid-Size to Large SMS Sites.

Smaller sites (under 500 clients) using primary site servers should have a quad channel RAID controller installed. They should also support at least seven drives. This will allow a disk mirror (RAID 1) to be configured for the system disk and the SQL installation. RAID 5 can be configured for the SMS application files and the SMS database. A disk mirror can be configured for the distribution point and transaction logs and SMS logs. With this configuration, every SMS component has a reliable fault-tolerant disk subsystem.

For servers that are SMS Site Systems configured only as distribution point roles, the hardware RAID and disk speed minimums indicated in the previous paragraphs should be observed. Distribution points can be created on hard disks included in RAID Level 10, RAID Level 5, or RAID Level 1 configurations. If it is not possible to place the distribution point on a disk included in one of these RAID level configurations, be sure to create multiple distribution points for that site. This will provide fault tolerance as well.

Assess and Baseline Existing SMS Servers

A great way to determine the performance capacity of your system is to use the Windows Performance tool. The Windows Performance tool is composed of two parts: System Monitor and Performance Logs and Alerts. With System Monitor, you can collect and view real-time data about memory, disk, processor, network, and other system components. Also, application-specific counters are added during the installation. For example, there are SMS Server and SQL Server counters added when these products are installed. Performance Logs allow you to create a history log based on the performance counters. Alerts allow you to set notifications to contact you if specific thresholds are met based on the performance counters.

It makes sense to monitor an existing SMS server with these tools prior to setting up software distribution to see how much tolerance is left on a system before hitting critical metrics. It will also give you a good baseline for use after distribution is implemented. Monitoring should be performed periodically, after setting up software distribution, to be sure performance is still acceptable.

To access the Windows Performance tool, choose the **Start**⇨ **Control Panel**⇨ **Administrative tools**⇨ **Performance** menu item. The Performance MMC interface will appear.

Viewing Real-time System Monitor Data

To view real-time system performance data from a chart, follow these steps from the Windows Performance tool interface:

1. Select **System Monitor** from the left pane; and from the menu buttons in the right pane, select the **View Current Activity option**.

2. Select the **Add** (+) button and begin adding counters. Click the **Explain** button for explanations of each counter. See Table 2.2 later in this chapter for some helpful counters. Figures 2.1 and 2.2 show the System Monitor **Add Counters** sheet and the **Explain Text** box.

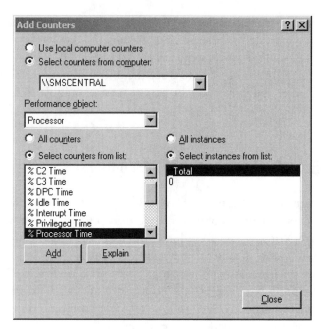

Figure 2.1: Adding Counters to System Monitor.

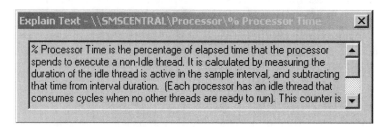

Figure 2.2: Viewing Counter Explanations.

3. After the counters are added, you can save the chart settings to make it easier to start monitoring the same counters during future sessions (see Figure 2.3). To save chart settings, select **Save As** from the **Console** menu; then select the location to save to. Keep in mind that viewing current activity does not log the session for viewing at a later time; you must set up a counter log to save a monitoring session.

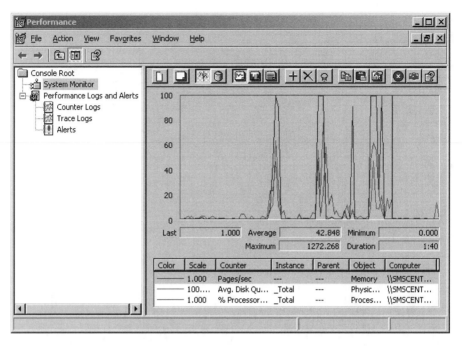

Figure 2.3: Viewing Current Activity with System Monitor.

Saving Monitoring Data to a Log File

Monitoring data can be saved to a log file. To log monitoring data, do the following in the Windows Performance tool interface:

1. From the left console pane, right-click on the **Counter Log** and select the **New Log Settings** menu item. The dialog box depicted in Figure 2.1 will appear.

2. Click the **Add (+)** button to add the counters that you want to monitor.

3. Select the **Log Files** tab. Choose the location and name for the log.

4. Select the **Schedule** tab. If desired, provide customized schedule information.

5. Click the **OK** button to close the **Counter Logs** property sheet.

6. The new log icon will appear in the right pane (see Figure 2.4).

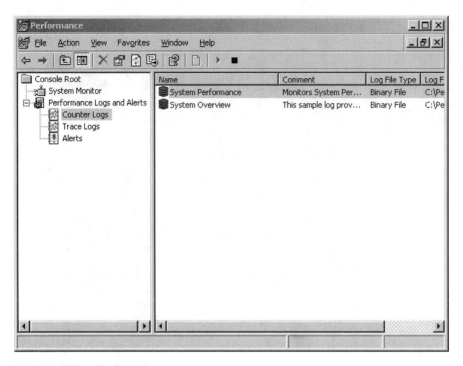

Figure 2.4: Adding a New Counter Log.

Viewing Log Data

To view logged data, follow these steps from within the Windows Performance tool interface:

1. Go back to the **System Monitor** tree.

2. From the right pane, click the **View Log File Data** button. If the log is still collecting data, you will need to close and then re-open the log. This will enable you to see new collection data and keep the chart current.

3. To start and stop logging, select **Counter Logs** from the left pane. Select the log that you want to stop or start from the right pane. Click the **Stop** or **Start** buttons from the menu in the right pane.

4. Click the **View Chart** button.

System Monitoring Considerations

There are a few considerations for performance monitoring:

- Performance Monitor should be used to monitor remote systems. This monitoring tool consumes a considerable amount of system resources. If Performance Monitor is run locally on the system that is being monitored, the end result will be inaccurate due to the additional load to the server from the tool itself.

- Disk counters are disabled by default. To turn on all disk counters, run `Diskperf -Y` from a command line on the server, then reboot.

- Before you begin monitoring, set some goals. Determine what time frame you want your data to represent, then set the sampling interval and schedule to meet these goals. These options are configured in the **Log** properties.

Recommended Counters

The counters in Table 2.2 were included with the Windows Performance Tools and shipped with Windows 2000, XP, and Server 2003. A best practice approach to implementing SMS software distribution includes monitoring an existing system and analyzing it for performance issues.

Object	Counter	Comment
System	Processor Queue Length	This is the number of processes in the queue waiting to be carried out. Less than 3 is acceptable.
System	% Total Processor Time	Represents the average percentage of time the processor is busy with non-idle processes. Sustained periods over 90% point to a problem.
Physical disk	% Disk Time	This is the percentage of elapsed time the disk is servicing read or write requests. Greater than 80% indicates unacceptable disk performance.
Physical disk	Current Disk Queue Length	This is the number of read or write requests waiting to be performed. Subtract the number of disks from the number of queued requests. A result less than 2 is acceptable.
Memory	Committed Bytes	The amount of committed virtual memory in bytes. A resulting value twice the size of your physical RAM is too high.
SQL Server	Cache Hit Ratio	A value greater than 98% is acceptable.
Memory	Page Reads/sec	This is the number of times the disks were read per second to resolve hard page faults. Consistent readings above 5/sec is a warning sign.

Table 2.2: Performance Monitor Counters.

Optimize Existing SMS Servers

Administrators at organizations that have existing SMS implementations must consider additional factors. Before implementing software distribution, you will need to focus on a few areas. Cleaning up trouble areas now will improve your chances of success once you begin distributing software. There are several areas you will want to investigate when optimizing:

- **FREE SPACE ON HARD DRIVES THAT MAY BE USED FOR DISTRIBUTION POINTS** — You will want to clean up any unnecessary directories or files. If there are no drives or arrays with enough disk space, you will need to add some. Review the "Distribution PointDisk Space" section of this chapter to find out how to determine how much space you need.

- **ANALYZE SYSTEM PERFORMANCE WITH SYSTEM MONITOR** — Use the Performance Monitor counters described earlier and the counters at the end of this section. Document each of the counters prior to the SMS or software distribution implementation. This practice will help to uncover any trouble areas and give you a server performance baseline to use for monitoring after a software distribution implementation.

- **BE FAMILIAR WITH ANY SITE STATUS MESSAGES WITH A STATUS OF ERROR OR WARNING** — You are asking for failure if you move forward with any SMS upgrades or configuration changes when the server is experiencing errors that have not been investigated. To check this, open the **System Status** tree, and then open **Site Status** and **Component Status** (see Figure 2.5).

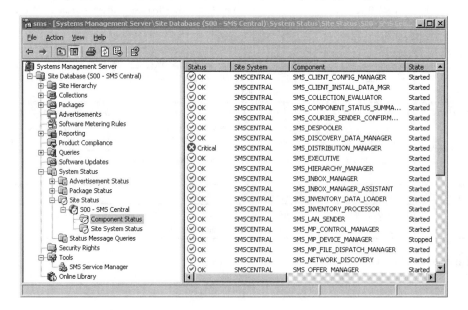

Figure 2.5: Site Status Messages.

- **SEARCH SMS LOGS FOR ERRORS OR WARNINGS** — This can be done with the use of a GREP tool or by simply using any Windows operating system search function. GREP tools return entire lines from log files based on a search criterion. Search the SMS\Logs directory for files containing the text "Error" or "Warning." Next, open the logs that contain the "Error" or "Warning" text and begin to investigate the issue. It would not be prudent to continue without investigating the cause of any errors.

Counters for SMS 2003 Servers

There are 22 Performance Tool objects specifically available for SMS site systems. All of these objects and counters could be useful at some point. Many are only helpful in a troubleshooting scenario. In this case, readings can be taken when performance appears to be degraded and then a comparison can be made to a baseline reading that was taken in the past or provided to Microsoft Product Support Services. The counters listed in Table 2.3 are recommended for monitoring prior to implementing software distribution on an existing SMS infrastructure.

Object	Counter	Comment
SMS Discovery Data Manager	DDRs Processed/minute Total DDRs Processed	Any site will have a few bad DDRs processed occasionally from incidental corruption. A percentage based on Bad DDRs / Total DDRs, will show the wasted processing resources.
SMS Software Inventory Processor	Bad SINVs Processed Total SINVs Processed	Any site will have a few bad SINVs processed occasionally from incidental corruption. Figuring a percentage based on Bad SINVs / Total SINVs will show the wasted processing resources.
SMS Standard Sender	Total Bytes Failed	Resending data can be costly to performance. This counter provides resends that have occurred since monitoring began.
SMS Status Messages	Corrupt	There should only be a few corrupt status messages from time to time. Start out using the Total Instance. If a problem appears to be occurring, turn on individual instances to narrow the problem down.
SMS Inventory Data Loader	Bad MIFs Processed Total MIFs Processed	Any site will have a few bad MIFs processed occasionally from incidental corruption. Figuring a percentage based on Bad MIFS / Total MIFs will show the wasted processing resources.
SMS HINV Retry Mgr	Failed Reports	This counter tracks the number of reports that failed during processing due to problems like not enough disk space or memory.
SMS MP Status Mgr	Failed Reports	This counter tracks the number of reports that failed during processing due to problems like not enough disk space or memory.

Table 2.3: Performance Counters for SMS Servers.

Utilize Microsoft's SMS Planning Tools

Infrastructure capacity planning for SMS is dependent on many different variables. In this chapter, we are covering infrastructure capacity planning as it relates to implementing software distribution. Microsoft offers additional tools for several aspects of SMS infrastructure implementation planning in the form of documentation and a Microsoft Excel application. While some aspects of these tools cover software distribution, they are really more general in nature—but they can still be helpful during the planning process. The goal here is to help you become familiar with your computing environment, especially as it relates to software distribution. After you are familiar with your environment, these tools will help to provide a starting point for implementing the SMS 2003 software distribution feature or even an entire SMS infrastructure. Here are a few helpful tools, available at `http://www.microsoft.com/smserver/techinfo/productdoc/default.mspx`.

- SMS 2003 Capacity Planner

- Scenarios and Procedures for SMS 2003: Software Distribution and Patch Management

- SMS Technical FAQ: Planning and Deployment

Optimize the Local Area Network

Software distribution has the potential to have adverse effects on network bandwidth. Imagine copying a 500-MB directory from a file server at your site to a workstation—not so bad. Now imagine everyone at your site copying the 500-MB directory to his or her workstation. Many installations can be that large. During the process of creating and distributing a package, source files will need to be copied to each distribution point and then, of course, each workstation will install the files. Prior to implementing software distribution, check your infrastructure for possible bottlenecks. This section focuses on a few areas where network bottlenecks can occur, gives you some network optimization recommendations, and provides an overview of Microsoft Network Monitor.

There will be some obstacles that may limit your choices for network optimization, including: size of the organization, design of the facility, existing network infrastructure, network management decisions, and of course, availability of capital. Regardless of the obstacles you may face, you still need to do your homework in this area. It may be necessary to make a business case for a network hardware upgrade. It is best to do this before the implementation, because if you wait until afterward, you could be viewed as making excuses for a failed implementation. For obvious reasons, it is best to have the proper network infrastructure in place, so you can get off to a flying start. If the network infrastructure remains a problem, there are some additional solutions available to help you avoid network bottlenecks:

- Phased deployments can be used to target groups of users or machines at different times. Reducing the number of installations that occur simultaneously helps to avoid over-utilization of the network.

- Package design can be performed in such a way to reduce the file size as much as possible.

- Strategic planning of distribution points and SMS sites allows the conservation of bandwidth utilization over slow links.

Look for Network Bottlenecks

Let's consider your network infrastructure. As a minimum, a site of 400 or more users should have servers connected to a powerful *layer-three backbone switch* in the server room. Also known as *core switches*, layer-three backbone switches are designed to allow sustained high volume network traffic from the entire organization. They also provide routing features. It is preferred that the backbone switch be connected to workgroup switches (also known as *closet switches*) via fiber optic cable. These switches are generally designed to handle the traffic from one workstation per port. There should be a Gigabit uplink connection between the backbone switch and each workgroup switch. Finally, workstations should be patched to the closet switches using enhanced Category 5 Ethernet cable. You will need to scale this a bit for your organization. Larger sites may need large layer-three switches on each floor. Smaller sites may not even need a layer-three switch. Generally speaking, organizations with less than 100 users do not need to invest in a layer-three switch. Sizing for the switches discussed in this section varies according to vendor and model. It's best to consult the vendor for your specific scenario.

Check to see if any of your sites contain any of the following items. If so, I recommend monitoring these hardware devices for network utilization issues:

- **HUBS** — These are bandwidth-sharing devices. A 100-MBPS connection coming into a hub will be divided among the number of workstations connected to the hub. Replace hubs with switches that will provide 100-MBPS, full duplex connections.

- **COAXIAL CABLING** — This technology only supports a 10-MBPS connection.

- **TWISTED PAIR CABLING RATED LESS THAN CATEGORY 5** — Only Category 5 twisted pair cabling will support 100-MBPS connections. Categories of network cabling are described in the EIA/TIA-586 standard. This cabling contains 4 pairs of wires protected by an outer layer of insulation and plastic. The connectors look similar to those that connect to a telephone. See EIA.org or TIAonline.org for more information.

- **SWITCHES THAT DON'T SUPPORT 100-MBPS FULL DUPLEX TRAFFIC** — Even though data is primarily moving in one direction during a distribution, operating at half duplex will not provide optimal results.

- **SWITCHES THAT ARE CONFIGURED FOR 10/100 AUTO-SENSING** — Auto-sensing is a switching feature that provides the switch with the ability to detect the speed of the network interface at the other end of the connection. If auto-sensing is switched to On, workstations can inadvertently connect at 10 MBPS, due to driver problems. If this occurs, it will most likely go unnoticed; it would be better to configure the switch for 100 MBPS, if all connections at the other end are known to be 100 MBPS.

To round out the list, network cards and drivers can also be an area for concern. All workstations and servers should have 10/100-MBPS or 100-MB network adapters as a minimum. The most recent drivers should be used on installations and images. Even though 10/100-MB cards are used, it is possible that the machine is only connecting at 10 MBPS. This can be verified by viewing the switch management software; there will be an option to monitor port speed. Look at each switch to verify that all workstations are connecting at 100 MBPS. After you verify that all workstations are connecting at 100 MBPS, it would be a good time to turn auto-sensing Off. Configure the switch in 100-MBPS mode only.

Analyze Your Network

Use protocol analyzers to look for negative trends in your network environment. A protocol analyzer is a tool that can be helpful when looking for unwanted network activity that could be occurring in the communications between existing SMS servers and other systems on your network. Before implementing SMS software distribution, it's a good idea to verify that communication between SMS servers and other systems in your environment is clean. There are several protocol analyzers on the market, using different approaches, so determine your needs before making a purchase. An example of a protocol analyzer is Microsoft SMS Network Monitor.

SMS Network Monitor

SMS Network Monitor (NetMon) is included with the SMS installation software and is a more advanced version than what is available with Windows Server Family installations. The version included with SMS can monitor remote network cards, while the Windows Server Family version only monitors the machine where NetMon is installed.

Network Monitor supports capturing data units for all the common protocol standards. *Capture* is the term used for gathering network packets. The term *packet* is used loosely within the confines of this product; technically, packets are only layer-two data units. Using NetMon, packets are captured from the network data stream of the target Network Interface Card (NIC). Packets are placed in the memory buffer of the target computer until they are saved to a file. Using the Frame View window, the frames can be analyzed. Details such as Protocol, source address, destination address, and frame size can be viewed. In Figure 2.6, these panes are visible: Graph, Total Statistics, Session Statistics, and Station Statistics.

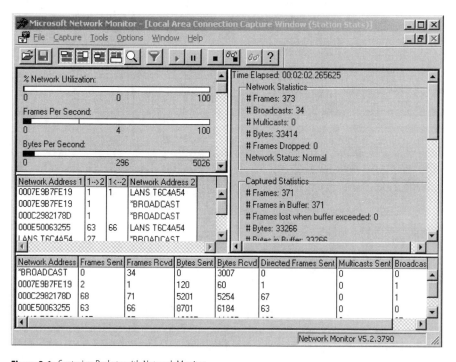

Figure 2.6: Capturing Packets with Network Monitor.

One example of using Network Monitor to look for negative trends is to analyze a capture for retransmitted TCP frames. Such an event could be concerning if it were a trend among multiple SMS clients attempting to communicate with an SMS site server. This would indicate over-utilization at a point between the client and the site server (or at the site server itself) that needs to be investigated. Using the *Experts* tools can help you get up and running, even if you don't have a background in network engineering. Experts are automated tools to help you interpret the network capture data. There is a set of six Experts included with the advanced version of NetMon that ships with SMS (see Figure 2.7). You can find **Experts** located under the **Tools** menu item. For the Experts option to be visible, you will need to start and stop a capture.

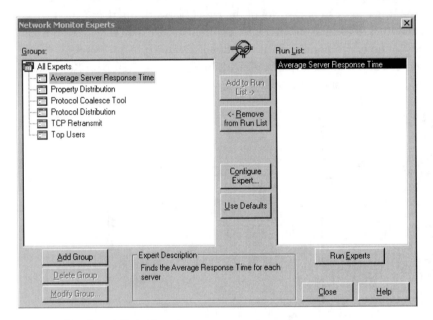

Figure 2.7: Using Network Monitor Experts.

Filters

Filters are used to narrow the amount of network packets included in a capture. Details like source address, destination address, NetBIOS name, or IP address can be added to the filter. Display Filters can also be used to narrow the amount of data that can be viewed. Filters can be complicated at first. When you begin using a protocol analyzer, it would be helpful not to apply a capture filter, as you may inadvertently exclude valuable data. After the capture is complete, apply a display filter to narrow the data down.

Consider Slow Network Links—The WAN Dilemma

Slow network links are obstacles that will need to be considered when implementing software distribution. Advanced Clients at remote locations must be able to download source files for advertised programs without negatively impacting the Wide Area Network (WAN). SMS 2003 has features to help it overcome issues surrounding remote sites connected by slow network links. Packages are automatically compressed when they are replicated between SMS site servers over a WAN connection. Optional SMS bandwidth throttling gives an administrator the ability to limit the percentage of network resources it will consume. A new feature in SMS 2003, Delta Package Replication, allows for sending only the new files added to a package between package update cycles. And when visiting remote sites, Advanced Clients that are roaming can access local distribution points to avoid pulling package files from their installed site. Unfortunately, there are no features to limit WAN impact if a client at a remote site is targeted with an advertised program but does not have a local distribution point to access source files.

Picture a scenario where you have 15 users in a remote office using a 128Kbs connection. You need to distribute an application to them, which requires 500 MB of disk space. Each workstation must pull that 500-MB installation over the WAN. Several of them may attempt to run the install simultaneously. Let's check the math: 500 MB x 15 users = 7500 MB that must come across the WAN link. This equals 7.680.000 Kb. 7680000 KB/128kbs = 6000 seconds or 100 minutes. Multiply that by 8 to convert to bytes and you get about 15 hours—that's if your connection was completely utilized, which would not allow any other communications to pass. Is it worth spending the money for an additional site server, which will provide the features necessary to distribute software over a WAN? That question should be considered during the planning process.

Test Your SMS Implementation

One area that is overlooked far too often is proper testing. Whether you have an existing implementation of SMS or not, testing the impact of implementing major changes, such as software distribution, is critical. SMS in general, and software distribution specifically, are powerful tools. If proper testing is performed, your implementation stands a much better chance of success. Taking the "Let's turn on software distribution and see what happens" approach is asking for failure. Software distribution is one SMS feature that has a higher profile, because end users are more likely to interact with it. Advertised programs wizards and interruptions from successful and unsuccessful installation programs usually force them to interact. With software distribution, you have the ability to help many users by providing clean, smooth installations. You also have the ability to upset a lot of users quickly, by wrecking their machines. Building a simple, useful test lab will give you the environment to properly test changes before implementing them into production, allowing for more success.

It is best to have a permanent lab that remains available for testing at any time. This will help you quickly implement changes in the future, and help you avoid having to skip the testing process, because you have to build a lab from scratch. It is best to have servers and workstations in your lab that resemble your production environment as closely as possible. Having the exact hardware in the test lab will enable you to notice possible problems with drivers or other programs provided by hardware vendors. If that is not financially possible, a lab that is comprised of high-end workstations turned into SMS servers will still be quite helpful. If your production network includes child sites, then your test lab should have at least two networks and two servers. This will allow you to simulate the SMS processes that occur between parent sites and child sites. See at Chapter 5 for more information on testing.

Try Virtual Computing for Creating Test Labs

Virtual Computing is a great alternative to traditional test labs. This technology uses software to create multiple virtual machines or guest systems on one hardware platform. Virtual machines are environments that are independent of the host Operating System (OS), but use the same hardware. Applications are available that take advantage of virtual machines and allow you to allocate hard drive and memory resources to specific virtual machines. OSs can then be installed to the virtual machines. Virtual computing differs from creating multi-boot systems because virtual machines can be launched in a separate window while the host OS is running, but without affecting it. Multi-boot systems, of course, require a reboot before entering a separate OS. In the past, virtual computing was used primarily by software developers, but there are many uses within the realm of systems management for this technology.

Setting Up a Virtual Test Lab

An application to create and manage virtual machines is loaded onto a system. This is considered the *Host system*. These applications can be purchased from vendors, such as VMWare or Microsoft. Once the application is loaded, a virtual machine can be created. This is a simple step that allows you to configure the amount of hard drive and memory resources that are dedicated to the particular virtual machine, along with several other resources. Once this step is completed, an operating system can be loaded onto the virtual machine, using a process very similar to loading an OS on a physical machine. This new OS is considered to be a *Guest OS*. Once the OS is loaded, the virtual machine is ready for use. I was also able to load one of our company's standard Ghost images onto the virtual machine—very handy.

Here are some helpful features of virtual machines:

- **Undoable disk** is a configuration setting that allows you to remove any changes to a virtual disk after a session. This is great for testing scripts and repackaging software. The original virtual machine can remain intact.

- **Networking configuration** allows some pretty complicated configurations. Virtual machines can be configured to use the existing NIC to communicate with other systems on the LAN, only the host, Network Address Translation (NAT), or no networking.

- **Multiple virtual machines** can be installed and run simultaneously on one computer.

- **Cloning** allows for the duplication of existing virtual machines. The copy requires significantly fewer system resources, but requires the original virtual machine to be running while the clone is operating.

- **Virtual Machine Teams** are groups of virtual machines that are connected. Commands and options can be set simultaneously for the entire team.

System Requirements for Virtual Machines

The most obvious system requirements are the amount of free memory and free hard disk space. There must be enough of these resources for the host machine and each virtual machine that you plan to run simultaneously. You also need to have a high-end processor. The system requirements pretty much depend on how many and what type of host OSs you need to run.

Virtual Machine Products

The three main products in this category are VMware Workstation 5.0, Microsoft Virtual PC 2005, and Virtual Server 2005. They are very similar, but there are a few differences. When considering your purchase, it really depends on what you want to do with the product. I recommend downloading an evaluation version of each and seeing which one you prefer. If you are interested in the Virtual PC or Virtual Server products, have a look at *The Rational Guide to Microsoft® Virtual PC 2004* and *The Rational Guide to Scripting Microsoft® Virtual Server 2005*, both available from www.rationalpress.com.

I personally prefer VMware Workstation. I've been using the product since version 3.0 and have been very happy with it. I have used each version of Microsoft Virtual PC, even before Microsoft owned the rights. I have always felt that VMware was more advanced and provided a better product. Virtual computing is a great addition to any administrator's tool kit, regardless of the vendor you choose.

NOTE

Virtual computing can only be used when testing procedures can be performed on hardware platforms that are dissimilar to your production environment. If you require testing a scenario that includes hardware drivers, virtual computing is not an option.

Software Distribution Team Members

Preparing the software distribution team is just as important as preparing the infrastructure. Good software distribution administrators tend to be very detail oriented. They don't mind repetitive tasks and enjoy communication and coordination with customers of the software distribution team. Customers of the software distribution team would be internal customers from within the organization. This would be anyone who requests services from the software distribution team. This role is critical in the success of the entire SMS operation. Of all the SMS features, end users tend to have the most interaction with software distribution. Mistakes anywhere in the process can be serious, but many find the results to be rewarding.

Train SMS Support Staff

SMS can be a complicated system to implement and administer. Acquiring the proper training and information will help your organization to move through the learning curve. It would be great if everyone involved with SMS support could obtain some hands-on training to get a "jump-start" on learning the various SMS features and components. Because of cost considerations, that usually doesn't happen. Sometimes at best, the lead SMS administrator will attend a class and disseminate the knowledge to the other support staff (referred to as "Train the Trainer"). Proper information, coupled with time in the lab, can actually be better than instructor-led classes. Instructor-led classes can generally introduce an administrator to various topics, but books such as this one can focus on specific SMS features. A good book will allow SMS support staff to have a reference that can be accessed many times over. In addition, books frequently bring more real-life experience to the administrator. Another way to obtain SMS information is through online resources. Learn Systems Management.com is one vendor that provides online training (http://www.learnsystemsmanagement.com).

Free SMS Support Resources

Here are a few free resources that can be of great help to you:

- **MICROSOFT'S SMS HOMEPAGE** — `http://www.microsoft.com/smsmgmt/default.asp`. This site contains a multitude of SMS white papers, including some on software distribution.

- **MYITFORUM** — `http://myitforum.com`. I consider this site an SMS portal. This is the place to go for articles, forums, and links to other resources. This third-party support site is managed by Rod Trent. Rod, and many other SMS administrators in the field, make significant contributions to this site.

- **THE SMS EMAIL LIST SERVER** — `mssms@lists.myITforum.com`. myITforum supports this service. The list is very active and is monitored by many knowledgeable SMS administrators. It is quite a community effort. You can subscribe or just read the threads from the Web site. More information about the email list is located at `http://www.myitforum.com/Lists.asp`.

- **DANA DAUGHERTY'S SMS SUPPORT WEB PAGE** — `http://myitforum.com/contrib/default.asp?nm=Dana%20Daugherty&cid=171`. This page contains a biography and links to all the articles that I have contributed to myITforum. Many of my articles are on the topic of software distribution.

Summary

Implementing SMS software distribution in your environment requires a considerable amount of planning. The information in this chapter helped to prepare you for implementing SMS software distribution into your enterprise. For some support staff, implementing software distribution also includes implementing SMS for the first time. To prepare for the deployment of the software distribution feature, the following topics were discussed: determining usage plans, becoming familiar with your environment, performance monitoring, optimization of servers and LANs, testing the implementation, and training support staff. Following the guidelines recommended within this chapter will increase your chances of a successful implementation.

DID YOU KNOW?

The next version of SMS is named System Center Configuration Manager (SCCM). In addition to the software requirements of SMS 2003, SCCM will require Microsoft SQL Server 2005 and Windows Server 2003 SP1 (or later) or Windows Server 2003 SR2. Clients will require Windows 2000 SP4 or later.

SMS Security Planning and Configuration

Systems Management Server software distribution is a powerful feature that gives administrators the ability to install software with elevated system rights or user rights. It is because of this power that we must ensure that SMS is properly secured. Microsoft takes security very seriously and so should you. This chapter will help you to plan and configure SMS security from a software distribution perspective. You will learn the best practice approach for securing the SMS infrastructure and the software distribution product feature. This chapter also discusses SMS administrator access security, including object security, planning, and configuration.

SMS Infrastructure Security

SMS infrastructure security means securing those SMS components that are responsible for supporting the entire SMS implementation. SMS infrastructures can be quite complex, including inter-site communications, IIS, site servers, management points, SQL Server and client access, to name a few. We will limit our discussion in this section to recommendations for SMS 2003 Advanced Security, because the vast majority of SMS implementations are configured in this way. Prior to analyzing your environment for SMS-related security issues, ensure that basic Windows Server security fundamentals are in place. The following recommendations are considered best practices for the highest possible level of security for SMS implementations. Keep in mind that each organization must consider the balance between security and cost when determining the feasibility of any security recommendation. These considerations can be made by utilizing risk management practices to help you to determine your level of acceptable risk.

Security Foundation

This section focuses on general Windows security configuration, which is a foundation for the SMS site server.

Here are some basic recommendations:

- Use SMS 2003 advanced security rather than standard security. Standard security utilizes domain user accounts to run services and to connect to other SMS site systems. Advanced security uses machine accounts to access remote resources and Local System to run local services. SMS 2003 advanced security requires the following:

  - The SMS site must reside in an Active Directory domain.

  - The SMS site server and all SMS site systems must be running Windows 2000 Server SP2 or later installled.

  - Management points must have Windows 2000 SP3 or later installled.

  - Site servers must have SQL 2000 or later installled.

  - A site with SMS advanced security cannot report to a parent site with standard security.

- Upgrade all sites and all clients to the latest SMS 2003 service pack. As in the case of SP1, new security features are often added to service pack releases.

- Use the Advanced Client rather than the Legacy Client. Advanced Client primarily uses machine accounts to access remote resources and Local System to run local services, but the Advanced Client Network Access Account can also be utilized. For details about this special account, see the "Advanced Client Network Access Account" section later in this chapter.

- Extend the Active Directory schema for SMS and enable Active Directory publishing. Management points can publish their certificates and their location in Active Directory. This allows clients to identify authorized management points from a trustworthy source.

- Apply non-SMS service packs and security-related hotfixes as they are released. Obviously, this is a good practice.

SMS Hierarchy

These recommendations focus on security configuration within the SMS hierarchy.

- Do not allow SMS sites to span Active Directory forests. This type of site design is not supported by SMS 2003. The SMS site server requires administrative access to all site systems. To grant administrative access to an SMS account from one forest to a site system in another forest would violate the use of separate forests as a security boundary. There must be at least one SMS site in each forest. Design the site so that it does not span forests.

- Install SMS on a Member Server instead of a domain controller. Domain controllers do not have a local Security Accounts Management (SAM) database other than the domain database. If SMS is installed on a domain controller and SMS becomes compromised, then all the accounts in the domain are also compromised.

- Avoid interoperating with SMS sites that cannot sign their data. Pre-SMS 2.0 SP5 sites are unable to sign their intersite communication. This could allow an attacker to push unauthorized data to a parent site using a rogue child site. This should be considered a significant risk.

- Avoid installing other services that use Local System on the SMS site server, because this would limit the use of enhanced privileges of the system's computer account, thereby limiting access to SMS data by other systems.

SMS Communications

These recommendations focus on security for intersite communications.

- Use IPSec to encrypt communications between site systems and the site server. Use IPSec to guard against unauthorized systems impersonating a valid system to gain access to the site server. Run IPSec between site servers and servers that contain separated roles, with the exception of distribution points and MPs. Also exclude domain controllers.

- Require Secure Key Exchange. The default primary site configuration uses a less secure key exchange algorithm. If the Active Directory (AD) schema has been extended with the SMS extensions, enabling this option will allow SMS to utilize AD to exchange keys. When this option is used, pre-SMS 2.0 SP5 sites won't be able to send data to parent sites. Plan to upgrade the site as soon as possible.

SMS Site Systems

This section focuses on security for SMS site systems.

- Use Windows Server 2003 for all site systems. This Windows Server version is much more secure due to Microsoft's recently increased attention to security.

- Use a role separation strategy on site systems. Where feasible, separate SMS site systems onto separate server hardware. Isolating different SMS roles on to separate hardware reduces the chance that all roles will be compromised in the event of a successful attack on the vulnerabilities of one role. The exception to this recommendation is for the SMS database role. It is preferable to maintain this role on the same physical hardware as the SMS site server.

IIS Server in SMS Infrastructures

These recommendations focus on securing IIS server.

- Disable unused IIS functions. Install only the minimum IIS features that are required by the server role being supported. To enable or disable IIS features for Windows Server Family systems go to **Control Panel**⇨**Add or Remove Programs**⇨**Add/Remove Windows Components**. Select the **Application Server** check box and then click the **Details** button. Next select the **Internet Information Services (IIS)** window item and then click the **Details** button (see Figure 3.1).

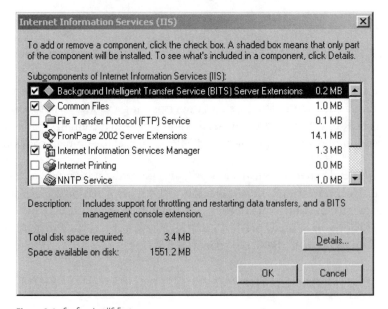

Figure 3.1: Configuring IIS Features.

- Use Windows Server 2003 with IIS 6.0 (the most secure release).

- Follow the SMS IIS Hardening Checklist. The SMS 2003 Security checklist includes a checklist for hardening IIS when used with SMS site systems (see Figure 3.2). The link to the SMS IIS Hardening Checklist is located at the end of this chapter.

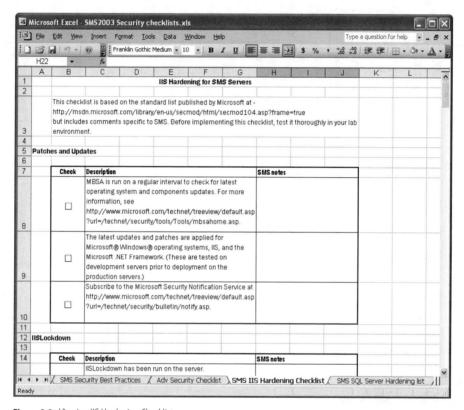

Figure 3.2: Viewing IIS Hardening Checklist.

- Run IIS Lockdown Wizard and URLScan. Run the SMS IISLockd.ini if your site system is running Windows 2000 Server and IIS 5.0. It also includes URLScan. The results include disabling unused features and restriction of some types of HTTP requests. IIS 6.0 has the IIS Lockdown feature integrated, but still requires the URLScan to be run. References and links for these tools are part of the SMS Toolkit documentation (see Figure 3.3) available for download at `http://www.microsoft.com/smserver/downloads/default.mspx`.

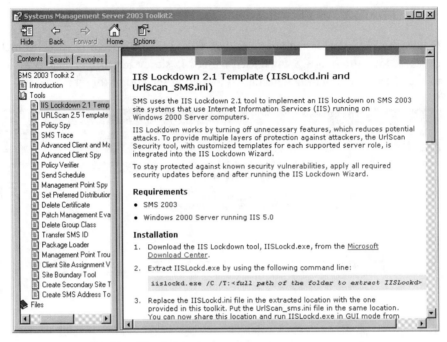

Figure 3.3: Viewing IIS Lockdown Wizard Information.

- Do not install the site server on a server with IIS. The site server has local and remote administrative access, while IIS has a history of exploited security vulnerabilities. Together, they make a dangerous combination. Plus, if all SMS site components are on one server, the entire site can be at risk if the server is attacked.

SMS Site Server

Follow these recommendations for SMS site servers.

- Use **Run As** when starting the SMS Administrator Console from a remote workstation rather than logging on to the workstation with SMS Administrator rights. In general, it's a bad idea to log on to any workstation with any account that has administrative privileges on server systems, because it provides powerful rights that an attacker can use to exploit the workstation's vulnerabilities. To use **Run As** right-click on the **SMS Administrator Console** short-cut applet⇨ **Run AS.** The **Run As** popup box will appear (see Figure 3.4). Select **The following user** radio button and input an account with access to the SMS Administrator Console. Avoid logging on to the workstation with an account with SMS administrative privileges in case the workstation is attacked.

Figure 3.4: Using Run As to Access the SMS Administrator Console.

SQL Server in SMS Infrastructures

Follow these recommendations for SQL Server in SMS infrastructures.

- Install SMS and SQL Server on the same server. This allows SMS to have the highest level of control over the SQL Server security configuration. This simplifies the SQL Server security configuration for the administrator, and reduces the possibility of security configuration mistakes.

- Configure SQL Server to use Windows Authentication mode, which is more secure than SQL Authentication mode.

- Follow the SQL Hardening for SMS Servers checklist. The SMS 2003 Security checklists include a checklist for hardening SQL when used with SMS site systems (see Figure 3.5). A document called "Scenarios and Procedures for SMS 2003: Security" includes the SMS 2003 Security checklists. See the "Microsoft SMS 2003 Security Documentation" section at the end of this chapter for the link to the SMS SQL Hardening Checklist.

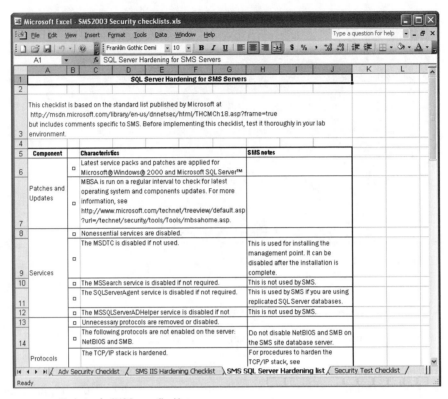

Figure 3.5: Hardening for SMS Servers Checklist.

- Configure the SQL Server service to run with a domain user account. Avoid using Local System for other applications when using SMS 2003 Advanced Security.

- Use a dedicated Microsoft SQL Server for each SMS site, as opposed to a shared SQL Server for multiple SMS sites. This ensures that service outage from an attack is limited to a single site.

SMS Software Distribution Feature Security

This section focuses on securing SMS object access, which is mainly done through the SMS Administrator console. (This section, like the rest of this book, discusses the SMS Advanced Client but not the Legacy Client).

Running Programs with Administrative Rights

Running a program with administrative rights is not part of the default SMS configuration. To enable this option, follow these steps within the SMS Administrator console:

1. Open the **Packages** tree.

2. Open the package that you need to configure.

3. Open the **Programs** tree, and then open the properties of the program you wish to configure.

4. Select the **Environment** tab (see Figure 3.6). Check the **Run with administrative rights** radio button. This feature works with or without a user being logged on. This option utilizes Local System until the installation is complete or until the system is rebooted. See Chapter 6 for details about program creation and each of these options.

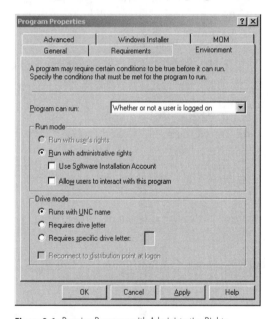

Figure 3.6: Running Programs with Administrative Rights.

Advanced Client Network Access Account

SMS 2003 product documentation is unclear about the way that the Advanced Client uses the SMS Advanced Client Network Access Account. This option provides an alternative for software installation in scenarios where neither the SMS client host machine account nor the logged-on user account has access to the program's source file location. The program source file location can include an SMS distribution point or a network file share. Unlike the Legacy

Client Software Installation Account, SMS Advanced Client Network Access Account cannot be used to launch a program from a DP and then access network resources from another file share where the logged-on user or the host system computer account does not have access.

Examples where this option could be useful include:

- Network file shares containing program source files where the host computer account and logged-on user do not have access.

- When the Advanced Client is roaming among locations where the DPs are in different domains or forests, while its host computer account and logged-on user do not have access to the local distribution point.

- The installation is unattended. *Unattended programs* are advertised programs that are configured to run when no users are logged on. Unattended installations can occur if the following SMS program options are selected: **Only when no user is logged on** or **Whether or not a user is logged on**. The computer account will be tried first, and then the Advanced Client Network Access Account.

The following steps must be completed to use the SMS Advanced Client Network Access Account:

1. You must first create the proper account. This must be a domain account with rights to access the necessary files. Use a descriptive name, like client access. Also, include a description that indicates what the account is used for.

2. Configure SMS to use this account:

    a. Open the Hierarchy tree and drill-down to the site where you will be distributing the package.

    b. Open the **Site Settings tree**⇨ **Component Configuration tree** (see Figure 3.7).

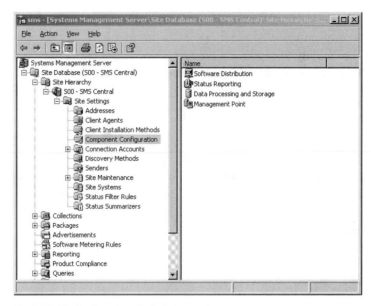

Figure 3.7: Viewing Component Configuration.

c. From the right pane, open **Software Distribution** (see Figure 3.8). Under **Advanced Client Network Access Account**, select **Set**; then add the domain account that you created in Step 1.

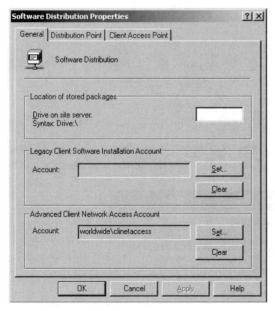

Figure 3.8: Adding the Advanced Client Network Access Account.

If the Advanced Client Network Access Account is properly configured, the Advanced Client runs the advertised program and attempts to run the program executable, using either the logged-on user's account or the Local System, depending on how the SMS program is configured. The SMS client will attempt to use the Advanced Client Network Access Account when trying to access a DP or file share where the user account (when appropriate) or computer account do not have access.

It is a best practice to create an Advanced Client Network Access Account maintenance cycle. The idea is to proactively reset the password for the account prior to having it get locked out due to domain account policies. This would cause a software distribution to fail if it was depending on the Advanced Client Network Access Account. If your domain does not have a policy that requires changing passwords on system accounts such as this one, regularly changing the password is even more important.

Package Access Accounts

Package access accounts allow you to set permissions to specify users and user groups that can access a package folder on distribution points. These accounts are utilized by all users and SMS components to access distribution points. By default, SMS makes the folders located on the DP available to all users, but if sensitive data exists, the folders can be restricted to specific users or user groups by using these accounts. The following generic accounts are created by default for each package:

- Administrator = Full Control

- User = Read

- Guest = Read

Generic access accounts are mapped to Windows Server Family local (for member servers) or domain (for domain controllers) user or group accounts on the individual DPs. Table 3.1 shows the mapping of the default generic access accounts to the actual Windows Server accounts.

SMS 2003 Account	Windows Server Family
Administrator	Local Administrator
User	Local Users
Guest	Local Guest

Table 3.1: Account Mapping.

Additional package access accounts can be added by following these steps:

1. In the **Packages** tree, open the package that you want to configure.

2. Right-click **Access Accounts** and choose the **New** menu option. Select the proper type of account.

3. The **Access Account** properties screen will appear (see Figure 3.9). Add the proper account and permissions information; then click the **OK** button. Accounts can also be deleted from the right pane. Never delete the Administrator package access account. It is needed to update distribution points.

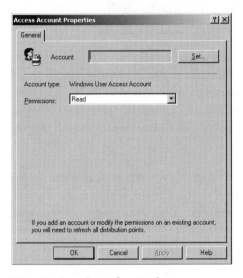

Figure 3.9: Access Account Properties Screen.

The idea behind package access accounts is to give sufficient permissions to the user or group accounts that will be in the target collection, while denying access to everyone else. This process is only necessary and possible in certain situations. Let's say there is sensitive information in a particular package, and the package will only be distributed to a few individuals. It may make sense to create your own package access accounts and map them to existing accounts in your domain. On the other hand, if this same package will be distributed to all users or machines in your domain, it is impossible to restrict the package—because any user in a target collection must have at least read access to a DP in order to install a program from it.

Software Distribution Accounts Checkpoints

If you think a problem with user rights is causing an SMS package to fail, check execmgr.log located on the client in %Windir%\system32\ccm\logs. Look for "access denied"-related errors when the client tries to access the source files for the advertised program. If a user rights problem exists, follow these guidelines:

- If an SMS program is configured to run when no one is logged on, or if end-users don't have administrative rights to the local machine, you will typically need to select **Run with administrative rights** from the **Environment** tab in the program properties.

- Don't delete the Administrator package access account. SMS components need it to update DPs.

- All machines or users in a target collection must be included in a package access group account. By default, packages allow read access to the local groups listed in Table 3.1. In turn, the local groups typically include Domain Guest and Domain Users group accounts. If someone has changed these account permissions, or removed these accounts from SMS, users may not have access to DPs when attempting to run programs from that package.

- If an SMS advertised program is configured to run an executable file from a file share or distribution point where either the logged-on user or the host computer account lacks access, then the Advanced Client Network Access Account needs to be configured.

Packaging Security

Using the powerful SMS Software Distribution feature, an administrator could intentionally or unintentionally harm all the computer systems in an organization very quickly. An SMS administrator could knowingly package harmful programs in a plan to damage targeted systems. It's also possible for an administrator to create a software package that accidentally includes a virus. One way to reduce this risk is through standard procedures that govern package creation, testing, and distribution workflow. The procedures should include package creation standards and a hand-off from the administrator who created the package to a tester, and then to the administrator who will deliver the package. The package should be monitored closely for suspicious activity during the testing phase.

SMS Administrator Access Security

Let's discuss the foundational concepts of SMS administrator access, and then utilize this information to plan and administer access security. SMS uses a three-layer security approach for administration. To be granted access, an SMS administrator must pass through these security layers:

- Windows Authentication, including Windows Management Instrumentation (WMI)

- SMS Object Security

- SQL Server Authentication

Initially, an administrator must be authenticated on a Windows Server Family network and that account must have access privileges to the site server. When opening the SMS Administrator's console, a connection is made to the SMS WMI Provider. Next, the administrator's cumulative permissions for SMS objects are verified by the SMS Provider. Finally, SMS connects to the SQL Server database, and is authenticated using the account that was provided during the initial site setup process. This section will zero-in on the WMI/SMS Provider layer. (SMS security rights can be modified by accessing WMI through the use of scripts or other tools. While this topic has merit, we won't touch on it here).

SMS Object Security

SMS Object Security is enforced by the SMS Provider and includes two types of objects: *classes* and *instances*. Instances are contained within classes. For example, an administrator could have read access to the **collections** class, which would actually give him read access to all collections. The administrator could also have read access to an instance of the **collections** class, which is a collection named **All Windows XP Computers**.

- *Class security* is applied to all instances.

- *Instance security* is applied to a specific instance only.

SMS Object Security Classes

Within this level of security, there are three object classes where an administrator's permissions will affect his or her ability to distribute software:

- **ADVERTISEMENT** — Each advertisement that is created at a specific site represents one instance of the advertisement class.

- **PACKAGE** — Each package that is created at a specific site represents one instance of the package class.

- **COLLECTION** — Each collection that is created at a specific site represents one instance of the collection class.

SMS Administrator Security Planning

Before you begin configuring security, it's best to come up with a security plan. The needs of your organization and IT support staff must be taken into account. Security needs can be addressed best if you have a plan outlining software distribution for your organization. Here are a few points to consider:

- A centralized approach for software distribution usually works best, making it easier to apply standards. There is less chance of "recreating the wheel" where packages are concerned.

- Only administrators with the responsibility of distributing software should be granted the security rights to do so. SMS software distribution can be one of the most powerful tools in your organization. Providing this access to everyone can lead to major problems.

- If you have a large organization, a group of administrators may be required to work together to achieve the organization's software distribution goals. If this is the case, creating a domain security group for software distribution can reduce administrative overhead.

Software Distribution Organizational Structures

There are various methods for organizing software distribution teams. The most common structure would be to use a centralized approach, where the SMS team handles all aspects of SMS operations and software distribution. This approach would probably not require the level of flexibility offered by the SMS security rights model, because most of the members of this team have the SMS access rights to perform all the SMS administrative functions.

Another approach is to have a general SMS operations team. These folks would be responsible for all aspects of the SMS infrastructure and administration and also perform the software distribution role. A separate team would be responsible for the creation of the software package. This team would complete the software package based on the specifications of the internal customer, and then the SMS operations team would distribute it. This approach most likely would not require the use of the various SMS security rights.

A slightly different approach would again have an SMS operations team that would handle all SMS infrastructure and administration issues. Software distribution would be performed by a separate team called a software release team. These folks would handle all aspects of software packaging and SMS software distribution. The software release team would actually be internal customers of the SMS operations team. With this structure, the SMS operations team would be required to provide the proper level of SMS access rights to the software release team. Using the right combination of class and instance rights will allow the software release team to perform their role without jeopardizing the security of the SMS infrastructure. See the next section to learn about the software distribution class and instance rights.

Software Distribution-Related Security Class and Instance Rights

Knowledge of software distribution-related object classes and instance rights is required to begin planning security access for SMS administrators. Use Tables 3.2 through 3.7 below for details about these object classes and instances and their descriptions.

Advertisement Class Security Rights	Description
Manage Folders	Allows a user to create folders and add advertisements into the folder.
Delegate	Allows users to give advertisement object access to other users.
Create	Allows a user to create advertisements. The user will also have the advertise right for the target collection.
Administer	Allows a user to administer security for all advertisements.
Delete	Allows a user to delete all advertisements.
Modify	Allows the user to modify to all advertisements.
Read	Allows the user to read the properties of all advertisements.

Table 3.2: Advertisement Class Security Rights.

Advertisement Instance Security Rights	Description
Delete	Allows the user to delete a specific advertisement.
Modify	Allows the user to modify a specific advertisement.
Read	Allows the user to read the properties of a specific advertisement.

Table 3.3: Advertisement Instance Security Rights.

Collection Class Security Rights	Description
Delegate	Allows users to give collection object access to other users.
Read Resources	Allows the user to view the contents of all collections.
Create	Allows a user to create collections. If the administrator also has the Read Resource class right, they can add any resource from the site into a collection they create. It is necessary for target collections to be created for advertisements. The user can also modify collections that he or she has created.
Delete Resource	Allows a user to delete the members of a collection.
Administer	Allows a user to administer security for all collections.
Modify Resources	Allows a user to modify a resource in a collection.
Advertise	Allows the user to advertise to all collections.
Read	Allows the user to read the properties of all collections.

Table 3.4: Collection Class Security Rights.

Collection Instance Security Rights	Description
Read Resources	Allows the user to view the contents of a specific collection.
Delete Resource	Allows a user to delete the members of a collection.
Modify Resources	This right actually has no effect. It is not possible to modify resources through the SMS Administrator Console.
Advertise	Allows the user to advertise to a specific collection.
Read	Allows the user to read the properties of a specific collection.
Delete	Allows the user to delete a specific collection.
Modify	Allows the user to modify a specific collection.

Table 3.5: Collection Instance Security Rights.

Package Class Security Rights	Description
Manage Folders	Allows a user to create folders and add packages into the folder.
Delegate	Allows users to give package object access to other users.
Create	Allows the user to create packages. The user can also modify the packages that he or she has created.
Administer	Allows the user to administer security for all packages.
Distribute	Allows the user to distribute all packages.
Delete	Allows the user to delete all packages.
Modify	Allows the user to modify all packages.
Read	Allows the user to read the properties of all packages.

Table 3.6: Package Class Security Rights.

Package Instance Security Rights	Description
Distribute	Allows the user to distribute a specific package.
Delete	Allows the user to delete a specific package.
Modify	Allows the user to modify the properties of a specific package.
Read	Allows the user to read the properties of a specific package.

Table 3.7: Package Instance Security Rights.

SMS Administrator Security Configuration

SMS security is configured from the SMS Administrator Console. The **Security Rights** tree is located near the bottom of the left pane of the console. Select this tree to see the right pane populate with security information. The information in the section "SMS Object Security" in this chapter is useful when attempting to configure SMS security. There are several possible methods to use when administering security for users:

- **SMS USER WIZARD** — This tool allows the addition of new users and groups. It is a tool for adding, removing, or modifying any class or instance security right for users or groups.

- **NEW CLASS SECURITY RIGHT** — This tool provides a property screen for assigning class-level rights to users or groups.

- **NEW INSTANCE SECURITY RIGHT** — This tool provides a property screen for assigning instance rights to users or groups.

- **CLONE SMS USER** — This tool allows administrators to copy the SMS rights of an existing user or group to a new user or group.

- **OPEN THE PROPERTIES SHEET OF AN INSTANCE OR CLASS OBJECT OF A USER OR GROUP** — This allows for the modification of class and instance rights for existing users or groups.

SMS User Wizard

When administrating security for the first time, the SMS User Wizard may be the most helpful. This tool can be accessed by right-clicking the **Security Rights** tree in the left pane, and choosing the **All Tasks⇨ Manage SMS Users** menu item. When the wizard starts, click the **Next** button. You can choose to modify or delete existing users or groups, or add a new user or local NT security group (see Figure 3.10).

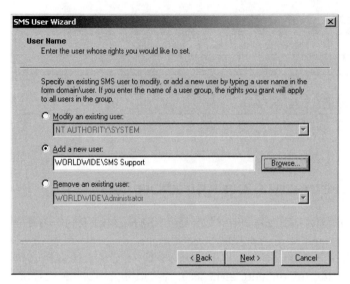

Figure 3.10: Managing Administrator Access with SMS User Wizard.

After making a selection, click the **Next** button. The **Rights** screen will appear, listing the rights that are currently available for the user or group (see Figure 3.11).

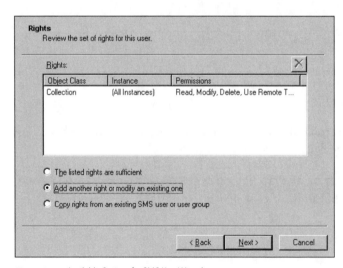

Figure 3.11: Available Options for SMS User Wizard.

These are the available options:

- **THE LISTED RIGHTS ARE SUFFICIENT** —This is the default. Unless another option is selected, clicking the **Next** button will cause the wizard to close.

- **ADD ANOTHER RIGHT OR MODIFY AN EXISTING ONE** — Selecting this option will bring up the **Add a Right** screen, which includes two drop-down boxes that contain collection and instance options (see Figure 3.12). Select the appropriate rights; and click the **Next** button. If you need to administer rights for more than one class or instance, you must click the **Back** button, and then go through the process again. In other words, only the rights that are selected for the class or instance (the ones that you can view when you click the **Next** button) will be entered into the database. Click the **Finish** button to accept the changes that you made.

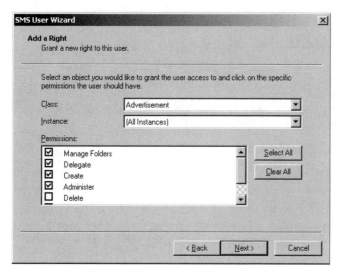

Figure 3.12: Adding a Right with SMS User Wizard.

- **COPY RIGHTS FROM AN EXISTING SMS USER OR GROUP** — This option will bring up the Copy Rights screen, which includes one drop-down box that contains existing SMS users, and a window that lists the user's rights. You will need to select a user or group from whom you want to copy rights. The rights will then be applied to the user or group that you selected at the beginning of the wizard. Click the **Finish** button to commit the changes that you made.

Configuring New Classes and New Instances

New class and new instance security rights can be added without the SMS User Wizard. These options are only available for existing SMS users. To use this method of administering rights:

1. Right-click on the **Security Rights** tree, and then select **New**.

2. Select either the **Class Security Right** or the **Instance Security Right** from the drop-down box (see Figure 3.13).

3. Make the appropriate selections, then click the **OK** button.

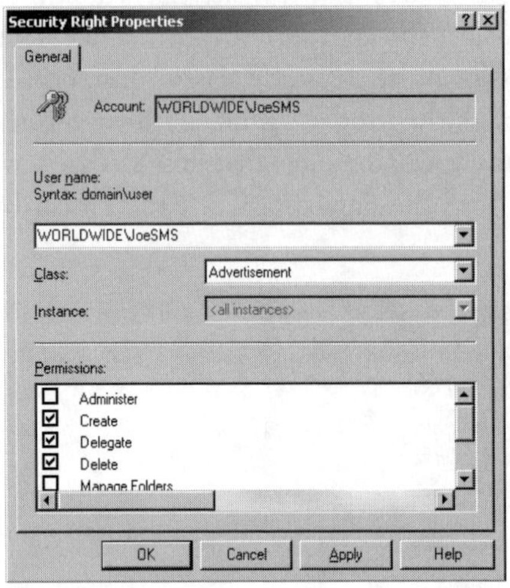

Figure 3.13: Configuring New Classes and New Instances.

Cloning Users

To copy class or instance rights from an existing SMS user to a new user with an existing NT account, use the **Clone SMS User** option. To access this option:

1. Select the **Security Rights** tree from the left pane; the right pane will enumerate with security objects.

2. Right-click an object from a user that you want to clone, and choose the **All Tasks⇨ Clone SMS User** menu item.

3. Enter the domain and user or group account. Select **Class security rights** and/or **Instance security rights** (see Figure 3.14).

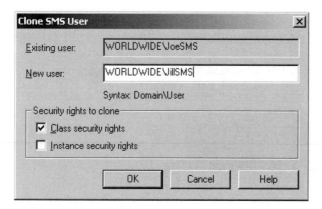

Figure 3.14: Cloning Users.

Configuring an Existing Class or Instance Right

Administering a class right or an instance right for a user or group can be performed on the properties sheet of the class or instance. Select the **Security** tree in the left pane. From the right pane, open the properties of a class right or instance right (see Figure 3.15). Here, you can only add or remove rights for that particular class or instance.

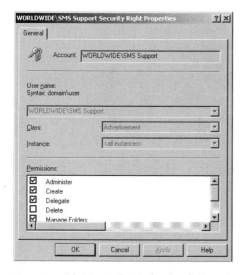

Figure 3.15: Administering Security for a Specific Class or Instance.

This action can also be performed by accessing a class or instance via a component tree located in the left pane of the console. For example; from the left pane, select the **Advertisements** tree (see Figure 3.16). Right-click an advertisement and choose the **Properties** menu item. Then select the **Security** tab (see Figure 3.17). Configure the **Security** tab properties to provide the proper access to administrators.

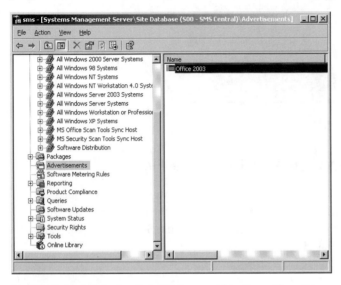

Figure 3.16: Administering Security through Component Advertisement Properties.

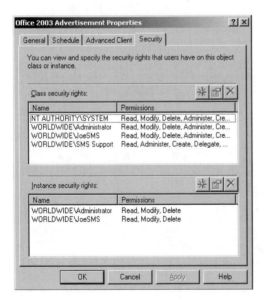

Figure 3.17: Configuring the Advertisement Security Tab.

Considerations for Administering SMS Security for Software Distribution

To minimize administrative overhead, apply SMS security to local groups, and then add users and global groups to the local groups where possible. If you were to apply the rights to all the users, or even to all the global groups, a significant amount of redundant administrative tasks would be required. Also Microsoft recommends this as a best practice approach for administering security.

Follow these recommendations:

- Avoid granting the Administer right for any SMS class or instance, whenever possible. *Administer* is an SMS right that can be assigned to SMS administrators that gives them the permission to change the rights of other SMS administrators. Limiting the use of the Administer right will allow better access control over your implementation.

- Be careful about granting class rights. Class rights are inherited by all instances within that class.

- For one administrator to build and distribute a package, he or she must have permissions to create packages and advertisements. The administrator will also need the rights to read the resources and distribute software to the collection. If a new collection will need to be created, he or she must also have the permissions to perform that task.

- To have the ability to connect to the SMS Provider with the SMS Administrator Console, a user must be a member of the *SMS Admins* security group. If the site server is on a member server, this will be a local group; otherwise, it will be a domain security group. Users and groups are automatically added to this group when they are provided with rights under the **Security** tree within the SMS console. If a user is inadvertently removed from the SMS Admins group, they will no longer be able to connect to the SMS Provider.

Microsoft SMS 2003 Security Documentation

Security is becoming serious business for most companies. Because of the many different Microsoft products that SMS utilizes, security configuration for an SMS implementation is quite complex. For more details regarding SMS 2003 security, download and read SMS security related documents such as "Scenarios and Procedures for Microsoft Systems Management Server 2003: Security" from the Systems Management Server 2003 Product Documentation Web page at http://www.microsoft.com/smserver/techinfo/productdoc/default.mspx#EDJAC.

Summary

This chapter showed that there are many security aspects to consider when administering SMS, because several Windows applications and services are utilized. You learned how to secure the SMS software distribution feature, and the best practices for securing the SMS infrastructure. This chapter also discussed SMS administrator access security, including object security, planning, and configuration. Finally, the chapter covered additional considerations for administering security for software distribution.

Configuring and Optimizing Software Distribution

The initial SMS setup process automatically installs the components that are required for software distribution, but they still must be configured properly. Configuration for these components is based on the number of clients, the network environment, and the size of the packages that you intend to distribute. Configuration of these settings is also determined by how your organization plans to use software distribution. In this chapter, you will learn to enable and configure the proper client agent for software distribution, create and configure distribution points, and minimize network bandwidth usage. You will also discover ways to transfer configuration settings between SMS 2003 sites.

 **NOTE**

The term *client* used in this chapter and throughout the book refers to the Advanced Client and not the Legacy Client.

Configuring the Advertised Programs Client Agent

Following a setup of an SMS 2003 site server, the Advertised Programs Client Agent will be disabled by default. In order to distribute software, you will need to configure this client agent's properties.

Follow these steps to view the properties:

1. From the SMS Administrator Console, open the Site Hierarchy tree and then open the site where you plan to implement software distribution.

2. Select the **Client Agents** tree from the left pane (see Figure 4.1).

3. Right-click the **Advertised Programs Client Agent** from the right pane and select the **Properties** menu item to view the properties sheet.

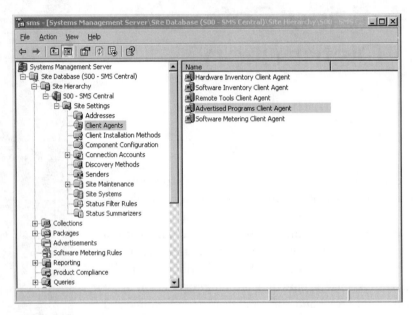

Figure 4.1: Viewing Client Agents in the SMS Administrator Console.

Agent Settings

The following is a list of Advertised Program Client Agent properties that you will need to configure, along with a few considerations:

- **General** tab (see Figure 4.2)

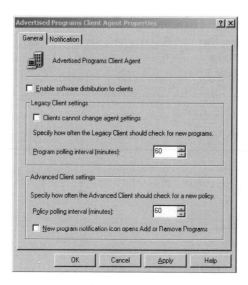

Figure 4.2: Configuring the General Tab.

- **ENABLE SOFTWARE DISTRIBUTION TO CLIENTS** — In order to have the Advertised Programs Client Agent enabled on the clients at a particular site, this option must be selected.

- **CLIENTS CANNOT CHANGE AGENT SETTINGS** — Legacy Client setting.

- **CHECK FOR NEW PROGRAMS EVERY <XX> MINUTES** — Legacy Client setting.

- **SPECIFY HOW OFTEN THE ADVANCED CLIENT SHOULD CHECK FOR A NEW POLICY** — The default for this option is 60 minutes, but it can be set as high as 9999 minutes. There is a tradeoff here: checking for new programs more often will cause a little more network traffic. The other aspect of configuring this option with a lower number is that clients will install new programs closer to the time when they become available. In turn, the entire distribution will be competed more quickly. This will cause higher network utilization over a shorter period of time, which may be a bad thing, depending on your environment.

- **NEW PROGRAM NOTIFICATION ICON OPENS ADD OR REMOVE PROGRAMS** — When selecting the new program notification that appears in the notification area of the taskbar, the user will be taken to **Add or Remove Programs**, where the advertised program is displayed. If this option is not selected, the **Run Advertised Programs** dialog box will automatically open when a new advertised program arrives. The good thing about this is that it is SMS–

specific, providing only the optional programs being offered by SMS. **Add or Remove Programs** takes a bit more effort to navigate, because it generally has more options. On the other hand, if users are new to receiving SMS-optional advertised programs, the **Run Advertised Programs** dialog experience will be new to them. If users are already familiar with **Add or Remove Programs**, it may make more sense to stay with that applet.

- **Notification** tab (see Figure 4.3)

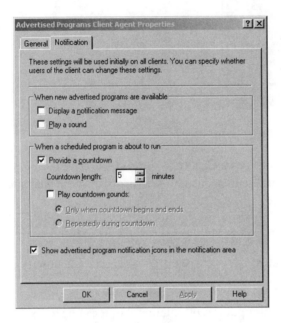

Figure 4.3: Configuring the Notification Tab.

- When new advertised programs are available:

  - **DISPLAY A NOTIFICATION MESSAGE** — The message notifies the end-user about new optional advertised programs that are available. Even though this option is selected, its action can be controlled later on a program by program basis from the **Program Properties**⇨**Advanced** tab. To cause the notification not to appear, select the **Suppress program notification**. option.

  - **PLAY A SOUND** — Be careful when using this option. The sound is repetitive and can become quite distracting to users. If a user is away from his or her desk when a new program becomes available, the noise will continue to sound.

- When a scheduled program is about to run, provide a countdown, with or without sounds.

  ◆ **COUNTDOWN LENGTH: <XX> MINUTES** — This option accepts a range of 1 to 60 minutes. Setting the countdown timer to 5 minutes provides enough time for a user to save their work and allow the program to run. The start of the installation is more predictable to users when a short countdown length is used, rather than a long one.

- When a scheduled program is about to run, play countdown sounds:

  ◆ **ONLY WHEN COUNTDOWN BEGINS AND ENDS.**

  ◆ **REPEATEDLY DURING COUNTDOWN** — Keep your user environment in mind here. If you set a long countdown length and also select this option, users who sit near an absent employee could become annoyed by the beeping workstation.

- **SHOW ADVERTISED PROGRAMS NOTIFICATION ICONS IN THE NOTIFICATION AREA** — This setting allows users to control the display of the notification icon in the system tray. If both the **Display Notification Message** option on the **General** tab and this option are selected, then both will occur. The message will appear in the taskbar notification as well.

It is best to notify users of optional programs that are available to them by displaying the notification message. Depending on the user environment, it may also be helpful to play a sound when the message appears. When users are logged on, always notify them when a scheduled program is about to run on their PC that will interrupt their work or require input from them. Selecting the countdown timer (from the bottom section of the **Notification** tab), is the easiest way to accomplish this.

Keep in mind that any option you select in the **Advertised Programs Client Agent properties** dialog box will be applied to all the clients that report to that site. There are no methods in the SMS Administrator Console to configure the properties for individual clients. The client configuration changes that are initiated in the console are immediately translated into a policy and placed on the Management Point (MP). Changes to client agents will be propagated to existing clients based on the policy refresh interval (every 60 minutes by default). During the refresh interval, the Advanced Client contacts the local MP, in order to update its configuration with any client configuration changes that may have been made on the site server. New clients automatically apply the changes during installation.

Transfer Site Settings Wizard

If there are multiple sites in an SMS implementation, using the SMS 2003 Administration Feature Pack Transfer Site Settings Wizard can save a considerable amount of time. This wizard is part of the SMS 2003 SP1 Administration Feature Pack and is available as a free download at `http://www.microsoft.com/smserver/downloads/2003/adminpack.mspx`. The Transfer Site Settings Wizard provides the ability to export site settings, collections, and packages from one SMS site and then import them to any number of other sites. Settings can be copied directly from an object, such as a package, from one site to another through the use of an XML template. Additionally, the template can be saved for use at another time. The Transfer Site Settings Wizard streamlines the process of setting up SMS sites.

Accessing Site Properties Manager

Before you can access Site Properties Manager, SMS 2003 Administration Feature Pack installation files must be available from the SMS site server where you plan to perform the installation. After downloading it from the Internet, extract the downloadable file, called SMS2003SP1_AdminFP_Enu.exe, into a folder. Included with the setup file are a help file and a release notes file. From the site server, browse to the folder where you extracted the files and then open the folder named TransferSettings. In this folder, run TSSsetup.exe. Close any open instances of the SMS Administrator Console and perform the installation. When the installation is complete, you will notice a new option when you use the right-click contextual menu on objects that can be exported.

To transfer the Advertised Programs Client Agent settings, follow these steps:

1. Open the SMS Administrator Console. Right-click on any collection or package object or any site server object under the Site Hierarchy tree. Select **All Tasks**⇨ **Transfer Settings**. The Transfer Site Settings Wizard will appear (see Figure 4.4).

Figure 4.4: Starting the Transfer Site Settings Wizard.

2. Select **Transfer site configuration settings** and then click the **Next** button.

3. Select **Create a configuration template** and then click the **Next** button.

4. Select the SMS site that you plan to use as the source and then click the **Next** button.

5. Within the wizard, open the **Client Agents⇨ Advertised Program Client Agent** tree item (see Figure 4.5).

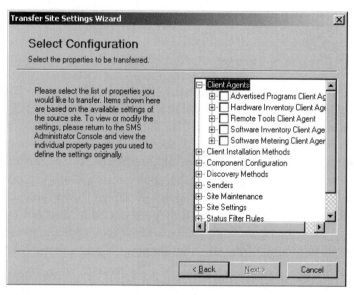

Figure 4.5: Viewing Advertised Programs Client Agent Properties.

6. View the available properties that can be transferred. Make your selection and click the **Next** button.

7. Select the target site to directly transfer the settings to the target site and click the **Next** button.

8. Select the **Include current values for each setting** option to transfer the existing settings values from the source.

9. Click the **Finish** button.

NOTE

Be sure to read the release notes that accompany the setup files. There are a few known issues to be aware of.

Using Distribution Points

The SMS Distribution Point (DP) contains the installation source files that are required to install an SMS advertised program. SMS clients must access a DP in order to install advertised programs. Selection of site server hardware should be based primarily on disk space and disk I/O, due to the resource demands of SMS and SQL Server. DPs are also heavily resource-intensive during software distributions. Therefore, it's best to create DPs on non-SMS site servers.

Distribution Point Prerequisites

BITS-enabled distribution point prerequisites include the installation of Windows 2000 SP2 or later, Background Intelligence Transfer Service (BITS), and Internet Information Server (IIS). BITS and IIS must also be enabled. BITS and IIS allows Advanced Clients to utilize bandwidth throttling and checkpoint restart features. Bandwidth throttling allows the client to become aware of available bandwidth at the client network interface and adjust the utilization of the download so that the user is not disrupted. Checkpoint restart allows the download to begin where stopped in cases where the download gets interrupted. Bandwidth throttling and checkpoint restarts are not utilized when the **Run program from distribution point** advertisement property is selected (see Figure 4.6). Suffice to say, it is best practice to use BITS-enabled DPs and the **Download program from distribution point and run** property wherever possible.

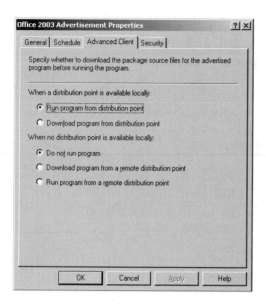

Figure 4.6: Configuring the Properties of an Advertisement.

Protected Distribution Points

Use protected distribution points (PDP) to restrict access to a DP to Advanced Clients in specific site boundaries. The **Enable as a protected distribution point** property is available on the **Distribution Point** property tab of any site system (see the section "Adding Distribution Points to Existing SMS Site Systems" later in this chapter). This option also forces clients that reside in PDP boundaries to only download content from these PDPs using the algorithm described later in this section. One point of caution: when an Advanced Client resides in the boundaries of PDPs, it will ONLY attempt to access this list of PDPs. In this scenario, the client cannot fail over to another available DP as it normally would.

Locating a Distribution Point

In order to run an advertised program, an Advanced Client must first locate a DP. Advanced Clients utilize built-in intelligence to select a distribution point, initiating the following algorithm:

- On the Advanced Client, the Location Services CCMExec.exe thread queries the management point (MP) for a list of DPs. This is called a Content Location Request.

- The MP returns the path of the content on each available distribution point (DP) to Location Services (called the Content Location Response), using the following metrics:

- If the client is included in protected distribution point (PDP) boundary(s), the MP will verify that the content is available at the PDP(s). If the content is available, only the PDP(s) will be provided to the client. If no PDP(s) are available, then the content will not be downloaded.

- If the client is not included in a protected distribution point boundary, the MP will attempt to provide a local DP—first on the same subnet, then within the AD Site, then any DP local to the client, and finally, a remote DP within the SMS site.

- If the Advanced Client cannot contact a DP in its resident site, it will contact the DP again with the same request. The MP will then return a list of all assigned MPs. The client then chooses a DP from the list at random.

Viewing Existing Distribution Points

To view existing DPs, follow these steps:

1. Open the Site Hierarchy tree from within the SMS Administrator Console.

2. Drill down to the site where you want to configure a DP and open it. In the left pane, select the **Site Systems** tree. The right side will become populated with all the site systems.

3. Expand the width of the **Roles** column. Look for any systems that are designated as DPs. By default, the SMS site server will be configured as the only DP during installation (see Figure 4.7). The DP will be placed, as a hidden share, on the disk drive with the largest amount of free space. The hidden share name will be smspkg<DriveLetter>$.

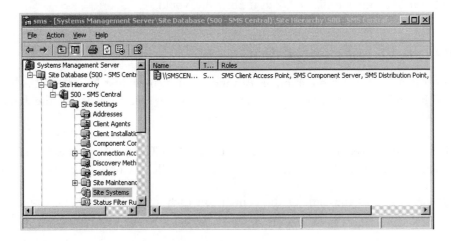

Figure 4.7: Viewing the Site Systems Roles Column.

Best Practices for Adding Distribution Points

Before adding additional DPs, you should observe these best practices:

- In scenarios where Advanced Clients are configured to download source files from BITS-enabled DPs prior to executing the program, fewer server resources are generally used. An example when this may not be the case would be a large package containing a year or more of archived software updates. In this case, the Advanced Client would only install the required updates. If the client were to download the entire package and use only a few packages, it would make more sense to run the program from the DP. When deploying small (2-3 MB) packages, there should be one DP per every 3500 - 4000 clients. If larger packages will be distributed, one DP should be available for every 1500 - 2000 clients. More DPs will afford a quicker rate of completion.

- Even though there are new features in SMS 2003 to help with Wide Area Network (WAN) traffic, DPs function best when they are located on the same LAN (Local Area Network) as the site server where they were created.

- Be careful not to remove all the DPs for a site where packages are distributed from. If this scenario should occur, an SMS recovery will have to be performed. And, if an SMS recovery doesn't resolve the issue, all of the packages will need to be recreated. SMS recovery involves completing several tasks that result in returning the SMS server to the condition it was in prior to a failure. These tasks include, but are not limited to, actions such as restoring registry keys and files to their proper location and synchronizing jobs between child and parent sites.

- Multiple DPs will serve to distribute the client load to multiple servers. They will also serve as a form of fault tolerance, allowing for the availability of source files even when one or more DPs are unavailable.

- Use protected distribution points (PDP) to restrict access to a DP to Advanced Clients located within specific site boundaries. PDP(s) also offer a preferred DP scenario.

- Use BITS-enabled DPs and the **Download program from distribution point and run** advertisement property wherever possible.

Adding Distribution Points to Existing SMS Site Systems

To add a new distribution point to an existing site system, follow these steps:

1. Open the properties of the existing site system.

2. Select the **Distribution Point** tab, then select the **Use this site system as a distribution point** property (see Figure 4.8).

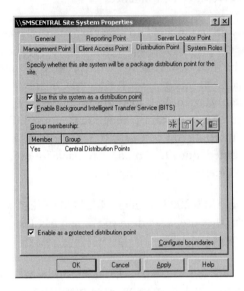

Figure 4.8: Adding a Distribution Point.

3. Select the **Enable Background Intelligence Transfer Service (BITS)** property to allow Advanced Clients access to the DP using the Download and Run feature.

4. Select the **Enable as protected distribution point** if you desire to restrict Advanced Client access to this DP to certain boundaries. Also, click the **Configure boundaries** button and specify the site or roaming boundaries where you want to permit access.

Distribution Point Groups

Distribution point groups are collections of multiple DPs grouped together to allow for easier management. Distribution point groups can be assigned to packages with a single selection. This can save a considerable amount of time if an administrator is responsible for many DPs.

To create a distribution point group, follow these steps:

1. Open the properties of a site system.

2. Select the **Distribution Point** tab.

3. Select the **Add** symbol to the right of the **Group Membership** label.

4. Provide a name for the group in the **Name** box.

5. Repeat steps 1 through 4 on other DPs that you want to add to the group.

 NOTE

Distribution point groups do not flow down the SMS hierarchy to child sites. They will need to be recreated if you want them to appear on child sites.

Adding Distribution Points to Non-Site Systems

To add a new distribution point to a non-site system using an existing share, follow these steps:

1. In the left pane, right-click on the **Site System** tree.

2. Choose the **New**⇨ **Server Share** menu item.

3. Click the **Set** button and add the server share name. Click the **OK** button (see Figure 4.09).

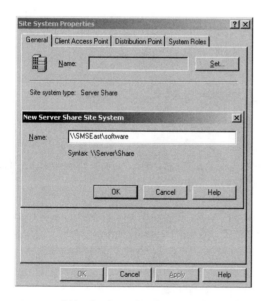

Figure 4. 9: Adding Distribution Points to Non-Site Systems.

4. Select the **Distribution Point** tab, and then select the **Use this site system as a Distribution Point** property. Also select any additional properties that you require.

5. Click the **OK** button.

Assigning Distribution Points to Packages

Once a package is created, distribution points will need to be selected so clients can access the installation programs. To select distribution points where package source files will be copied, follow these steps:

1. From the left pane, open the **Packages** tree, and then open a package where you want to configure distribution points (see Figure 4.10).

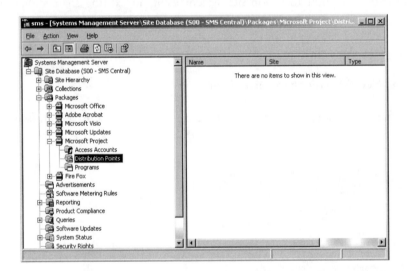

Figure 4.10: Viewing the Package Tree.

2. Right-click on the **Distribution Points** tree and choose the **New⇨ Distribution Points** menu item. The **New Distribution Point** wizard will appear.

3. Click the **Next** button. View the list of available distribution points where package source files can be copied (see Figure 4.11). Make your selection.

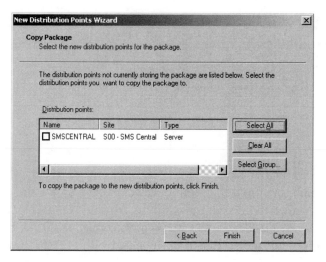

Figure 4.11: Assigning Distribution Points to a Package.

4. When you click the **Finish** button, the source files will immediately be copied to all the distribution points you added.

Updating Distribution Points

After creating distribution points, you might need to update or refresh them periodically. Updating distribution points pulls a new copy of the source files to the compressed source files on the site server. It also copies the new source files to the local DPs. The DPs at the child sites are then updated from the new version of compressed source files, located on the site server. The need to update DPs occurs when the source files change. For example, if you make a change to the installation executable for a package, this change needs to be propagated to all the DPs.

To update distribution points, follow these steps:

1. From the left pane, open the **Packages** tree, and then open a package where you want to configure distribution points.

2. Right-click the **Distribution Points** console item, then select the **All Tasks**⇨ **Update Distribution Points** menu item. The **Confirm Update Distribution Points** dialog box will appear.

3. Click the **Yes** button at the dialog box (see Figure 4.12).

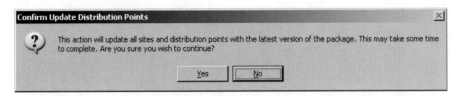

Figure 4.12: Confirming Update Distribution Points.

Refreshing Distribution Points

Refreshing distribution points pulls files from the compressed source files on the site server to the DP. Any files that have been added to the compressed source files but are missing from the DP will be copied to the DP. Because the files use a local compressed copy, this is not resource-intensive for the network or server, but the package is not updated with the latest changes to the source files.

To refresh a distribution point, follow these steps:

1. From the left pane, open the **Packages** tree, and then open a package where you want to configure distribution points.

2. Select the **Distribution Point** tree. From the right pane, right-click on a distribution point.

3. Select **All Tasks** and then select the **Refresh Distribution Point** menu item. Click the **Yes** button on the dialog box.

Using the Manage Distribution Points Wizard

The Manage Distribution Points wizard provides options for administering distribution points. Among the options are refreshing distribution points, updating distribution points, copying files to new distribution points, and deleting distribution points.

To start the Manage Distribution Points wizard, follow these steps:

1. From the left pane, open the **Packages** tree, and then open a package where you want to manage distribution points.

2. Right-click the **Distribution Points** console item, and then select the **All Tasks**➪ **Manage Distribution Points** menu item. The Manage Distribution Point wizard will appear. Click the **Next** button to view the options (see Figure 4.13).

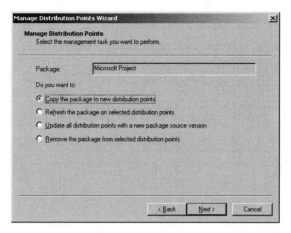

Figure 4.13: Managing Distribution Points Wizard.

Tips for Using Distribution Points

Here are a few additional considerations to help you avoid problems when you are configuring distribution points:

- DPs generally only need to be updated when you have made changes to the package source files.

- DPs only need to be refreshed if the source files they contain have been corrupted in some way.

- There is a known issue where SMS site servers can detect a change in the archive property of the package source files and erroneously send the entire package file to all child sites. In this case, SMS site servers may send a full size package source file when it should be sending a delta package file. The file archive property can be changed by some types of backups. The Microsoft Knowledge Base number is 872943 and there is a hotfix for the issue.

Configuring the Software Distribution Component Property

The Software Distribution component item contains several configurable options that could prove to be helpful for optimizing software distribution in the SMS site hierarchy. This item is located in an inconspicuous place. To find it, open the Site Hierarchy tree in the SMS Administrator console and then open a site server of your choosing. Select the **Site Settings Component Configuration** node from the left pane and then open the **Software Distribution** console item from the right pane.

Look at the **General** tab shown in Figure 4.14.

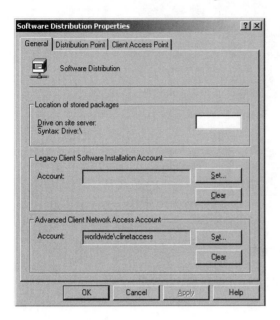

Figure 4.14: Configuring General Tab.

Below the **Location of stored packages** label, you input a value for **Drive on site server**. This option is for configuring the location where the site server stores a compressed version of the source files. This option would be used if you needed to place the compressed version of the source files at a location other than the default. The **Legacy Client Software Installation Account** and the **Advanced Client Network Access Account** can also be configured. (Due to the focus of this book, we won't go into detail about the Legacy Client.) The Advanced Client Network Access Account is covered in detail in Chapter 3.

Look at the **Distribution Point** tab shown in Figure 4.15.

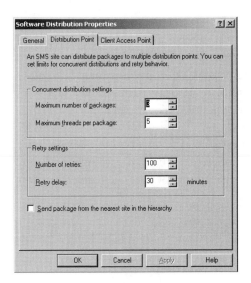

Figure 4.15: Configuring the Distribution Point Tab.

Below the **Concurrent distribution settings** label are the options to configure the maximum number of packages that will be distributed at one time and the maximum number of *threads* allocated to each package. An instruction is the basic unit of execution in a processor, and a thread is the object that executes instructions. Every running process has at least one thread. With multiple threads, a process can execute multiple instructions at once. Reducing the **Maximum number of packages** value will minimize the network bandwidth being consumed when copying multiple packages, but will increase the amount of time it will take if the number of packages to be copied is greater than the setting. Setting the value higher will cause the opposite effect. Lowering the **Maximum threads per package** value will remove SMS site server resources from processing packages and offer them to other server activities, causing a slowdown in the time it takes to process a package. Raising this value will designate more server resources to processing SMS packages, causing them to be processed more quickly.

Under the **Retry settings** label are the options to configure the number of retries that will occur when the distribution manager attempts to copy source files to a distribution point and the amount of time between each attempt. The **Send package from the nearest site in the hierarchy** check box can be selected to cause distribution points to receive source files directly from the parent site. Lowering the **Number of retries** value will cause the site server to stop retrying a package copy sooner when a DP is unavailable, saving system resources for other activities. You may want to keep this number higher if you have DPs that are commonly unavailable for a period of time. If it is more of a priority for you to have the site server copy files to the DPs than it is for you to conserve server resources, then you may want to reduce the **Retry delay** value.

The **Send package from the nearest site in the hierarchy** option can save network resources when it is selected. In this case, when the DP is targeted to receive a new package or to receive a package update, the site server where the package originates notifies the closest parent site (to the DP that has the proper version of the compressed package) to copy the source files to the DP. This will be helpful if the site where the package originates is located across a slow link from the targeted DP, but the DP's parent is not located over the slow link.

In the **Client Access Point** tab, below the **Retry settings** label, the distribution manager retry behavior can be configured. Options include the number of times that a source files copy operation will be attempted and the time delay between each attempt. The client access point is utilized by Legacy clients only.

Minimizing Bandwidth Usage

Software distribution consumes the most network bandwidth of any SMS feature. Because of the bandwidth requirements, there is a need for SMS servers to be installed on each LAN. Fortunately, Microsoft included features to minimize the interruption of business operations while configuring network communications between SMS servers. The bandwidth minimizing features include compression, scheduling, direct connection to a grandchild site, and bandwidth throttling.

Compression

Compression squeezes out any free space that may be present, leaving the package smaller in file size. This process occurs on the primary server where packages are created. It happens automatically when a package is sent to a distribution point at another SMS site. By default, the compressed files are stored in a directory named SMSPKG, located on the drive that contains the SMS_<SiteCode> directory. The compressed files are formatted with a name that matches their corresponding source folder located on the distribution point. The file extension is .PCK. Compression rates vary depending on the type of files that are included in the source folder. Keep in mind that most installation source files are already compressed. After source files are compressed by an SMS primary server, you can expect to see a 10% to 15% reduction in size. A compressed version of the package can still be created, even though a package may not be configured to use a distribution point at another site. To do this, right-click on a package in the SMS Administrator Console and select the **Properties** menu item. The package property sheet will appear. Select the **Data Source** tab, then select the **Use a compressed copy of the source directory** property (see Figure 4.16).

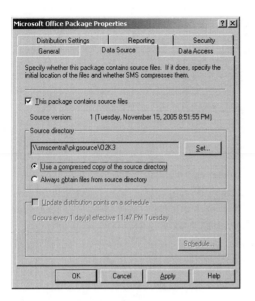

Figure 4.16: Configuring the Data Source Tab.

This option could be useful if you are creating a package from a CD. The CD that contains the package source files will eventually be removed, causing the files to be unavailable for refreshing or updating distribution points. By using a compressed copy of the source files, they will always be available to the SMS site server.

Scheduling

Scheduling is the procedure for configuring a time when bandwidth usage can be consumed by an SMS server. This task allows an SMS administrator to restrict bandwidth usage during certain times. Scheduling can be configured on the properties sheet of a package or on the properties sheet of an address—specifically, on the **Data Source** tab of a package properties sheet, and on the **Schedule** tab and **Rate Limit** tab of an address properties sheet. SMS senders use information from the addresses to find other SMS sites. *Senders* describe WAN technologies that can be used to access another SMS site. Addresses hand off specific SMS site information to senders, so that a connection to that site can be completed.

On the **Data Source** tab of a package properties sheet, select the **Update Distribution Points on a schedule** property, then select the **Schedule** button. Then, you can schedule DP updates to occur after business hours, if necessary (see Figure 4.17). Only in a rare case, when the source files of a package change often, would it be necessary to update a distribution point on a regular basis. Typically, this is done manually when the software distribution administrator updates the source files of the package.

Figure 4.17: Configuring the Package Schedule.

To access the properties addresses for a site, open the Hierarchy tree, and then open the site that you want to modify. From the left pane, select **Addresses**; in the right pane, open the properties sheet of the address that you want to modify. From the **Schedule** tab, select timeframes when you want to limit certain SMS traffic. Every object that is sent using this address has a priority. You can configure the priority of status messages and packages.

Let's look at an example. On Wednesdays, you only want to send objects to a certain site with a priority of High between the hours of 8 a.m. and 5 p.m. Don't forget about checking the object's priority configuration. Within a package's properties, there is an option for sending priority on the **Distribution Settings** tab (see Figure 4.19). By default, a package priority is set to Medium. So, leaving the address schedule configuration and package distribution configuration as they are in Figures 4.18 and 4.19, DPs will not be updated by this package on Wednesdays between 8 a.m. and 5 p.m. Source files for any packages that have been set to a priority of Medium will not be sent to this address on Wednesdays between 8 a.m. and 5 p.m. The **Unavailable to substitute for inoperative addresses** property (see Figure 4.18) refers to situations where there may be more than one address configured for a site. Notice, on the package properties on the **Distribution Settings** tab, that there is the option for specifying a sender (see Figure 4.19).

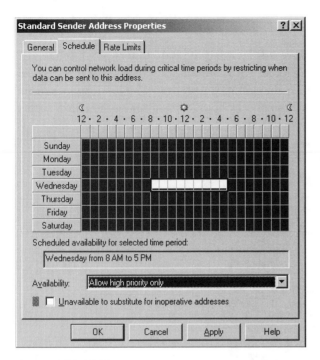

Figure 4.18: Schedule Tab.

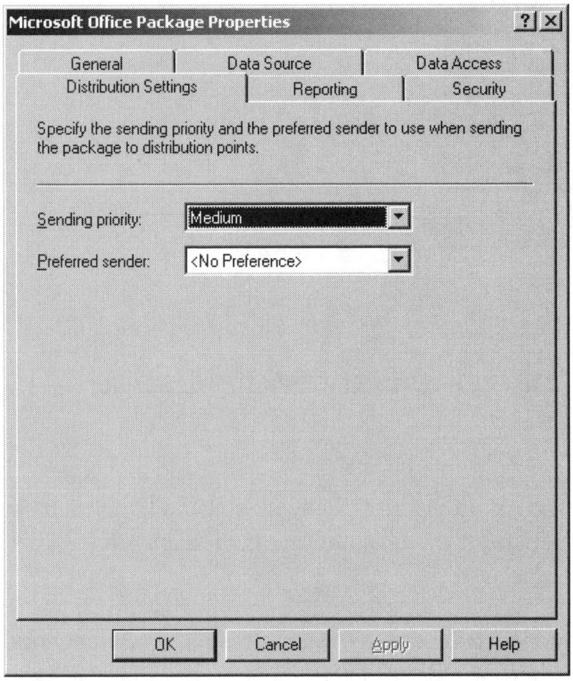

Figure 4.19: Distribution Settings Tab.

Bandwidth Throttling

Another way to restrict traffic on SMS addresses is by using the **Rate Limits** property tab (see Figure 4.20). This feature provides throttling for all SMS communications that use the specified SMS address. Select the **Limited to specified maximum transfer rates by hour** radio button, and then configure the percentage of bandwidth usage by hour. The total amount of SMS traffic, from the site you are configuring to the specified address, will be limited to the percentage that you select during the hours that are selected.

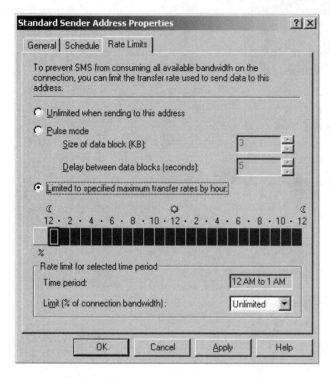

Figure 4.20: Rate Limits Tab.

Points to Consider When Minimizing Bandwidth Usage

Keep the following points in mind:

- Be careful when restricting addresses based on priority. Remember that all objects have priorities. If this is the only link to a particular site, some status messaging and other SMS communication will be restricted as well.

- Communicate your plans for bandwidth usage to your organization's network management team. Together, you should be able to determine a replication plan that everyone can live with.

- For best performance, install a site server at remote offices that connect to the central office across a WAN link. A secondary site server is a good alternative for sites that contain fewer than 1000 clients. There are some variables to consider when determining whether to install a primary site or a secondary site. The main consideration is support staff. If there is support staff located at the site in question, and the staff members will use SMS to manage systems at the site, they will realize improved performance if a primary server is located locally. Other considerations include cost, an additional MS SQL Server (if a primary site is installed), and SMS features used.

- Consider the size of the package you will be sending across a WAN link. All files and subfolders located in the source folder (which you configure in the properties of a package) will be sent to DPs that you select.

- Configure packages to only use distribution points for sites that will install the package. Otherwise, the source files must be copied to distribution points unnecessarily.

- Be aware that BITS does not perform bandwidth throttling between SMS sites or between site servers and DPs. This is a common misconception. BITS manages bandwidth utilization at the Advanced Client network interface only. The benefit of the bandwidth throttling aspect of BITS is limited to situations where the Advanced Client is connecting to the corporate network over a slow connection.

Summary

In this chapter, you learned how to set up and optimize software distribution. Setting up software distribution requires administrators to enable and configure the Advertised Programs Client Agent, to configure distribution points, and to configure the SMS Software Distribution Component properties. These settings are located under the **Site Settings** tree within the Site Hierarchy. Configuration changes applied to the Advertised Programs Client Agent are translated into policies and copied to the management point, where Advanced Clients access them during the policy refresh interval. After configuring distribution points, administrators must select them when distributing packages. Once configured, the Advanced Clients Network Access Account is used by SMS to gain access to files located on networked resources when the logged-on user does not have access.

Optimizing SMS for software distribution includes configuring a site to operate in a way that best fits the needs of your organization. Minimizing bandwidth utilization can be accomplished by using features such as scheduling and bandwidth throttling. These features allow an administrator to schedule DP updates when network usage is low and limit the amount of bandwidth that SMS will use when replicating packages over WAN links. Protected distribution points allow administrators to restrict distribution point access to Advanced Clients that reside in specific boundaries.

DID YOU KNOW?

The next version of SMS, System Center Configuration Manager (SCCM), will include a site server role called *branch distribution points*. This new role will allow workstations to host packages without requiring a site server. Branch distribution points allow for bandwidth control settings that utilize BITS. This feature will offer a cost-effective approach to distributing SMS package source files to small branch offices.

Software Distribution Public Relations

Public relations are a key concern in the world of Systems Management Server administration. SMS implementations and administrators tend to receive more than their fair share of blame for issues from server crashes to network outages to mysterious disappearing files. By focusing on the quality of the products that are being delivered and using good communication practices, you can help to improve the opinion of end-users regarding your work. After reading this chapter, you will understand the impact that planning, testing, communication, and a distribution process standard have on any SMS project, especially software distribution. You will discover how the balance of planning and testing can be applied to improve the quality of your work. You will also learn various communication strategies that will help to improve your image. This chapter also demonstrates the important functions that test labs provide for SMS projects, and the need for creating software distribution standards.

Planning

In general, any project you are working on should have a written plan in place. This provides several benefits to you. It will help to keep you focused and make it easier to share your plan with management and co-workers. Management is more likely to "buy in" to a written plan. If you receive your manager's blessing to begin your project, the plan can then serve to protect you. As long as you follow the plan, the burdens of any unfavorable outcomes (including political fallout) can be shared, since the pre-approved specifics will be clear. Written plans also allow you to reflect on a project, building on its successes and making improvements to avoid repeating its failures.

Creating a Formal Project Plan

Formal project plans should include certain sections. While a plan may use different headings or organization, the content should typically include these basic components: overview, general approach, scope of work, testing plan, implementation plan, implementation team, schedule, budget, a completion evaluation, and an executive summary. Here's a brief description of each:

- **Overview** is a very general description of your project. This may include background, reasons for the project requirements (including plenty of details), and what you want to accomplish. Also include the benefit your organization will receive by completing this project.

- **General Approach** should be a more detailed description of how you are going to accomplish the goals of the project. This is not as detailed as the Implementation Plan. A manager who has a high-level knowledge of SMS should be able to read this and understand the tasks that need to be performed in order to complete this project.

- **Scope of the Work** should include all the systems and staff that will be affected in any way by the implementation of your project. Also include details regarding why and to what extent the systems and staff will be affected.

- **Testing Plan** is a very detailed outline of what you will test, why you will test it, and in what order the testing will occur. There should also be a detailed description of your test environment.

- **Implementation Plan** is a detailed plan describing the tasks necessary to implement your product and in what order the implementation tasks must take place. Include a rollback plan in case the implementation should fail. Also include any other tasks that must be performed for the rollout to be successful. Finally, add a verification process to provide proof that the project was successful.

- **Implementation Team** includes anyone who has involvement with the implementation of the product.

- **Schedule** should include starting and completion dates for testing, implementation, and the completion summary for your project. Be as realistic as possible, so you don't have to change the schedule. It's good *public relations* (PR).

- **Budget** should include *all* expenses necessary for your plan. Don't forget to include consulting services, additional third party software, software licensing, maintenance, and travel.

- **Completion Evaluation** should be done after some pre-determined period following implementation, and can be extremely valuable for future reference. Here, you want to include a description of the outcome of this project on each level. It's important to include both positive and negative results. This will allow you to repeat the things that went well and change the things that did not.

- **Executive Summary** re-emphasizes the main points of your plan (in plain English for the non-esoteric).

The recommendations thus far will be useful for the vast majority of organizations because most companies develop project plans around a specific technology. Some companies have adopted the *Microsoft Operations Framework (MOF)* or *Microsoft Solutions Framework (MSF)* project methodologies. These are solutions-based approaches that develop processes in an effort to solve a specific problem, or fill a business need. In general, these project methodologies require considerably more manpower to operate than the standard project planning approach, but are also more flexible, allowing the organization to "plug in" any tool that will do the job. Many companies find it difficult to adopt this approach because of its complexity and the amount of resources that they must commit to the project.

Processes Requiring a Project Plan

Now that we've explored the content of a formal project plan, let's look at some of the types of processes requiring one.

- SMS add-on components

- Adding new sites

- Service pack upgrades

- Server rebuilds

- Product evaluations

- Some software distributions

Software distribution scenarios that need a formal project plan include:

- **LARGE SOFTWARE DISTRIBUTIONS** — These should be treated like projects, especially those that require formal application testing. In many distribution scenarios, there is no need for a formal plan, but some sort of written plan should be crafted. The plan should have a section that includes distribution notes to outline any special issues or tasks that must be performed. This will aid in troubleshooting and with similar future installations. It's in your best interest.

- **APPLICATIONS REQUIRING INTEGRATION TESTING** — For example, most organizations formally test the Microsoft Office upgrades. Test not only for the success or failure of the install, but also for integration problems that could occur with other programs installed on machines and existing documents. Testing is especially important for large organizations, or those that rely heavily upon the application being targeted for the upgrade.

- **LARGE ORGANIZATIONS** — Especially those that have multiple SMS administrators involved in a distribution.

- **VERY COMPLICATED INSTALLATIONS** — It can be helpful to have a specific plan for more complicated installations.

Testing

Acquiring a proper SMS testing environment, isolated from production, is invaluable. The need for testing many aspects of SMS is critical and should be an ongoing process. By having a dedicated testing lab, you will not be as likely to skip the testing process. This lab can be as simple as one primary server, one child server, and a few clients. In some scenarios, even virtual computing technologies could be utilized.

Critical tasks that require testing, before they are released into an existing SMS production environment, include:

- Software distribution

- Service pack rollouts

- Feature and component configuration changes

- SMS server hardware migration or OS/SQL upgrades

- Troubleshooting

Software Distribution Should Be Tested

Software distribution is a bit different than other tasks. Most organizations distribute software on a regular basis. When you are first learning to create and distribute packages, use an isolated testing environment to practice. It is quite easy to inadvertently send a package to the entire company. While in the test environment, you can experiment without the stress of accidentally sending advertised programs to a production machine. Properly constructed labs should provide a comfortable learning environment. If software distribution is new to your organization, begin to create standard software distribution processes while in the testing environment. After you are comfortable with the process, document it. Then try it out on a few production machines. If you have existing distribution processes at your organization, become familiar with these processes while in the testing environment. Once comfortable with it, move into production, but follow the approved processes.

SMS Service Pack Rollouts Should Be Tested

SMS service packs are quite different than service packs for other Microsoft products. SMS servers need to be upgraded in a specific order, beginning with the top-most server in the hierarchy. Due to the dependency that SMS has on other Microsoft applications and services, upgrades are more complicated. Clients will generally require an advertised program to perform the upgrade. It is not prudent to perform an SMS service pack upgrade based on information that other administrators are posting on Internet news groups and forums. These are excellent resources for finding pitfalls that others have found, but you can't rely totally on their reports. It is not possible to be sure exactly what will happen in your organization, unless you run the upgrade in a simulation of your own production environment.

Feature and Component Configuration Changes Should Be Tested

Component configuration changes can produce some unexpected results. SMS is a powerful application that has the ability to cause a company to experience a loss in revenue due to system downtime. Misconfiguring SMS in a production environment could get an administrator into serious trouble. However, in the proper testing environment, configuration changes can be performed and then monitored prior to attempting them in the production environment.

SMS Server Upgrades

Server hardware and software upgrades that affect SMS or the operating system can be quite complicated. There are multiple items to consider, such as client access, parent and child access, loss of data, and synchronization. By properly planning for these issues and testing the plan in the lab, your chances of success are much greater.

Troubleshooting

Lack of a suitable lab is the primary reason many organizations purchase Microsoft technical support calls. A lab can give you the ability to recreate problems and try solutions without disrupting your users. A company benefits in two ways when they supply the proper equipment for a lab:

- SMS administrators become more knowledgeable and more efficient.

- Technical support calls are reduced dramatically.

Creating an SMS Testing Lab

There are a few variables to consider when building the lab:

- **HOW SIMILAR TO YOUR SMS PRODUCTION IMPLEMENTATION DO YOU WANT THE LAB TO BE?** — At times, to properly test certain scenarios, some hardware in the test environment should be identical to the hardware in the production environment. Specifically, OS upgrades require this. Upgrading from Windows 2000 Server to Windows 2003 Server is a good example of the need to have identical software. Having identical hardware is most critical for SMS primary servers.

  Most SMS scenarios can be properly tested on hardware that is not identical to your production environment. Your lab should mirror the types of SMS servers and the design of the hierarchy in your production environment.

  For example, a certain production environment has a central server, 20 primary servers, and 30 secondary sites. All sites are separated via WAN links. Clients include Windows 2000, Windows XP, and Windows Server Family. A proper test lab for this implementation will include:

  - **INFRASTRUCTURE SERVERS** — These should include domain controllers, DHCP and DNS.

  - **ONE SMS CENTRAL SITE SERVER** — The hardware needs to be capable of supporting domain controller services and, of course, SMS and SQL. The same OS, Service Pack (SP), SMS SP, and SQL SP as the production server should also be installed.

  - **SMS PRIMARY SERVERS** — One to represent each OS and SMS version and SP that is in your production environment.

- **SMS SECONDARY SERVERS** — One to represent each OS and SMS version and SP that is in your production environment.

- **OTHER SMS SITE SYSTEMS SERVERS** — You should include standalone MPs and DPs if they are in your production environment.

- **ROUTING DEVICE** — This network hardware needs to have the ability to create multiple networks. The idea is to simulate the network addressing that is provided on your production network. A layer-three switch with the ability to create Virtual Local Area Networks (VLANs) is ideal.

- **CLIENTS** — Provide one system for each OS that is in the production implementation. Simulate production OSs and service packs.

- **WHAT IS YOUR BUDGET FOR THE LAB?** — Of course, this is the most limiting factor. You may find it necessary to utilize desktop machines as test lab servers. New high-end desktops are capable of running OS\SMS\SQL server software in a lab environment. If it is necessary to negotiate with someone for your lab equipment, there are some items that you *must* have to perform proper testing:

  - **THE ROUTING DEVICE** — This is necessary if you have multiple sites with multiple network addresses and you must test roaming scenarios. It would be preferable for testing software distributions, but is not a requirement.

  - **ACCESS TO IDENTICAL HARDWARE FOR SOME PROJECTS** — It is not necessary to have identical server hardware on a daily basis, but when performing server hardware and software upgrades and migrations, it is a necessity.

- **HOW MUCH SPACE WILL BE AVAILABLE?** — If limited space is available for a test lab, consider purchasing a Keyboard Video Mouse (KVM) switch. This will reduce the need for multiple monitors. Also, explore purchasing rack mount equipment.

- **WILL THE HARDWARE BE SHARED WITH OTHER SUPPORT TEAMS?** — Cost could be a factor, but rally for a dedicated SMS network. It can become problematic if other support engineers are adding or removing systems and software from your lab. However, you may find it necessary to share hardware that is identical to your production primary or central servers. Try to schedule this equipment to be available to you throughout the duration of a project that requires it.

As indicated earlier in this section, the test lab environment must sometimes mirror your production servers in order to recreate a problem. In order to *really* see how an SMS server is going to react in a given situation, you must simulate the production machine as closely as possible within the test environment. There are a couple of ways to approach this. You can attempt to back up the production server, and then restore it to the test server. Or you can build the test server, paying close attention to each detail. Below are a few tips for each method.

Building a Primary Test Server

There are several methods for building a test server. Your approach depends on how similar your test server will be to its production counterpart.

- **FRESH INSTALL** — There aren't many stipulations on building this type of server. If your goal is to simply learn about a basic SMS process or feature, this is a good approach. If there is any serious testing to be performed, make sure to install the same OS and SP along with the same SMS SP as the server's production counterpart. This build isn't recommended for any troubleshooting or in-depth testing.

- **RESTORE A RECENT SMS BACKUP FROM THE PRODUCTION COUNTERPART OF THE TEST SERVER** — This approach will allow you to restore a test server so that its SMS-related databases, files, components, and registry settings mirror the server's production counterpart. This option provides a relatively simple way to recreate a production server in an isolated test environment. This approach can be used for systems that are exact hardware replicas of the production SMS server. It will also provide a mirror installation of a production SMS server on a desktop test machine. This option provides a test server build that is sufficient for most scenarios.

- **VIRTUAL COMPUTING TEST BEDS CAN BE USED WHERE IDENTICAL HARDWARE IS NOT REQUIRED** — This is a software solution that allows multiple OSs to run on the same hardware simultaneously. The benefits are cost savings and a rollback technology that allows the administrator to restart the system and discard the changes.

- **SMS RECOVERY EXPERT** — Microsoft only supports the recommendations in the *SMS Recovery Expert,* which is included with the SMS 2003 installation. The Recovery Expert is designed to help you restore and synchronize a failed SMS site. While this tool is quite helpful, it doesn't cover every situation. For situations not covered in the SMS Recovery Expert, view the **All SMS Recovery Tasks** list, also located in the SMS Recovery Expert documentation, to determine what items need to be performed.

Restoring a Test Server with the SMS Site Repair Wizard

This procedure works best when attempting to restore an SMS central site server into a lab situation with a single site. The procedure will work in a multiple SMS site hierarchy, but the setup becomes a bit more complicated, requiring the parent and child sites also to be restored from the production environment and to be resynchronized with each other. If you wish to restore a test server using the SMS Site Repair Wizard, perform these tasks:

1. Build the test server.

2. Perform a full backup of the production SMS server with the SMS Backup task.

3. Notice what items the SMS Backup exports.

4. Verify that the backup was successful.

5. Copy the entire *<SiteCode>* directory.

6. Utilize the SMS Site Repair Wizard to restore the test site with production data.

Let's look at the detailed steps of each of these tasks.

First, build the test server, using the same name and domain as the production server where the SMS backup will be performed. It is important for the SMS hierarchy in the test lab to mirror the SMS hierarchy in the production environment prior to attempting this procedure; otherwise, you may experience unexpected results. For best results, use the same versions of the following software components that were installed on the production counterpart of this server:

- OS and service pack

- Microsoft SQL Server and service pack

- SMS and service pack

Next, perform a full backup of the production SMS server with the SMS Backup task, by following these steps:

1. In the SMS Administrator Console, open the Hierarchy tree from the left pane, and then open the site where you will perform the backup.

2. Open the **Database Maintenance** tree and select **Tasks.** You will see the tasks enumerated in the right pane (see Figure 5.1).

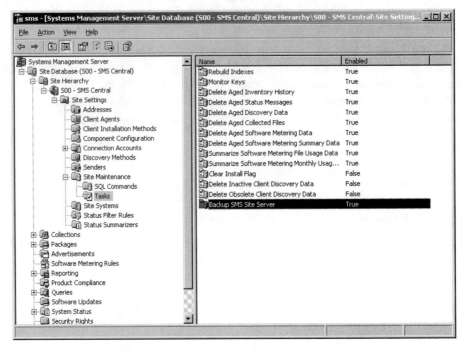

Figure 5.1: Viewing Database Maintenance Tasks.

3. Open the **Backup SMS Site Server** task (see Figure 5.2).

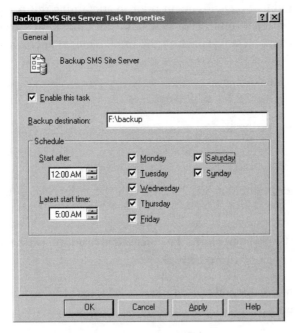

Figure 5.2: Configuring Backup SMS Site Server Task.

4. Select the **Enable** check box.

5. Supply the path to the location where you want the backup files to be placed. Use Universal Naming Convention (UNC) paths, such as \\SMSCentral\Backup, or local machine paths, such as F:\backup.

6. Configure the schedule to occur at a certain time by supplying the necessary information. Schedule backups to occur when the server is not being used and when it is not being backed up by your third party server backup software (if one is being used).

7. Start a backup session immediately by going to **Control Panel**⇨ **Computer Management**⇨ **Services and Applications**. Right-click **SMS_Site_Backup** (see Figure 5.3) and then choose **Start**.

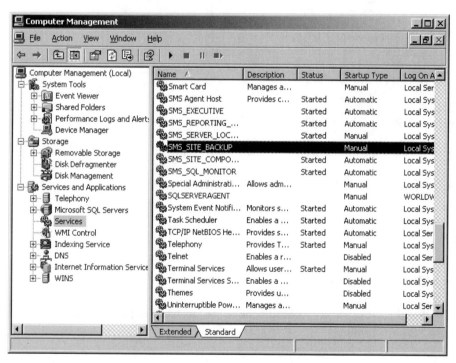

Figure 5.3: Starting a Manual SMS Backup.

The backup export package is located at the path that you entered in the SMS site backup task (see Figure 5.4). A folder named with the site code is created with two sub-folders for the site database server, and site server. Each sub-folder is filled with registry keys and files.

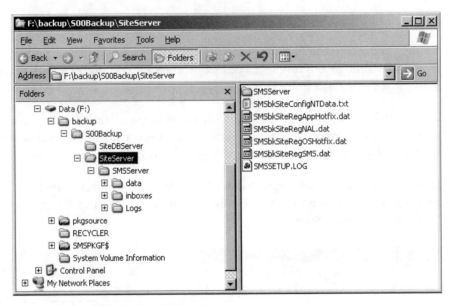

Figure 5.4: Viewing SMS Backup Export Package.

Notice what items the SMS Backup exports:

- SMS database information including SQL Configuration and SQL data

- All files located in \\<*SiteServerName*>\SMS\inbox and \\<*SiteServerName*>\SMS\Logs

- SMS-related registry keys

- SMS configuration data

- SMS backup log file

To verify that the backup was successful, check the Smsbkup.log in the <*SiteCode*> directory at the backup export location.

Next, copy the entire <*SiteCode*> directory from the backup package into the test lab.

Utilize the SMS Site Repair Wizard to restore the test site with production data, by following these steps:

1. Choose the **Start⇨ Programs⇨ Systems Management Server⇨ SMS Site Repair Wizard** menu item to bring up the wizard shown in Figure 5.5.

Figure 5.5: SMS Site Repair Wizard.

2. On the **Welcome** page of the wizard, verify that the name of the site server that you are repairing appears in the **Site server to be repaired** input text box. If so, click the **Next** button.

3. On the **Access Rights and Permissions Required** page of the wizard, ensure that the account displayed beside the **Current user account** label has the rights and permissions required to perform the repair process (see Figure 5.6). If so, click the **Next** button.

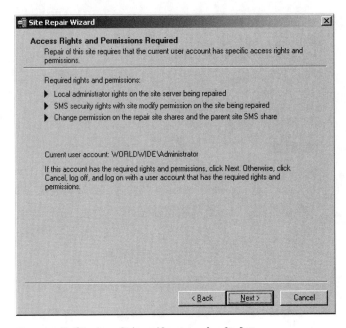

Figure 5.6: Verifying Access Rights and Permissions for a Site Restore.

4. On the **Site Restore Steps** page (see Figure 5.7), browse to the site backup export package that you previously copied to the lab (when you copied the entire *<SiteCode>* directory). Click the **Next** button.

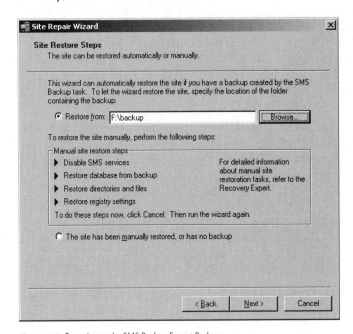

Figure 5.7: Browsing to the SMS Backup Export Package.

5. On the **Restore Database** page, select **Restore the database from SMS backup** (see Figure 5.8), and click the **Next** button.

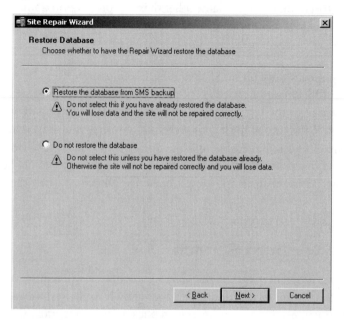

Figure 5.8: Restoring the Database from SMS Backup.

6. Complete the remaining pages in the wizard based on the specifics of the SMS site and hierarchy that exist in your test lab.

Full Restore of the Production Server to a Test Box

This restore method is required only if you need to restore an exact replica of the production SMS server to identical hardware, such as situations where you want to test OS upgrades or driver issues. The outcome will be an exact replica of the production server. This restore requires a complete backup of the production server using Windows Backup or third-party backup software, such as ArcServe or Backup Exec. The test lab requires the same domain name as the production domain.

 **NOTE**

This backup and restore method is not supported by Microsoft for production servers.

If you are fortunate enough to be able to transfer a backup job from your production network to an isolated test network, you can save the steps required to build a server from scratch. If your server is going to be placed into a domain with a name other than the production domain, you'll need to do some additional "hacking." This book doesn't provide any recommended procedures for this.

Prior to initiating the backup process, disable all SMS and SQL services. The test server will, of course, need to have the same OS and service pack as the production server that you are backing up. Restore the production server to the test box. Be sure to include the registry and overwrite files with the same names. Once the restore to the test server is complete, you must remove the server from the test lab domain and rejoin it, because the *Security Identifier* will change. The Security Identifier is a unique descriptor that is associated with the computer name. Security Identifiers are created during OS installation and stored in Active Directory when the system joins the domain.

Building a Test Server from Scratch

This method is tedious, but in a different way than the previous method. It will require you to go through each OS configuration on the production server and apply it to the test server. Again, this method is required only if you need to restore an exact replica of the production SMS server to identical hardware, such as situations where you want to test OS upgrades or driver issues. The outcome will be an exact replica of the production server. Applications, including service packs, hot fixes, and drivers need to be applied in the same order as on the production server. Once the OS is configured, you can take advantage of the SMS Site Repair Wizard. It's not necessary to configure SMS components to match the production machine—this will happen automatically in the restore process. Once the test server is a mirror of your production server (with the exception of the SMS configuration), go to the "Restoring a Test Server with the SMS Site Repair Wizard" section in this chapter. Start the restore process for a backup performed by the SMS backup task on the production server that you are trying to simulate. It may seem like "overkill" for you to spend so much time on your test server. For many scenarios it is, but not all. OS upgrades are one such exception. For example, earlier in my career, I was the project lead for migrating a primary server to a new hardware platform, a new OS, and a new version of MS SQL Server. This server had an earlier version of SMS installed, but the concept is applicable for today. I planned to move the data to the new box using SMS backup. This would require moving the data from a Windows NT 4.0 and SQL Server 7.0 platform to a Windows 2000 and SQL Server 2000 platform. It seemed more logical to upgrade the existing production server to Windows 2000 and SQL 2000 prior to performing the SMS backup task. Before trying the upgrade on my production primary server, I tried it on an exact replica in my isolated test lab.

The Windows 2000 upgrade rendered the machine useless. The upgrade didn't like the RAID controller driver and insisted on a Windows 2000 driver. We downloaded one from the vendor's Web site and followed the directions. On the reboot, the machine would not even boot and eventually had to be rebuilt. Without a proper test server, the production primary server—at the top of my production hierarchy—would have suffered that same fate.

Virtual Computing Test Beds

There are some newer software products on the market that take advantage of virtual machines. *Virtual machines* are computing environments that run independently of the host machine's operating system. The virtual machine makes use of the host machine's hardware, but does not affect its OS or files in anyway. Within the virtual machine, OSs and other applications can be installed and operated simultaneously with the host system and even other virtual machines. Figure 5.9 shows an example of a Virtual Machine interface.

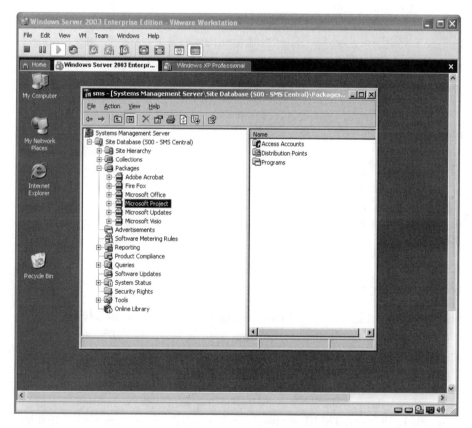

Figure 5.9: Virtual Machine Guest Interface.

Making use of the host machine's NIC, the virtual machine can connect to networks and communicate with other systems. End-users access the virtual machines through a window, just like any other application.

Virtual computing provides multiple benefits to IT professionals. The most obvious benefit is a major cost savings on hardware. Bear in mind, the OS vendor's disk space and memory requirements still apply. These requirements must be satisfied on the host machine, but memory and disk space are pretty inexpensive these days. An entire test lab can be built on one system. Another benefit is the *undoable disk* feature. This allows changes to a system to be discarded when shutting down the system. This feature can save quite a lot of time. Now administrators and desktop engineers can enjoy the same advantages that virtual computing has been offering software developers for years. As long as you have plenty of memory and disk space, this technology can be a great option for a test lab where similar hardware is not a requirement. The price for a workstation application that provides this capability ranges from about $129 to $200.

There are two industry leaders in the virtual computing software market. VMware (`http://www.vmware.com/`) offers a product called VMware Workstion, along with other similar products. Microsoft offers Virtual PC and Virtual Server (see `http://www.microsoft.com/windows/virtualpc/default.mspx`). Both vendors offer free versions of the server product.

Communication

Practicing good communication will help you become a respected member of your company. Unfortunately, a few poor choices in this area can be quite hard to overcome. As SMS administrators, we have the responsibility of communicating with end-users and other IT staff members about SMS events that may affect them. It's important for this communication to be timely and professional.

From the User's Point of View

Any changes that are noticeable to the end-user require communication in advance. These changes could include, but are not limited to, software distribution, SMS software upgrades, and remote control.

When used carelessly, software distribution can adversely affect the productivity of an entire organization. Generally speaking, users don't appreciate having someone forcing them to install software in the middle of the workday. They also don't like to have their workstation disabled by an upgrade they didn't want in the first place. Users tend to dislike surprises of this nature.

If possible, distribute software after-hours. If it is necessary to distribute software during the day, send a preparation e-mail a few days in advance. Explain when the distribution will occur, what they will experience, and why it is necessary. Notify helpdesk personnel prior to releasing a software distribution. This will help them to better serve the end-user if problems arise and it can help them to notify the software distribution team more quickly if the distribution does not go as planned. This will help to prepare them for upcoming interruptions and to minimize complaints. When SMS software distributions could negatively affect system performance, end-users need to be notified. Don't just hope they won't notice. Go to the lab and find out what will happen. Then let users know—before they experience it. It's wise to find a way to minimize the effects, but at least communicate when you expect issues to occur. Even if end-users are unaffected, their view of your SMS team will be more positive. Creating and publishing policies that govern software distribution can also be helpful. This will help to clarify the standards that your team has in place for distributing software.

Develop standard company branding for installation programs that require a user interface. Something with the company logo and standard colors will help end-users feel more at ease when installation interfaces appear on the displays. They will be more willing to cooperate when they are assured that the software installation is approved.

Communicating with customers about the status of software distribution requests is also important. Customers include anyone who is requesting service from your team. It is wise to keep customers up to date on the entire software distribution process from the time they initiate a request until the conclusion of the distribution. Offering reports for requested software distributions is a helpful way to give customers a dynamic view of the distribution status.

Communication Vehicles

There are several methods that can be used to communicate between IT support staff and end-users. Some communication tools include: e-mail distribution lists, intranet sites, open issues documents, a status update, and Instant Messenger (IM).

Distribution lists are one method to keep your SMS staff members up to date. You can then archive the e-mails to the distribution list for documentation. The archive becomes a real time-saver when you need to refer back to previous issues. Many times, SMS support staff members are located at multiple sites. *Instant Messenger* can be used as a tool to communicate and can save an organization both time and money.

An SMS *intranet site* can be a great way to centralize support information. From such a site, links to SMS information and tools can be added, such as project plans, a list of available packages, support documents, training documents, and Web-based SMS tools. Web-enabled spreadsheets and documents can be available for support staff to enter and edit SMS-related information.

An *open issues document* can help you in many ways and should include an open issues section and a history section. For each entry, include a date for when the issue was opened and closed, which staff member was assigned, and a details section. Having this document helps to keep the SMS administrators focused on tasks that need to be completed. Other IT staff can look at the open issues document to see the status of issues that may concern them. Others can see progress that the team has made (great public relations). An open issues document provides good support for hiring more SMS staff and is handy to use during annual review periods as well.

Try sending a weekly *status update newsletter* to all your IT staff. HTML pages with links work really well. The content should include any information about upcoming SMS events, such as software distribution, SMS upgrades, support tools, policies, or any other changes that may affect them. The update should also highlight open SMS issues that the team has worked on in the last week and any new issues that have been added to the list.

Sending HTML pages to end-users via e-mail conveniently communicates SMS events that may affect them. This method allows for the use of plenty of dialog box screenshots for illustration, without becoming too large.

Distribution Process Standard

Another important component of public relations, in software delivery, is a distribution process standard. Such a standard will ensure that all parties involved in the software distribution process understand what will occur. A distribution process standard should include the following components:

- **REQUEST SUBMISSION** — This is the process for submitting software distribution requests. It is typically used by systems and IT staff members. If requests are made often, an online form should be created. Otherwise, an e-mail documenting the specifics of the request could be used. Specifics of the request will differ based on the services that are provided by the software delivery team. Requests should include:

  - What exactly is being requested

  - Who is requesting it

  - When it should be delivered

  - Why it is being requested

  - Where the source files are

  - Whether any packaging or wrapper scripts have been written previously

- Who the contact person is

The distribution team should provide a standard turnaround time for acknowledging requests. To qualify for good PR, the team should have a response within 2 to 3 days.

- **PACKAGE CREATION** — This is the process of building an SMS package, from start to finish. Create standard procedures for tasks such as:

  - Repackaging

  - Creating wrappers

  - Including scripts

  - Choosing the location of the SMS package source files

  - Choosing the location of any scripts created by the distribution team

  - Creating user interfaces for programs

  - Updating distribution points.

  - Creating Windows Installer (MSI) based packages. This introduces an additional consideration. If SMS clients must run MSI packages from a distribution point, then the package must be created to use a mapped drive or Universal Naming Convention (UNC) path to the folder where the MSI exists. Utilizing the download and run feature for MSI-based packages works fine.

  - Testing and verifying packages. A senior member of the distribution team, and/or the contact person for the request, should verify that the package performs as requested. (See the following bullet).

- **TESTING** — Determine if the SMS advertised program will run without failing or causing new problems on target machines. Here are some guidelines for testing software distributions:

  - The distribution should first be sent to 4-5 non-production machines at each site where the package will be distributed.

  - Create a test group from each SMS site. Send an e-mail that communicates the urgency for users to notify the distribution team of any errors that occur during or after the installation. Use voting buttons to automate the process. Give them a standard number of days to respond, indicating that if you don't hear from them, it is assumed that they have no problems.

- Follow up on any notifications of errors from the test group and document the results. *This is a critical step!* If any errors are reported, check them out thoroughly and address any necessary issues. If a major modification to the program occurs, it must be tested again. Also, monitor installation status messages for the program with status view or Advertisement Status Viewer. Advertised programs that are distributed with errors can severely damage public relations between the user population and IT staff. There are two types of errors: perceived and actual.

  Perceived errors include messages that the end-user may interpret as an error, but really do not affect the machine in a negative way. While you know that there is no true error, the message is causing a negative perception with users. Find these bogus error messages through testing and then suppress them.

  Actual errors are true errors that occur. They may not be obvious to the user at the time the program runs. Distributing programs that cause the end-user and IT staff problems will severely impact your effectiveness at your organization and the employees' general perception of SMS.

  Once all known errors occurring within the test group are investigated, you should document the following:

  - Users that reported errors

  - The results of your investigation of the errors

  - Solutions that were implemented for the errors

- **DELIVERY** — Includes the specifics surrounding the delivery of SMS advertised programs. Some points to consider:

  - Time of day when the deliveries will occur

  - End-user notification

  - Machine status at the time of delivery. Indicate how the advertised program will run (for example, only when a user is logged in, etc.).

  - What machines or end-users will be excluded from standard deliveries, such as Servers or Executives.

- **EVALUATION** — This is documentation that is available to the staff regarding the successes and failures of each distribution. We can all benefit from this information. *Percentage of Successful Installations* is a valuable statistic to include.

Summary

Because SMS interacts with nearly all the machines in an organization, public relations are an important aspect to consider when utilizing SMS features. Software distribution is one feature that is quite visible to the end-user. When planning SMS-related projects, consider the effect on end-users. Help to improve PR by properly planning, testing, and communicating. Software distribution standards need to be created and followed in order to minimally affect end-user productivity. By practicing the suggestions in this chapter, you will help to build better relationships with your customers. The end result will be users who are more willing to cooperate with future SMS projects, and more positive feedback that will make its way to your boss.

DID YOU KNOW?

The next version of SMS, Systems Center Configuration Manager (SCCM), will include a more intuitive SMS Administrator Console. The new console is multi-threaded, which allows multiple tasks to occur at the same time. For example, with the new console administrators can change the properties of multiple console objects simultaneously. Drag and drop functionality will also be available, something that was present in SMS version 1.0 but missing in version 2.0 and version 2003. A new search feature has been added to the Results pane of the console, allowing administrators to filter out unwanted results.

Part II

Using SMS to Distribute Software

Creating and Distributing a Software Package

Many times, when discussing SMS, the term "package" is used in very general terms. A *software distribution package* is only one part of a distribution, and contains the files that are necessary for an SMS advertised program to run. Configuration information for advertised programs, selected distribution points, and access accounts are also present in a package. This information is derived from the advertised programs, distribution points, and access accounts property settings within the package. After reading this chapter, you will have a better understanding of the package creation and distribution process of SMS software distribution. *Software distribution* is the process of automating various types of software installations and configurations from a central point. Successful software distribution occurs when SMS administrators follow best practice guidelines for creating and distributing software packages. In this chapter, you will learn, in detail, the steps that are necessary to create and distribute a software package. You will discover the considerations that must be made when distributing software to Windows operating systems. Finally, you will learn how to perform package management tasks that need to occur after a distribution has been initiated.

SMS software distribution is comprised of two major tasks: *distributing packages* and *advertising programs*. While the combination of these two processes results in the delivery of software to targeted SMS resources, they are very different. Package distribution is the combination of SMS processes necessary to move package source files to selected distribution points and to create programs that can be run by SMS clients. Advertisements are notifications to SMS user, group and system resources indicating that they are eligible to run a specific SMS program. This chapter describes the first of the two major tasks—distributing software. This chapter provides a detailed approach to creating and distributing software packages within the SMS Administration Console. The next chapter covers advertising programs.

Preparing to Distribute a Package

Before beginning the distribution process, there are a few preliminary items that should be completed:

- **DEVELOP AND TEST THE SOFTWARE PACKAGE THAT WILL BE DISTRIBUTED** — This should be done prior to creating the package, in order to conserve time and network bandwidth. Simply put, SMS software distribution is a delivery system. The package that is being delivered must work properly on its own.

- **MOVE PACKAGE SOURCE FILES TO A STANDARD LOCATION** — Sometimes this location is called the Master Software Repository (MSR). This isn't a critical step, but will make things much easier in the future. As multiple packages are created, administration will be greatly simplified if source files are contained in a standard network location with a standard naming convention. Looking in multiple locations will cause administrators to waste time, and could cause them to distribute the wrong source files.

- **CONFIGURE ADVERTISED PROGRAMS CLIENT AGENTS AND DISTRIBUTION POINTS** — For details on configuring the Advertised Programs Client Agent and distribution points, see Chapter 4.

SMS Package Creation Overview

Software distribution is initiated at the SMS site server, using the Systems Management Server Administrator Console. To distribute software, the SMS administrator must create a complete package, target collection, and advertisement. In this section, you will learn about package creation, including packages, programs, distribution points, and access accounts. This section outlines the steps to create these SMS objects, which are necessary to distribute software.

Creating a Package

To start the process of creating a new package, open the SMS Administrator Console and perform the following steps:

1. From the left pane, right-click the **Package** tree, and then select the **New ⇨ Package** menu item. You will see the **Package Properties** sheet appear. Just like in Figure 6.1, all text boxes will be empty.

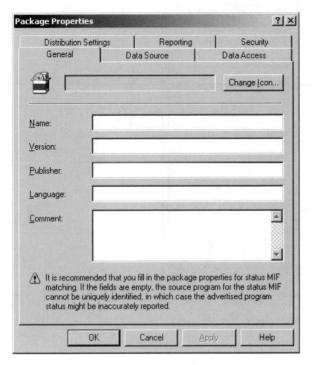

Figure 6.1: Opening the Package Properties Sheet.

2. On the **General** tab, **Name** is a required field. Enter as much information as possible in the remainder of the fields. Best practice is to include information such as who created the package, when it was created, for whom it was created, and any details that may help you or other administrators later, in case a troubleshooting scenario is necessary. This will help to avoid confusion if similar packages are created (see Figure 6.2).

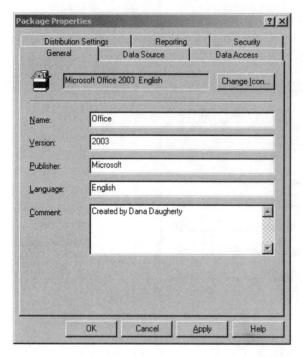

Figure 6.2: Configuring the General Tab.

3. Select the **Data Source** tab.

- Select the **This package contains source files** property, unless the executable is located on the machine where this package will run (see Figure 6.3).

- Click the **Set** button to browse to the source files, and choose a folder to serve as the source folder. This folder must contain the source files or a sub-folder that contains the source files.

- Choose the **Use a compressed copy of the source directory** property if you are creating a package from a CD. The CD will eventually be unavailable, but this option enables you to refresh the distribution points with the compressed version of the source files, which were originally on CD.

- Select the **Always obtain files from a source directory** property, which is the default, if source files will be modified.

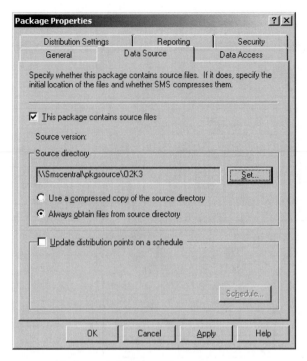

Figure 6.3: Configuring the Data Source Tab.

- Activate the **Update distribution points on a schedule** property if the source files change often. This option copies a new version of the source files at a specified time, and is helpful with scheduling network bandwidth usage.

4. Select the **Data Access** tab.

- Select the **Access distribution folder through common SMS package share** radio button. By default, it is the only option selected (see Figure 6.4). This setting refers to the standard way that SMS creates distribution points (<ServerName>\SMSPKG<DriveLetter>$\<packageID>).

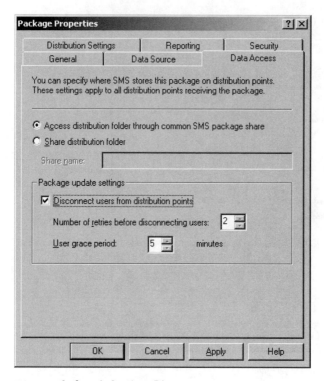

Figure 6.4: Configure the Data Access Tab.

- **Share distribution folder** allows the use of shares other than the standard SMS distribution point shares. One benefit offered here is that a share can be created on a drive of your choice and then be used as a DP, thereby giving you more control over the location of the SMS packages. This gives you the option of choosing a drive that has more free space or one that is underutilized. Another benefit is the ability for users to access the source files using a friendly name, rather than the letter and number combination that SMS assigns to the folder by default.

- Below the **Package update settings** label, enable the **Disconnect users from distribution points** option to avoid having package source files get locked in situations when a client may unexpectedly freeze up in the middle of running an advertised program. When this occurs, distribution points will not be able to update or refresh, because the client has the source files locked.

5. Select the **Distribution Settings** tab (see Figure 6.5).

- The **Sending priority** property works in conjunction with the **Availability** option on the **Schedule** tab, located on the property sheet of an address used for distribution points in a child site (see Figure 6.6). To access the properties of an address from within the SMS Administrator Console, open the Site Hierarchy tree from the left pane. Next, open the site where you want to view an address and open the **Site Settings**⇨ **Addresses** tree. From the right pane, select an address and open the properties sheet. These features are designed to work together to provide better control over bandwidth utilization. If both components are left at their default settings, package distribution points will not be restricted based on priority.

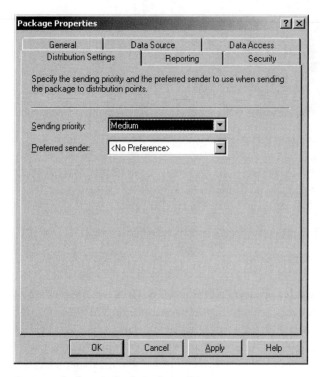

Figure 6.5: Configure the Distribution Settings Tab.

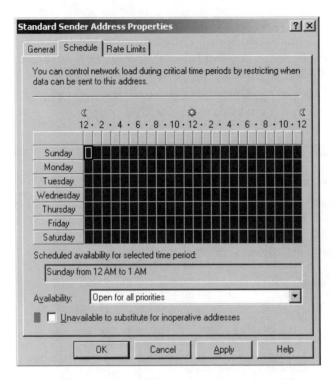

Figure 6.6: Configure the Schedule Tab

- The **Preferred sender** property corresponds to the available senders. Its configuration is necessary only if you have multiple WAN connections to child sites. To access the properties of a sender, open the Site Hierarchy tree from the left pane. Next, open the site where you want to view a sender and open the **Site Settings**⇨ **Senders** tree. From the right pane, select a sender and open the properties sheet.

6. Select the **Reporting** tab. This feature will enable you to use custom installation status Management Information Format (MIF) matching. It is probably one of the most helpful but least utilized software package property options. *Management Information Formats* are text files with .MIF extensions that contain installation status information. Typically, at the beginning of an application installation, a MIF is written locally with a status of "Failed." If the installation completes successfully, the MIF is overwritten with a status of "Success." A standard format is used so that SMS can read the status information from a variety of application installations and insert it into the database, to be viewed by administrators. For detailed information about installation status MIFs, see Chapter 12.

- Select the **Use these fields for MIF matching** property, if you have a custom MIF that you want to match (see Figure 6.7).

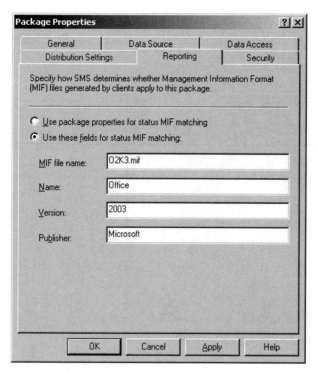

Figure 6.7: Configure the Reporting Tab.

- Add the name of the installation status MIF in the **MIF file name** field. This is the MIF that will be placed in the %WINdir%, %WINdir%\temp or %Temp% folders on the client by the installation program.

- Notice that **Name**, **Version**, and **Publisher** are optional fields. They are used to differentiate between two MIF files of the same name. Currently, most programs include the use of installation status MIFs. SMS advertised programs will return generic information based on the Package properties if you elect to use the default property setting, **Use package properties for status MIF matching.**

- To view installation status MIF messages that are returned to the site server, open the **System Status** tree, then open the **Advertisement Status** tree. From the left pane, open the advertisement where you want to view the MIF information. From the right pane, right-click on the site where the client reports, and choose the **All** menu item to see all status messages. If you have configured the **Reporting** tab to match a custom MIF file, and advertised programs run and gather a successful status MIF file, status messages with the ID of 10009 and 10007 will appear in the list. These messages will have the contents of the status MIF files.

7. Select the **Security** tab. The **Class security rights** window provides the ability to administer security rights for all packages (see Figure 6.8). The **Instance security rights** window provides the ability to administer security rights for the package that is currently being configured.

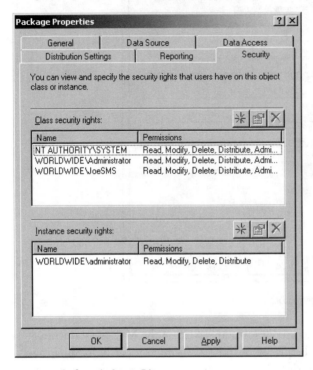

Figure 6.8: Configure the Security Tab.

8. Click the **OK** button. You will see your new package appear under the **Packages** tree (see Figure 6.9).

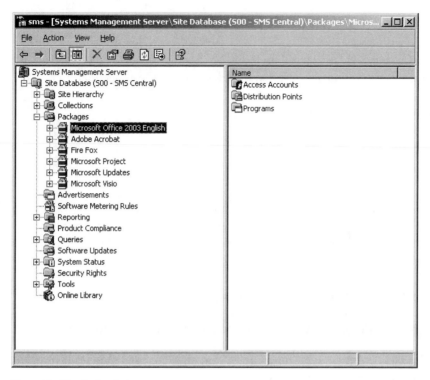

Figure 6.9: View the New Package.

Tips for Creating Packages

Source files should not be updated in the middle of a distribution. If this occurs, clients that complete the installation before the files are updated will receive different versions of the source files than those that complete the installation after the source files have been updated. When you determine that the source files need to be updated, the distribution should be stopped and new plans for installation need to be made. Clients may also receive errors because they will be contending for the same files as SMS Distribution Manager. In this case, the advertised program should be disabled. Do this within the SMS Administrator Console. Right-click on the advertisement and choose the **All Tasks**⇨ **Disable Program** menu item.

Providing class package rights affects all packages for the site—you should grant SMS administrators only the most necessary permissions to perform their responsibilities.

Package source files won't be updated when the **Sending Priority** property configured for a package is lower than the **Availability** property configured on the **Schedule** tab for a selected address.

Configuring Package Access Accounts

Package access accounts are used by all users and SMS components to access distribution points. The following generic accounts are created by default for each package that is created:

- Administrator = Full Control

- User = Read

- Guest = Read

As discussed in Chapter 3, generic access accounts are mapped to Windows Server Family local (for member servers) or domain (for domain controllers) user or group accounts on the individual DPs. Refer back to Table 3.1 in Chapter 3 for a mapping of the default generic access accounts to the actual Windows Server accounts.

Let's review the steps for adding additional package access accounts:

1. Open the **Packages** tree and open the package that you want to configure.

2. Right-click the **Access Accounts** tree from the left pane and select the **New** menu option. Select the proper type of account.

3. The **Access Accounts** properties sheet will appear (see Figure 6.10). Add the proper account and permissions information and click the **OK** button. Accounts can also be deleted from the right pane. Never delete the Administrator package access account. It is needed to update distribution points.

See Chapter 3 for more information on access accounts.

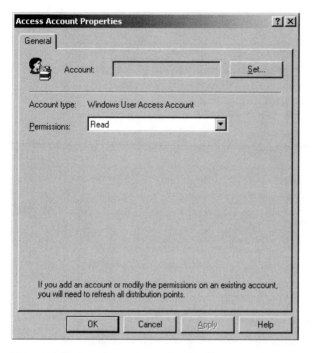

Figure 6.10: Viewing the Access Accounts Properties Sheet.

Assigning Distribution Points to Packages

Once a package is created, distribution points will need to be selected so clients can access the installation programs. To select distribution points where package source files will be copied, do the following:

1. From the left pane, open the **Packages** tree, and then open a package where you want to assign distribution points (see Figure 6.11).

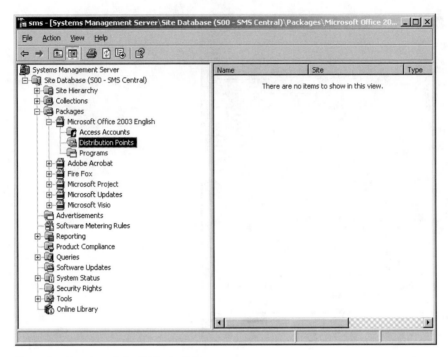

Figure 6.11: Preparing to Assign Distribution Points.

2. Right-click on the **Distribution Points** tree and select the **New**⇨ **Distribution Points** menu item. The **New Distribution Point** wizard will appear.

3. Click the **Next** button. View the list of available distribution points where package source files can be copied (see Figure 6.12). Make your selection.

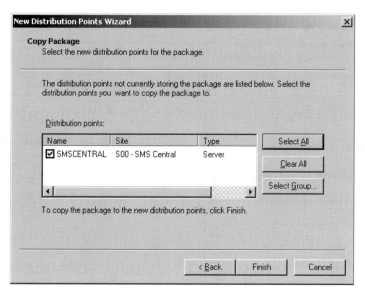

Figure 6.12: Assigning Distribution Points.

4. When you click the **Finish** button, the site server will begin the process of copying source files to all selected distribution points.

SMS Package Concepts

IT support staff members who are new to SMS software distribution may find it difficult to grasp the concepts of packages and advertised programs. Typically, a *program* is thought of as the executable that is responsible for the installation of the package source files to the client system. SMS advertised programs are a set of instructions that control package execution. In other words, advertised programs tell SMS clients *how* to execute a certain installation executable or script. The instructions presented to the client are beyond a simple pointer to an installation file. Other details, such as OS platforms, command line switches, disk space, logon state, user context, and rebooting are included in the instruction set. The next section will help you to select the proper configuration options when creating programs.

Creating an SMS Program

To create a program, select a package from the left pane. Then right-click the **Programs** tree and select the **New** menu item. The **Program Properties** sheet will appear, as shown in Figure 6.13. Let's look at each tab on this sheet in detail, and how to configure the options available on each.

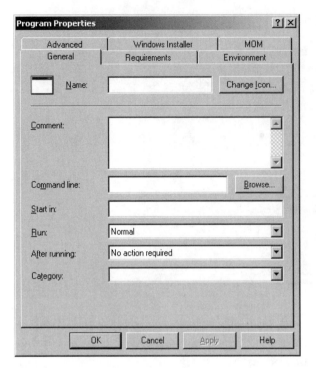

Figure 6.13: Program Properties.

The General Tab

On this tab, enter the program name and comments. Remember that the comments are visible to the users in the **Run Advertised Programs** dialog box, so they should be inoffensive and meaningful to the user. The program name must be unique within a package and cannot be changed later (see Figure 6.14).

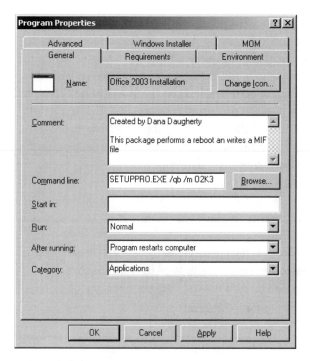

Figure 6.14: Configuring the General Tab.

Click the **Browse** button to bring up a dialog box that contains the folders and files located in the source folder. The source folder was configured on the **Data Source** tab in the **Package** properties (refer back to Figure 6.3). The source folder can contain different files than those available on distribution points if a distribution point update has not occurred since the files were added or removed from the source folder. By default, only files with an .EXE extension will be visible. To see other files, such as batch files, select the **All Files** option from the **Files of Type** drop-down box. After choosing a file, click the **Open** button to return to the **General** tab. Your selection shows up in the **Command Line** text box.

You can manually add the name of an installation program or script, located in either the package, the local Windows directory, the PATH statement, or the **Start in** text box to the **Command Line** text box. Switches and other command line syntax can be included as well.

The **Start In** property is an optional text box that helps the client to locate the installation directory. The entry can refer to the client or the distribution point.

The **Run** property allows administrators to configure the *program mode*. Program mode refers to the program interface size. The default is **Normal** mode. **Minimized**, **Maximized** and **Hidden** are also available. The **Hidden** option is especially useful for silent deployments. The options for this setting have no effect on the **Advertised Program Notification** dialog box, if it is configured to appear.

The **After running** property allows administrators to assign actions to client machines after the program completes successfully. The **No action** value is the default setting. **SMS restarts the computer**, **Program restarts the computer**, and **SMS logs user off** are also available values for this property. The **SMS restarts the computer** value causes the host computer to restart after the advertised program completes successfully. The **Program restarts the computer** value allows the program located in the software distribution package to restart the program. This is a helpful option for restarting clients based on the results of the software update installation program. Some software updates may require a restart, depending on the status of the file that needs to be updated. This approach will restart only the host computers that require it.

 NOTE

> The **After running** property setting on the **General** tab contains two options that require additional consideration: **SMS restarts the computer** and **SMS logs user off**. Each of these options occurs in a forceful manner; applications that are running may not close gracefully, and the status message may indicate that the program was interrupted before it was complete.

The **Category** property can be used to help end-users more quickly locate programs that are being advertised on an optional basis. The **Add or Remove Programs** and **Run Advertised Programs** interfaces include category fields to allow filtering. This allows users to shorten the list of available programs and more quickly access the programs they are interested in.

The Requirements Tab

Figure 6.15 shows the **Requirements** tab. None of the items on the tab are required. The **Estimated disk space** and **Additional requirements** properties are all items of information that are displayed on the **Advertised Programs Notification** dialog box. These entries do not restrict programs from being installed on machines.

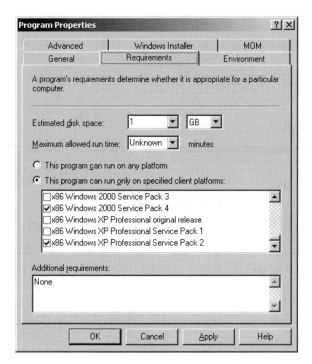

Figure 6.15: Configuring the Requirements Tab.

The **Maximum allowed run time** property controls how long the advertised program will be permitted to run on the client. The specified value appears in **Run Advertised Programs** in **Control Panel**. If a value of **Unknown** is selected, SMS stops the program on the Advanced Client if the program **Environment** tab is configured to **Run with administrative rights** and the **Allow users to interact with this program** setting is not selected. Otherwise, SMS stops monitoring the program after 12 hours if the maximum run time is **Unknown**. This option should be configured generously enough to allow all clients to run the program, but short enough to ensure that clients are not blocked from an emergency update if one should be required. It may take a couple of attempts to find a good balance. One approach to determining this number is to estimate the amount of time it will take a client to complete the advertised program, then add an additional hour or so for good measure. Monitor the deployment to see if any failure occured due to the time limit, then adjust your estimate accordingly.

The property called **This program can run only on specified platforms** restricts the program to the operating systems that are selected from the window. There is no differentiation between Windows 2000 Server and Windows 2000 Professional. This setting performs a client-side evaluation. Using this setting works better than using collections, because it takes until the next discovery or inventory cycle following an OS upgrade for this change to make it to the SMS database. For example, a Windows 2000 machine that is upgraded to Windows XP will still appear as a collection containing only Windows 2000 machines until the updated data records arrive from the upgraded system. On the other hand, by using this Program properties option, the evaluation will occur at program runtime.

NOTE

The property called **This program can run only on specified platforms** is very useful for distributing to specific platforms. Unfortunately, there are no SMS options to restrict a program from running on Windows 2000 servers that have the SMS client installed. However, this can be done using a script. Chapter 9 covers this topic in detail.

The Environment Tab

The **Environment** tab, shown in Figure 6.16, contains configuration settings that limit how the advertised program will run, based on the user login and system environments.

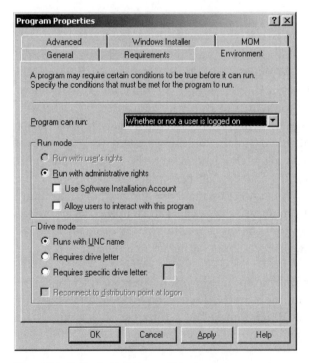

Figure 6.16: Configuring the Environment Tab.

The **Program can run** property seems pretty straightforward, initially. However, there are a few considerations to ponder before choosing an option from the drop-down list:

- The **Only when a user is logged on** default option is used for distributing to a collection of machines where you only want to run the program when someone is logged on. This option would be necessary if a program is being advertised that requires user interaction.

- The **Whether or not a user is logged on** option is very useful if you want the client to run the program any time, including during off-hours. The program runs under the local system account.

- The **Only when no user is logged on** option is good for situations where you want to avoid having any programs open. For example, when upgrading Microsoft Office, all Office applications must be closed.

The **Run mode** property options define the user context that the program runs under:

- The **Run with user's rights** option runs the program with the logged-on user's account and is only available when the **Only when a user is logged on** option is selected in the **Program can run** section.

- The **Run with administrative rights** option is designed for low-rights users who need to install programs requiring administrative rights on the local machine. This option provides a workaround that allows this type of user to install programs with the Advanced Client when typically they would not have permissions to do so. This option relies on the Local System account to run the specified program with administrative rights. This process occurs on the client without the low-rights user being logged off.

- The **Use Software Installation Account** option is for Legacy Clients only and will not be elaborated on here.

- The **Allow users to interact with this program** option is necessary when advertising programs that have interfaces that require user interaction, otherwise the interface will fail to be displayed, causing the program to fail. This check box is available only when the **Program can run** option has the **Only when no user is logged on** or the **Run with administrative rights** value is selected. There is a security issue to consider here. A program with malicious intent could be designed to hook into the user interface of the program that you are deploying. If that were to happen, the malicious program would be running with the same elevated rights as the program that is being distributed with SMS. By selecting the **Allow users to interact with this program** option you are choosing to accept that risk.

The **Drive Mode** property settings determine how the program will connect to distribution points:

- The **Runs with UNC** option is the default setting. It allows the program to connect using a path such as \\SMSCentral\SMSPkgF$\12300001.

- The **Requires drive letter** option is used for programs that require a mapped drive to run from a network location. This is rarely needed. It is intended for legacy programs that require traditional drive letters.

- The **Requires specific drive letter** option is used for programs that must use a specific drive letter for a mapped drive, in order to run from a network location. This is rarely needed. It is intended to legacy programs that require specific drive letters.

- The **Reconnect to distribution point at logon** option reconnects the machine to the network share, using a mapped drive, when a user logs on. This option is only available when the **Run with user's rights** radio button (located on the same tab) is selected. This option should be selected when the credentials of a logged-on user are required to access a network share.

The Advanced Tab

Let's review the various settings on this tab (shown in Figure 6.17).

The **Run another program first** property allows you to link two SMS advertised programs together, creating a dependent program. Select a package and a program from the drop-down box that you want to run prior to the program that you are currently configuring. Remember that the dependent program must complete successfully for the second program to run, otherwise it will be canceled.

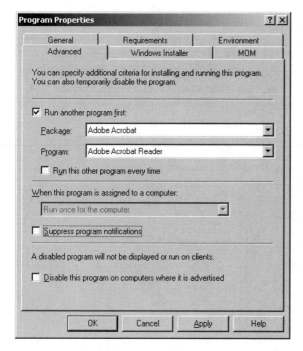

Figure 6.17: Configuring the Advanced Tab.

The **Run this other program every time** option controls possibility of the dependent program performing a recurring installation the next time this program is run.

The **When this program is assigned to a computer** property allows administrators to configure programs to run once, or to run once for each user that logs on. This option is useful when an installation needs to make changes to each user's profile. This option is only valid if the **Only when a user is logged on** option is selected from the **Environment** tab.

The **Suppress program notifications** property allows administrators to hide all messages related to the SMS program, causing the program to run silently to the end-user. Messages that are initiated by the software package will not be hidden.

The **Disable this program on computers where it is advertised** property disables any advertisements for programs that have this option selected. Remember this setting. If you need to disable a program in the middle of being distributed, this is a quick method of doing so.

 NOTE

When using the **Run another program first** option located on the **Advanced** tab, the first program must complete successfully in order for the second program to run. Also, be sure the **Run Mode** property is configured the same for both programs.

The Windows Installer Tab

The properties on this tab (shown in Figure 6.18) provide *installation source management*. Installation source management involves providing alternatives to the SMS client when the original source of the administrative installations for Windows Installer applications is no longer available. This is useful because it provides support for the dynamic features of Windows Installer for self-healing and install on first use.

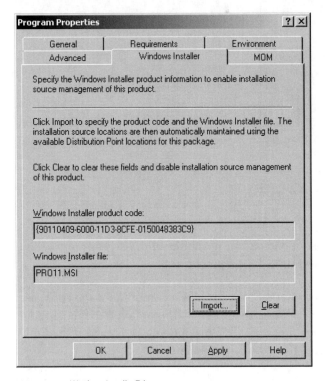

Figure 6.18: Windows Installer Tab.

The **Windows Installer product code** property is a Globally Unique Identifier (GUID) that is the principal identification of a Windows Installer application product. This field is updated only by importing a Windows Installer file (.MSI).

The **Windows Installer file** property is the Windows Installer file that is in the package source. This field is updated only by importing a Windows Installer file (.MSI).

The **Import** button opens a dialog box (shown in Figure 6.19) that allows you to browse to the source folder for MSI files.

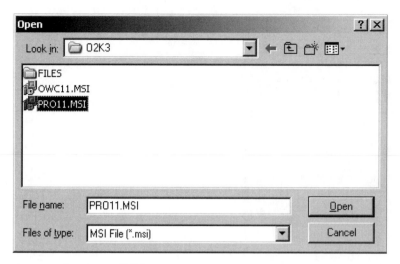

Figure 6.19: Browsing to an MSI File.

After selecting an MSI file, click the **Open** button to import the file information into the **Windows Installer product code** and the **Windows Installer file** property text boxes on the **Windows Installer** tab.

The MOM Tab

On this tab, configure the Microsoft Operations Manager (MOM) alerting settings (see Figure 6.20).

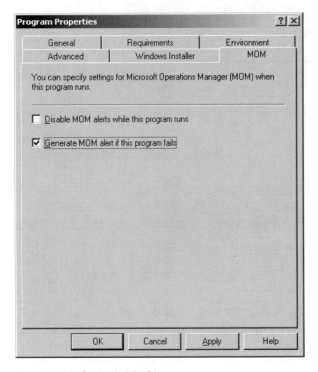

Figure 6.20: Configuring the MOM Tab.

The **Disable MOM alerts while this program runs** check box controls whether MOM alerting is enabled on a system while it runs the specified SMS program. This will avoid sending unwanted alerts caused by the advertised program activity on the system.

Selecting the **Generate MOM alert if this program fails** check box causes a MOM alert to be sent when the specified SMS program fails.

Managing Package Distributions

After a package has been created and sent to distribution points, there needs to be a certain amount of management involved to keep it on track. Various tasks will need to be performed, such as monitoring packages, updating distribution points, and (when finished) removing the package.

Monitoring Packages

To monitor packages, follow these steps:

1. Open the **System Status** tree, and then open the **Package Status** tree.

2. From the left pane, select the package that you need to monitor. In the right pane, compare the information displayed for each site. Each of the sites that you are distributing to should have the same information available. The distribution points for each site should have the same **Source Versions** listed, and eventually they all should have a value of **Installed** for the **State** property. DPs located across slower WAN links will take longer to receive the source files than those located across faster links. (see Figure 6.21).

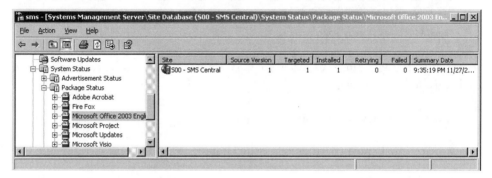

Figure 6.21: Viewing Package Status Details.

3. To see more detail about any site, right-click on the site and select the **Show Messages** ⇨ **All** menu option. The **Status Messages: Set Viewing Period** dialog box will appear. Make a selection, then click the **OK** button. A list of status messages will appear (see Figure 6.22). This information is quite helpful for troubleshooting.

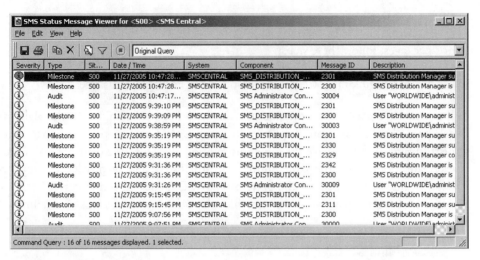

Figure 6.22: Viewing Package Status Messages.

These status messages can be exported to .CSV format, which can be read by Microsoft Excel. To do this, follow these steps:

1. Select the **View**⇨ **Options** menu item.

2. Select the **Export** tab, then select the **Comma delimited** option. Click the **OK** button.

3. Select the **File**⇨ **Save As** menu item. **CSV** will be the option viewable in the **Save as type** drop-down box.

4. Provide a name and location for the new file and then click the **Save** button.

The Manage Distribution Points Wizard

The Manage Distribution Points Wizard provides options for administering distribution points. The options include refreshing and updating distribution points, copying files to new distribution points, and deleting distribution points. It will be necessary to update distribution points if you make a change to the source files. Refreshing distribution points is only useful if one of the distribution point packages becomes corrupt for some reason. Refreshing recopies the compressed version of the source files to the specified distribution points.

Here's how to start the Manage Distribution Points Wizard:

1. Open the **Packages** tree from the left pane, then open a package where you want to configure distribution points.

2. Right-click on **Distribution Points** and then select the **All Tasks⇨ Manage Distribution Points** menu option. The welcome dialog box will open. Click the **Next** button to continue.

3. The **Manage Distribution Points** screen will appear (see Figure 6.23). Select an option and then click the **Next** button. Input the required information and continue through the wizard.

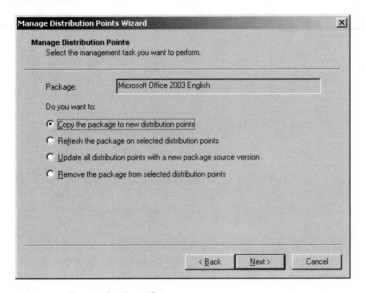

Figure 6.23: Managing Distribution Points.

Delete Package Wizard

When you are finished using a package, you will need to properly remove it from the system. To remove a package, follow these steps:

1. Right-click on the package (see Figure 6.24) and then select the **Delete** menu option.

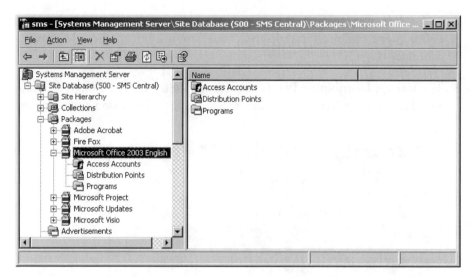

Figure 6.24: Selecting a Package for Deletion.

2. If you have been granted the Delete Package permission for this package, you will see the **Welcome to the Delete Package Wizard** screen (see Figure 6.25).

Figure 6.25: Deleting a Package.

3. Click the **Next** button, and then click the **Yes, I want to see more information** radio button. The wizard will show you all of the effects of deleting the package. The objects that will be deleted include advertisements, programs, access accounts, and security objects. Also, source files will be deleted from the distribution points.

4. Select the **Yes** radio button to delete the package or the **No** radio button to cancel and close the wizard. Click the **Next** button to confirm your choice. On the last page, click the **Finish** button to finalize your selections.

Summary

This chapter described the SMS package creation and distribution process. You discovered a list of preliminary items that must be completed prior to creating an SMS package. You learned software distribution "best practice" guidelines for creating and distributing software packages. While learning the steps that are necessary to create and distribute a software package, you also discovered the considerations that must be made when distributing software to various Windows operating systems. You also learned how to monitor the package creation and distribution process, and how to manage distribution points.

DID YOU KNOW?

myITforum.com is the largest online community for systems management professionals. The site receives about 1,300,000 page views each day and has over 20,000 members. myITforum offers downloads, blogs, a daily newsletter, technical articles, forums, and email discussion lists to help information technology professionals support various products offered by Microsoft and other vendors. The community uses a collaborative approach to help its members solve issues with various systems management products.

Creating Advertisements and Targeting Clients

Chapter 6 discussed the processes involved in creating and distributing a package. Once a package is created and copied to the distribution points, it must be sent to the Advanced Client to be installed on the host system. After reading this chapter, you will have a better understanding of the processes required for creating advertisements and targeting clients. *Advertisements* are notifications that are retrieved by Advanced Clients in the form of policies. Advertisements contain instructions about programs that are available for installation. Simply put, *collections* are a set of resources in a site. When creating an advertisement, you must select one collection as the target, known as the *target collection*. In this chapter, you will learn, in detail, the necessary steps to create advertisements and collections. You will discover the considerations that must be made when targeting collections with advertised programs. In addition, you will learn about special issues that remote users and roaming clients bring to an SMS implementation. Finally, you will learn how to perform advertisement management tasks that may need to occur after a distribution has started.

SMS software distribution is comprised of two major tasks: distributing packages and advertising programs. While the combination of these two processes results in the delivery of software to targeted SMS resources, they are very different. Package distribution is the combination of SMS processes necessary to move package source files to selected distribution points and to create programs that can be run by SMS clients. Advertisements are notifications to SMS user, group and system resources indicating that they are eligible to run a specific SMS program. This chapter covers, in detail, the tasks associated with creating advertisements and targeting users.

NOTE

In this chapter and throughout the book the term "client" refers to the SMS Advanced Client unless otherwise specified.

Creating Target Collections

SMS software distribution is simply a delivery vehicle for installation and configuration programs. By creating target collections, we give a destination to our delivery vehicle. *Collections* are sets of SMS resources that are grouped by common properties, using membership rules. SMS is built around the concept of collections as a method for managing clients. The only way to complete the final stage of distributing software is by sending it to a target collection via an advertisement.

Methods for Creating Collections

There are several methods for creating collections:

- Use Direct Membership rules.

- Use Query Membership rules.

- Use the Make Collection Tool.

To begin creating a new collection, follow these steps:

1. Open the **Collections** tree and right-click **Collections**. Select the **New**⇨ **Collection** menu item. The **Collection Properties** sheet will appear. If you right-click on an existing collection and perform the actions in this step, a *subcollection* will be created. Subcollections are collections that are associated with other collections in the SMS Administrator Console, appearing as though they are nested. As you will see in the "Creating Advertisements" section, advertisements can be configured to run on members of subcollections. Subcollections appear in a hierarchal view in the SMS Administrator Console, but they do not inherit the attributes of the parent collection. Also, actions performed on parents do not automatically occur on subcollections. A collection can appear many times as a subcollection to various parent collections. To link a parent collection to a subcollection, right-click on an existing collection and select the **New**⇨ **Link to collection** menu item. When the window opens, browse to the collection that you want to link to the parent collection.

2. Add values in the **Name** and **Comment** text boxes (See Figure 7.1). Entering descriptive text in the **Comment** text box will help to avoid mistakes for target collections and will aid with troubleshooting, if it becomes necessary.

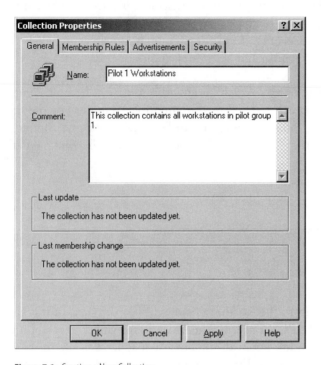

Figure 7.1: Creating a New Collection.

3. Select the **Membership Rules** tab. Both direct membership rules and query membership rules are created from this location.

Direct Membership Rules

The Direct Membership Rule Wizard is a graphical tool that adds resources to a collection one at a time. Creating membership rules that are based on User Resource and User Group Resource classes will allow you to distribute software to User and User Group accounts. When targeting User and User Group accounts, it can be tricky to limit advertisements to run on specific computers. End-users sometimes log on to multiple computers and may belong to multiple Windows security groups. For example, if a member of the server administration team is targeted with an advertisement for Microsoft Office, he would be surprised to see the Office installation starting on his domain controller. This could be avoided in a number of ways. If the servers are all running Windows 2003 and the workstations are all running Windows XP, then configuring the **Requirements** tab of the program properties sheet to only run on Windows XP computers would be a simple solution. The point here is that there are many unexpected scenarios that could occur when targeting users and groups.

Let's look at another example. Suppose you decide to target the HR user group with a new HR application and you make the required SMS configurations to initiate the deployment. On some occasions Jen, who normally works in HR, needs to log on to a PC in the Marketing department. If Jen completes this action while the advertisement is active, the HR application will be installed on the computer where she logs in. Within the properties of the collection, you could exclude users who are members of the Marketing group, but there would likely be many more employees who would have membership in multiple groups.

When users have multiple workstations, software product licensing can become complicated. Some products are allowed to be purchased and used on multiple computers by the same user without additional charges, while other products are to be installed on one computer only. Be sure to carefully read the licensing documentation for any product that will be used in the scenarios described here.

To create direct membership rules, follow these steps:

1. Click the **Direct Membership Rule Wizard** button.

2. Click the **Next** button on the first page of the wizard. From the **Resource Class** option, select **System Resource**.

3. Select the **Name** option from the **Attribute Name** drop-down box. In the **Value** text box, enter the name of the PC, or just use the % wildcard symbol to see all machines. You can also place the first few letters in the box, then append the % to the end (see Figure 7.2). Click the **Next** button. This is an example of only one way to use this dialog box. Other options exist in the drop-down boxes.

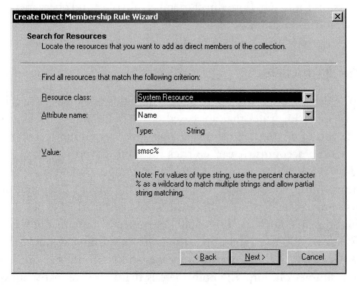

Figure 7.2: Creating a Direct Membership Rule.

4. Select the collections (on the **Collection Limiting** page) for which you have the proper permissions (if you do not have Read Resources permission for the entire Collections class). Click the **Next** button.

5. Select the PC(s) that you wish to add to the collection (see Figure 7.3), and click the **Next** button.

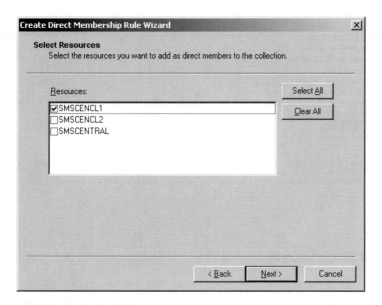

Figure 7.3: Selecting PCs for Direct Membership.

6. Click the **OK** button at the **Collection Properties** sheet. The new collection will appear in the list (see Figure 7.4). Select the new collection from the left pane to cause the collection members to appear in the right pane.

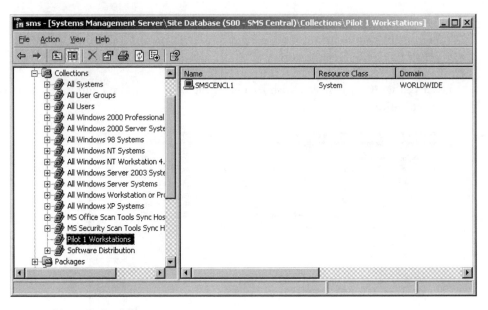

Figure 7.4: Viewing the New Collection.

Query Membership Rules

The Query Membership Rule Wizard is a graphical tool that allows you to use an existing query located under the **Query** tree, or to create a new *query rule*. Query rules dynamically add members to collections.

To create query membership rules, follow these steps:

1. Click the **Query Rule Wizard** button from the **Membership Rules** tab in the collection properties. Enter a value into the **Name** text box.

2. Click the **Import Query** button to browse to a query that has already been created, or click the **Edit Query Statement** button (see Figure 7.5) to open a new query for editing. The Query Statement properties property sheet will appear (see Figure 7.6) If you opt to browse a query that has already been created, you will actually import a copy of the query into the collection. You can then click the **Edit Query** button to modify the copy of the query. Collections based on existing queries will not change if the *WBEM Query Language (WQL)* is modified in the original query. WQL is a derivation of Structured Query Language (SQL), which is commonly used for accessing databases such as Microsoft SQL Server. It is used when accessing the WMI repository. Queries within the SMS Administrator Console use WQL to return information from the WMI repository on a primary server.

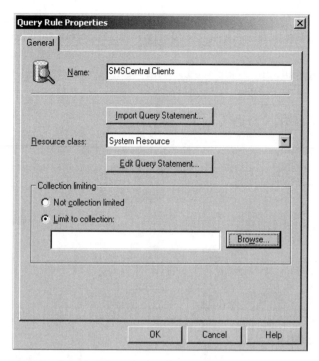

Figure 7.5: Using the Collection Limiting Option.

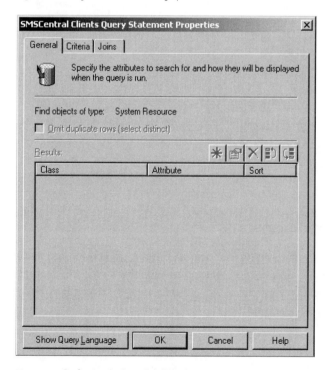

Figure 7.6: Configuring the Query Rule Wizard.

3. You can limit the collection that you are creating to an existing collection as an effective method of controlling a distribution. Go to the **Query Rule Properties** sheet, select the **Limit to collection** radio button, and then click the **Browse** button (see Figure 7.5). Select the collection that you want to use as a basis for creating your new collection.

Removing Resources from a Collection

To remove resources from a collection, always remove the membership rule that includes them. Select the rule that you want to remove from the **Membership Rules** tab, then click the **Delete** button (see Figure 7.7).

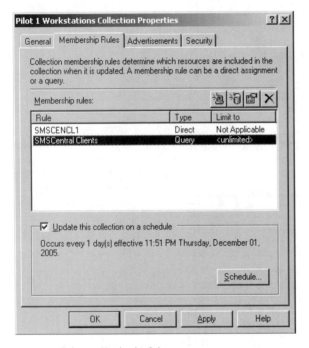

Figure 7.7: Deleting a Membership Rule.

Viewing Active Advertisements

Active advertisements are live advertisements that are targeting a collection. You should know what advertisements are targeting a collection before editing the collection membership or deleting the collection altogether. To view the active advertisements, select the **Advertisements** tab from the properties sheet of a collection.

Collection Security

To view the collection security, select the **Security** tab from the properties sheet of a collection. The **Class security rights** window lets you administer security rights for all collections. The **Instance security rights** window lets you administer security rights for the collection that is currently being configured.

The Make Collection Tool

There are plenty of situations that call for creating a collection of computers based on a list of NETBIOS names. You can use the Make Collection tool (MakeColl.exe) to create a new collection from a text file. The file can be a list of computer names or IP addresses. This tool can be very useful for creating large collections that would otherwise need to be made using the Direct Membership Rule Wizard. The code is located in the SMS 2003 Software Developers Kit (SDK), which can be accessed at: http://www.microsoft.com/smserver/downloads/2003/default.mspx. The executable is not available from Microsoft, but an example can be downloaded from this website: http://www.extendedtools.com/utilities/download.htm. I don't recommend using this utility in your production environment, because it was not posted by a well known source. However, you may want to use it in a lab scenario to give you a feel for what the utility can do.

Before using this tool, you must create a text file with a list of NETBIOS computer names or IP addresses. The list format needs to be one name or address per line. If your text file specifies IP addresses, use the -I option to have the Make Collection tool read the text file for IP addresses instead. The Make Collection tool requires MakeColl.exe and a text file that you create. It's best to first try using this utility directly on the site server where you want to create the collections, so that you can use fewer command line options.

Here is the syntax necessary to use the Make Collection tool:

```
MakeColl <filename> <collection> <server> [-I] [-Q] [-U:<user>
[<password> | *]]
```

Where:

- **[-S:<refresh schedule token>] [-C:<comment>] [-P:<collection name>] Filename** is the text-file list of computer names or IP addresses.

- The **Collection** option is the name of the collection being created.

- The **Server** option is the name of the site server where the SMS Provider resides.

- The **-I** option reads IP addresses, rather than machine names, from the text file.

- The -U **<User Password>** * option indicates a user and password for the server to create the collection. If this option is not selected, then the user and password currently logged on will be used. If implemented, this command line option must be specified last; otherwise, another command line option will be interpreted as part of the password. If you want to be prompted to enter a password, type an asterisk (*) after the user name. If no password is provided and an asterisk is not used, the password is interpreted as null. This is an optional switch. If your collection name includes spaces, enclose the collection name in quotation marks.

- The **-S** option sets the collection refresh schedule token (for periodic refreshing).

- The **-C** option specifies the comment field for the collection.

- The **-P** option specifies the parent collection name for the new collection.

VBS Script Version

There is also a VBS Script version of the Make Collection tool that is much easier to use but offers less in the way of features. This version requires you to add a few pieces of basic information into the script prior to run time. The script is purely designed to create a static collection of computer names. There are a few different versions of this script at myITforum.com. Here's the link to my favorite: http://www.myitforum.com/articles/1/view.asp?id=1309.

Advanced Collection Building

The effective use of query membership rules is a great way to limit collections. Using wildcard characters and query criterion types of subselected values or a list of values are advanced methods that can be used to limit collections to computers that you want to target with an advertised program. Table 7.1 shows wildcards and the characters they may represent. These values would commonly be used on the **Criterion Properties** sheet in the **Values** text box.

Wildcard	Description
%	Any string of zero or more characters
_ (underscore)	Any single character
[]	Any single character within the range or set (for example [a-f] or [abcdef])
[^]	Any single character not within the specified range (for example [^a-f] or [^abcdef])

Table 7.1: Wildcards.

To access the **Criterion Properties** sheet, open the **Query Membership Rule** wizard and enter a value into the **Name** text box. Click the **Edit Query Statement** button, and the **Query Statement Properties** sheet will appear. Select the **Criteria** tab and click the **New Criteria** button. The **Criterion Properties** sheet will appear. Configure the **Where** and **Operator** property options. In the Value text box, you can utilize the wildcard characters (see Figure 7.8).

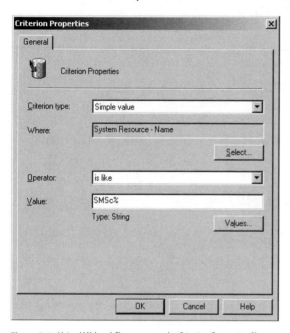

Figure 7.8: Using Wildcard Characters on the Criterion Properties Sheet.

Using the subselected query criterion allows you to limit collections based on another query or collection. To use this option, navigate to the **Criterion Properties** sheet as described previously in this section. In the **Criterion type** drop-down box, select the **Subselected Values** option. The properties sheet will change to accommodate your selection. Configure the **Where** and **Operator** text boxes. Click the **Browse** button to open a list of existing queries. You can select a query to import into this collection. Otherwise, you can paste WQL code into the **Subselect** text box (see Figure 7.9).

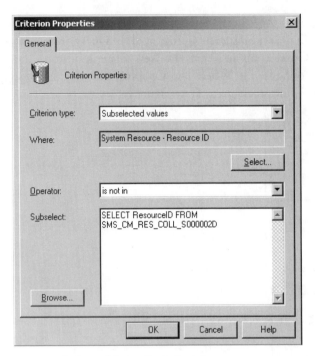

Figure 7.9: Configuring Subselect Criterion Properties.

You can base subselected values criterion properties on existing collections by entering the following line into the **Subselect** text box:

```
SELECT ResourceID FROM SMS_CM_RES_COLL_S000002D
```

S000002D is the collection ID. This is a good technique to use, because it can utilize collections that have already been created to quickly and easily exclude a collection from a software distribution. Generally, there are certain sensitive machines that you want SMS to exclude from software deployments. It could be a scenario where automated software installation is prohibited, or possibly the machines can never be rebooted with SMS. Using this technique, you can make collection S000002D an "exclusion" collection that can be easily be embedded into any target collection, protecting your sensitive machines.

Another aspect of this technique that you may want to consider is the *evaluation* of collection S000002D. Evaluation is when the SMS site server checks the membership of a dynamic collection based on the query embedded into the collection. Evaluation is enabled on the collection properties page on the **Membership Rules** tab using the **Update this collection on a schedule** check box. On busy SMS site servers, collection evaluation may not complete successfully or in a timely manner. This would be a problem, because excluding the proper machines from the software distribution depends on collection S000002D having an accurate list of members. If the list of sensitive machines will remain the same, then one option for preventing this problem from occurring is to use static membership for collection S000002D. Static membership rules do not require collection evaluation to occur.

The **List of values** option can also be selected on the **Criterion Properties** sheet. This option allows you to manually add a list of values as a way to include or exclude collection members. Configuring the **List of values** option is straightforward.

Tips for Creating Target Collections

Here are a few items to check when creating target collections in SMS.

- Notice the **Update collection on a schedule** check box, on the **Membership Rules** tab. Target collections with query membership rules should have this box checked. Otherwise, when new SMS clients are added to PCs, they will never enter the target collection.

- Create a Testing Collection that contains a few resources for testing. During the initial testing phase, point the advertisement to the test collection. You will usually need to make adjustments to the package prior to sending it to production machines. Using this step will help you to avoid bothering end-users or possibly corrupting their workstations.

- Update collections after making modifications that will result in a change in collection resources. This will cause the changes to take effect as soon as possible.

- Be careful when targeting a collection of users or user groups. Remember, users could use multiple workstations or servers. Also, users can be members of multiple groups, which could cause an advertised program to accidentally run on a computer that belongs to a user group that you are not targeting. Generally, it's much safer to target computers rather than users or user groups.

Preparing to Advertise a Program

Before beginning the distribution process, there are a few preliminary items that should be completed:

- CREATE AN SMS PACKAGE AND ASSIGN DISTRIBUTION POINTS — This must be done prior to creating the advertisement (see Chapter 6 for more information on creating packages). Simply put, the advertisement notifies the client that a program is available to be run. The SMS program is actually part of the package.

- **CONFIGURE ADVERTISED PROGRAMS CLIENT AGENTS AND DISTRIBUTION POINTS** — See Chapter 3 for details on configuring the Advertised Programs Client Agent and distribution points.

- **THERE MUST BE A TARGET COLLECTION AVAILABLE** — While creating the collection, you must provide the name of the target collection. See the "Creating Target Collections" section for more information about creating collections.

Creating Advertisements

There is one step remaining in the process of distributing software to SMS clients: creating an advertisement. *Advertisements* are the SMS objects responsible for notifying clients in a target collection that an SMS program is available to be run. You can send advertisements to a collection containing users, user groups, or systems.

To create an advertisement, right-click on the **Advertisements** tree, and choose the **New⇨Advertisement** menu item. A new **Advertisement Properties** sheet will appear. Let's review the tabs on this sheet and the options available in each.

The General Tab

The **General** tab is the default view in the **Advertisement Properties** sheet. Follow these steps to configure settings in the **General** tab.

1. Add descriptive text to the **Name** and **Comment** property text boxes (see Figure 7.10).

2. Select the package name that contains the program that you want to advertise from the **Package** drop-down box.

3. Select the program that you want to advertise from the **Program** drop-down box.

4. Click the **Browse** button, or just add the collection name to the text box. Clicking the **Browse** button will return a list of collections that may be slow to appear.

5. Configure the **Include members of subcollections** property check box with the appropriate setting. Choose this setting cautiously—be sure that you want to advertise the program to members of subcollections.

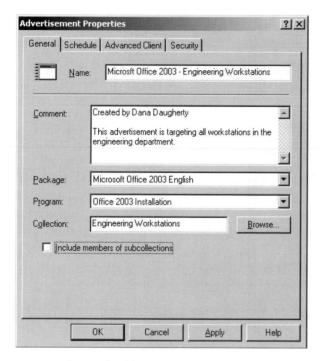

Figure 7.10: Creating a New Advertisement.

The Schedule Tab

Let's review the options available in the **Schedule** tab.

By default, the **Advertisement start time** property reflects the current time, but can be adjusted to future dates and times (see Figure 7.11). When the client machine's time reaches the advertisement start time, an optional advertisement will begin appearing, unless a mandatory assignment is configured, or the program is past the expired date. Also, if the **Download program from distribution point** option is selected on the **Advanced Client** tab, the download will begin at the **Advertisement start time**.

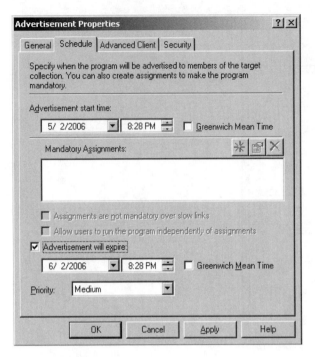

Figure 7.11: Configuring the Schedule Tab.

The **Greenwich Mean Time** option allows the advertisement to start at the Greenwich Mean Time (GMT) and date entered, regardless of the time zone where the SMS client is located. This option is useful when all clients need to have software updated or installed at the same time.

If you click the **Add Mandatory Assignment** button to add a mandatory assignment, the assignment **Schedule** dialog box will appear (see Figure 7.12).

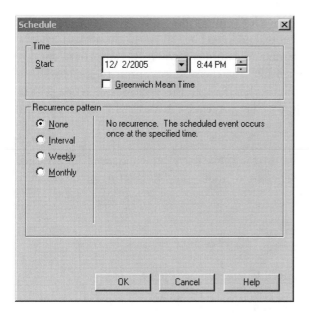

Figure 7.12: Configuring Schedule Dialog Box.

If no mandatory assignments are configured, this will be considered an optional advertisement. Optional advertisements are available for targeted end-users to run at their convenience. End-users invoke optional advertisements in the **Control Panel**⇨ **Run Advertised Programs** applet.

- Selecting the **Assign to the following schedule** radio button enables the **Schedule** button. Clicking the **Schedule** button causes the **Schedule** dialog box to appear, which includes options for setting the mandatory advertisement **Start** and **Recurrence Pattern** properties.

- Selecting the **Assign immediately after this event** radio button enables the drop-down option box that includes the following events: **As soon as possible**, **Logon**, and **Logoff**. If the current date and time are past, the **Advertisement will expire** property value invalidates the advertisement.

The **Assignments are not mandatory over slow links** property excludes clients that are connected at network connection speeds below 40 Kbps. This feature is set by default when a mandatory assignment is scheduled.

The **Allow users to run the program independently of assignments** property permits users to run mandatory assignments from the **Run Advertised Programs** applet in Control Panel or from **Add or Remove Programs**, depending on the configuration of the Software Distribution Client Agent properties. This option is only valid if the mandatory assignment is scheduled for a future date.

The **Advertisement will expire** option can be set for a future date or a past date. When the workstation reaches this date, the advertisement will no longer be valid. This feature won't stop a distribution as quickly as the **Disable this program on computers where it is advertised** option, located on the **Program Properties⇨ Advanced** tab. The client must contact the management point again to download the policies that contain this change. This cycle occurs based on the schedule that is configured in the **Site Settings⇨ Client Agents⇨ Advertised Programs Client Agent** property sheet.

The value set under the **Priority** option is used by addresses that are configured for sending communications to child sites. Addresses are located under the **Site Settings** console tree. **Medium** is the default setting.

The Advanced Client Tab

Let's review the options available in the **Advanced Client** tab (See Figure 7.13).

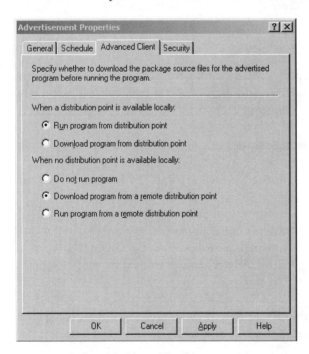

Figure 7.13: Configuring the Advanced Client Tab.

The **When a distribution point is available locally** property includes two options:

- The **Run program from distribution point** option causes the client to access the source files on the distribution point when running the installation program.

- The **Download program from distribution point** option causes the client to download the program source files to a local cache on the client. Either immediately after the download or at later time, the program will initiate. The DP must have Background Intelligent Transfer Service (BITS) installed.

The **When no distribution point is available locally** property is useful for Advanced Clients that are roaming or where local DPs are unavailable. You can choose from these options:

- The **Do not run program** option causes the program to stop if a local DP is unavailable.

- The **Download from a remote distribution point** option will cause the Advanced Client to access an available SMS management point to request a location for a remote distribution point. The DP must have Background Intelligent Transfer Service (BITS) installed.

- The **Run program from a remote distribution point** option causes the client to run the installation from the source files on the distribution point.

The Security Tab

In the **Security** tab (shown in Figure 7.14), the **Class security rights** window lets you administer security rights for all collections. The **Instance security rights** window lets you administer security rights for the collection that is currently being configured.

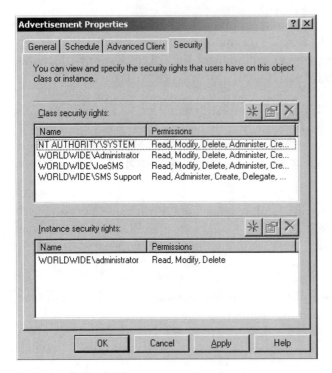

Figure 7.14: The Security Tab.

Tips for Creating Advertisements

Here are a few items to consider when creating advertisements:

- When adding the target collection name, on the **General** tab, select a test collection that contains only a couple of workstations in it. Most likely, you will need to make modifications to the package before sending it to production machines. This will avoid aggravating the end-user, and preserve your reputation.

- Be careful with the **Include members of subcollections** check box on the **General** tab. This is enabled by default, allowing all subcollections (below the parent collection that you are distributing to) to also receive the advertisement.

- It's a good idea to synchronize the time on your workstations with the site server that will be performing software distribution. The best way to do this is to use the **Net Time** command. To synchronize the computer's time with the current time on the domain, type the following command: `net time /domain /set`

  The options on the **Schedule** tab that contain start times will rely on the clock at the client machine.

- Before attempting to distribute a program to a dial-up user, be aware of the size of the installation program. Even with the new features of the Advanced Client, anything over 25 megabytes may warrant some type of workaround. These issues are discussed in the section "Overcoming Challenges of SMS Clients Connected Over Slow Links" later in this chapter.

- The **Priority** option on the **Schedule** tab must be equal to or lower than the **Availability** setting for child site addresses on the **Schedule** tab (located in the **Site Settings**⇨ **Address** tree) for the time period you want to advertise a program. Otherwise, the advertisement will not begin at the intended child site until the advertisement's assigned priority is available at that address.

- The Advertisement is the last step in the configuration process before sending the program to client machines. Before advertising to your entire enterprise, be sure to thoroughly test the application and the distribution process. Phasing the distribution to various groups of the user population is a best practice approach. Monitoring the initial phases of the distribution will provide an additional layer of testing in case you missed something in the test lab. Phasing will also provide a way of releasing the package over a longer time period to avoid over-utilizing the network.

Client-Side Advertisement Processes

This section explains how the advertisement process works at the Advanced Client level.

Program Execution Phase

Program execution is when the client attempts to execute the program source files in order to install the program. Here are the stages of the Program Execution phase:

1. The **Policy Agent** sends a policy request to the MP of its assigned site and, if authorized, downloads new policies. One policy contains the advertisement notification.

2. The **Policy Agent Provider** sends new advertised program notification to Execution Manager containing the properties of the advertised program. It records the program's properties and activity in WMI.

3. The **Scheduler** notifies Execution Manager when it is time to run the program.

4. The **Execution Manager** performs the following actions:

a. Sends informational status message ID 10002 to the MP after it receives the notification from Policy Agent Provider.

b. Creates an execution request for the new program (could be mandatory or optional). If the start time is set for the future, go to Step 4d later in this section and then return to this step and wait for the start time to arrive. Otherwise, go to Step 4c later in this section.

c.. If the program is configured as optional, the **Run Advertised Program** icon is displayed in the System Tray and the advertised program appears in the **Add or Remove Programs** applet.

d. Requests content location and the package source version from the **Content Access Service (CAS)** for the package (see "Content Access" later in this section).

e. Receives communication from CAS, including package information and content access status notifications.

f. Sends content access-related status messages to the MP, when necessary, with information or error text. Message ID 10035 indicates that the program will be run after the content is downloaded. Message IDs 10051, 10053, 10058, 10060, 10061, 10062, and 10065 indicate a content download problem.

g. Verifies the program is in the location identified by CAS.

h. Displays the **Advertised program is about to run** icon, if the program is configured to do so.

i. Runs the program after all package and advertisement configuration criteria have been met. These criteria are configured on the program property tabs and the advertisement property tabs. An informational status message ID 10005 is sent to the MP.

j. Monitors installation status MIFs at program completion. MIFs are Management Information Format files that use a standard format to store data. SMS uses MIFs to store the status of program installations as they occur on a client. The file is then sent to the site server by way of the management point. If there is no MIF file specified on the **Reporting** tab of the SMS package, Execution Manager monitors the program exit code.

k. Sends installation status messages to the MP with one of the following messages:

- Message ID 10009 for custom MIFs with a value of Success.

- Message ID 10007 for custom MIFs with a value of Failed.

- Message ID 10008 for the program exit code value of 0 indicates the installation succeeded.

- Message ID 10006 for the program exit code value other than 0 indicates the installation failed.

Content Access

Content access occurs when the Advanced Client finds the package source files and then downloads them to be executed during the program execution phase. The following steps occur:

1. **CONTENT ACCESS SERVICE**

   a. Checks the cache to see if the source files have been downloaded.

   (1) If so, it returns the package source version to Execution Manager.

   (2) If not, it creates a folder in the %Windows%\system32\CCM\Cache folder, based on the package ID, version, and context. It makes a request to **Content Transfer Manager** (**CTM**), including the package ID, version, and destination folder name (in the Cache folder).

2. **CONTENT TRANSFER MANAGER (CTM)** — Requests a list of DPs from **Location Services**.

3. **LOCATION SERVICES** — Queries the management point (MP) for a list of DPs.

   a. The MP returns the path of the content on each available DP to Location Services, using the following metrics:

   (1) If the client is included in protected distribution point boundary(s), the MP will verify that the content is available at the protected DP(s). A boundary is created based on subnet addresses and Active Directory Site names. If the content is available, only the protected DP(s) will be provided to the client.

(2) If the client is not included in a protected distribution point boundary, then the MP will attempt to provide a local DP—first on the same subnet, next within the AD Site, then any DP local to the client and finally, a remote DP within the SMS site.

(3) If the Advanced Client cannot contact a DP in its resident site, it will contact the MP again with the same request. The MP will then return a list of all assigned MPs. The client then chooses a DP from the list at random.

b. Returns the list of DPs to CTM.

c. If the MP doesn't reply, Location Services makes multiple attempts until it eventually fails.

4. **CTM** — Stores the DP locations in WMI and calls Data Transfer Service (DTS) to download package content from the first DP in the list.

5. **DTS**

a. Retrieves the list of files and folders from the MP.

b. Creates the sub-folder structure under the existing top-level source folder in the local Cache directory.

c. Attempts to contact a DP, starting from the top of the list. After a connection is made, it begins the download process.

d. If the DP is BITS-enabled, the client will begin a BITS session, under a **SvcHost** process. Otherwise, a FileCopy operation will be performed.

e. If a download error or timeout occurs, a connection with the next DP on the list will be attempted.

f. Notifies Execution Manager upon successful completion or failure of the download.

g. Return to Step 4F in the "Program Execution Phase" section.

Managing Advertisements

After an advertisement is created, there are a few management tasks that must be considered. Understanding how to perform such tasks as quickly disabling and resending advertisements can be helpful. Also, it is critical to know the risks associated with installing the Advanced Client on server systems.

Disabling SMS Advertised Programs

There are two methods of quickly stopping a distribution using the SMS Administrator Console:

1. Right-click the advertisement that you want to stop and select the **All Tasks**⇨ **Disable Program** menu item.

2. Select the **Advanced** tab from the properties sheet of the program that you want to stop. Then select the **Disable this program on computers where it is advertised** property option (see Figure 7.15). This setting stops SMS from offering the advertised program, rather than stopping a program from running that has already been installed on an SMS client.

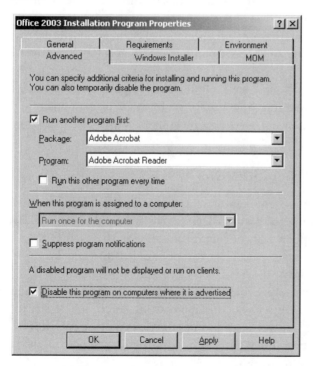

Figure 7.15: Disabling an Advertised Program.

Resending Advertised Programs

You can resend a mandatory advertisement to clients that have already received it. You can resend it to an entire collection, or on an individual basis.

To resend to an entire collection of clients, follow these steps:

1. Open the advertisement and verify that the target collection contains the resources that you want to receive the new mandatory advertisement. Make changes if necessary.

2. Select the **Schedule** tab and click the **Add** button.

3. Create a new mandatory assignment, then click the **OK** button.

4. To immediately trigger an advertisement to rerun, browse to the advertisement that you want to resend and right-click on the advertisement. Then choose the **All Tasks**⇨ **Rerun Advertisement** menu item. The advertisement must be configured with an existing recurring schedule, otherwise the program will not rerun if the SMS client has previously run the program successfully.

There is no built-in mechanism for targeting a single client to rerun an advertisement. However, there are console add-ins that have been developed to help with this task. One of these is offered free of charge on MyITForum.com by Corey Becht. After running a simple setup program, a new set of options appears when you perform a right mouse-click on an individual client or on a collection. There are multiple tools to choose from, one of which is **Re-Run Advertisement**. The tool can be downloaded at http://www.myitforum.com/articles/8/view.asp?id=7099. These tools require that the administrator have administrative rights on the remote machine that will be accessed. Also, be aware that these tools use methods of manipulating the SMS client that are not supported by Microsoft, but they are quite helpful.

SMS Clients Installed on Servers

SMS Clients that reside on server systems can present issues when distributing software. The main issue is accidentally installing software on servers that is intended for workstations. It doesn't look good for the SMS support team at your organization if Microsoft Office is installed on every production server. This type of accident can be avoided through the use of proper exclusion methods. With the release of the Advanced Client, more organizations are relying on SMS to manage server systems where previously it was rare to see this. The safest approach is to maintain a designated SMS site for servers. This approach makes it much easier to separate servers from workstations during software distribution activities. Another option is to place all servers into a special server collection and require SMS support staff members to always exclude the server collection from workstation software distributions.

Distributing Software to Remote Users and Roaming Clients

Remote users and roaming clients can definitely cause challenges for software distribution. *Remote users* are defined as those connecting to the corporate network by either a dial-up or a VPN connection. A roaming user visits multiple SMS sites in an organization. The difficulties to overcome include slow and unreliable connections, IP address changes, and SMS site location changes. In this section, you will learn about a few workarounds for these issues. There are two types of remote users:

- *Home-based* means they work from home 90% of the time and rarely visit a corporate office.

- *Occasionally work from home* indicates that they work from home once a week or so.

There are also two types of connections:

- *Dial-up access* is a connection type that also includes Integrated Services Digital Network (ISDN). It is highly likely that ISDN users are connecting directly to the office, using Multilink technology and Remote Access Authentication. Connection speeds will vary between 20Kbps to 112Kbps and may pose a problem. The IP address that the users receive may or may not be a problem.

- *High-speed access* users include anyone using cable modems, Digital Subscriber Line (DSL), or Satellite technologies. They will connect to their Internet Service Provider (ISP), and then use a VPN tunnel to connect to the office at speeds varying between 400 Kbps and 10 Mbps. The ISP is responsible for issuing the workstation IP address.

Overcoming Challenges of SMS Clients Connected Over Slow Links

For remote users, line speed is generally the most difficult barrier to overcome. Fortunately, the Advanced Client has built-in features to help alleviate some of these issues. Before the Advanced Client became available, distributions over 1 or 2 megabytes were likely to become corrupt, or cause workstations to time-out and drop the connection. This was very frustrating to the end-user who was attempting to do some work.

The Advanced Client provides *checkpoint restarts* and *bandwidth throttling* if BITS is enabled on the DP and on the client. Checkpoint restarts allow downloads to restart at the point where they were interrupted. Without this technology, interrupted downloads must start from the beginning. Some files are too large to download successfully without checkpoint restart technology. Bandwidth throttling allows the Advanced Client to monitor and adjust a download speed, providing enough bandwidth to avoid interrupting the end-user's work session. The truth is, even with these advanced features, it will take a very long time to install Microsoft Office over a dial-up connection. In most cases, an alternative will need to be provided. Obvious workarounds include having the user ship their laptop to the office, or sending them a CD containing the installation files.

Roaming Clients

The challenges for roaming clients occur when users travel from within a site boundary to a location outside of the boundary. Remember that a boundary is created based on subnet addresses and Active Directory Site names. Examples include an Advanced Client that does the following:

- Moves between subnets.

- Switches to a wireless LAN.

- Uses a dial-up connection.

- Moves between SMS sites.

- Moves outside the SMS site hierarchy.

SMS roaming was designed to support software distribution to Advanced Clients in as many scenarios as possible. SMS combines the roaming component with features of Active Directory to allow for more flexibility when targeting clients for software distribution. Let's look at these features in a bit more detail.

Roaming Boundaries

Within the SMS administration community, there has been much confusion about roaming boundaries, most of which comes from the names of the property tabs within the site properties. The **Site Boundaries** tab could easily be named "Legacy Site Boundaries," because this tab is not required for Advanced Clients. And the **Roaming Boundaries** tab could be renamed "Advanced Client Boundaries," because the settings on this tab do not affect the Legacy Client. A roaming boundary is created based on IP subnet addresses, IP subnet ranges, and Active Directory Site names. SMS provides roaming boundaries to help manage slow or unreliable links. With SMS, roaming boundaries are used to allow you to specify which subnets or IP addresses are *remote* to the site (slow, unreliable) and which are *local* to the site (fast, reliable). Roaming boundaries are so named because they support Advanced Client roaming. Any given boundary value should not be used at more than one site. Each boundary, whether it is an Active Directory site, an IP subnet, or an IP address range, should be included in only one SMS site. Roaming boundaries are configured in the site properties sheet, in the **Roaming Boundaries** tab (see Figure 7.16).

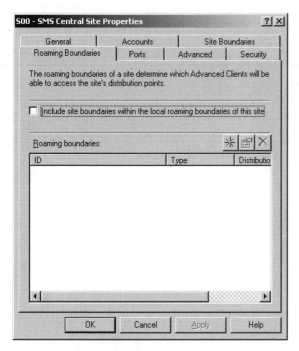

Figure 7.16: Configuring Roaming Boundaries.

Advertisements

While configuring an advertisement, you can determine how the advertised program will be treated, depending on whether the Advanced Client is local or remote to the available distribution point. First, determine if you want the client to run the program from the distribution point, or download the program first and then run it. Then decide if you want remote clients to run the program in the same manner when remote, or not run the program at all. For larger programs, (for example, Office 2003) the administrator could prevent the program from running when the client is remote. Configure these options on the **Advertisement Properties Advanced Client** tab (see Figure 7.17)

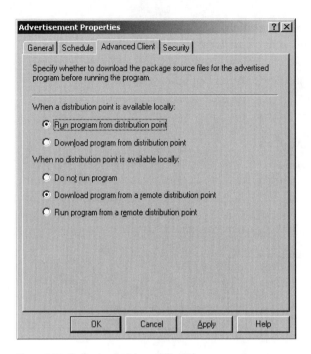

Figure 7.17: Configuring the Advanced Client Tab.

Management Points

From the point of view of a roaming client, the role of a management point is to locate an appropriate distribution point. The SMS management point provides the instructions for roaming clients to locate and run programs. From the client view, a management point might be its *assigned management point*, a *proxy management point*, or a *resident management point*. Assigned management points are associated with the Advanced Client during the client installation process. Proxy management points are used in secondary sites to direct Advanced Clients to a parent site where the client is assigned. Advanced Clients are never assigned to a proxy management point. Resident management points exist when SMS 2003 Active Directory schema extensions have been configured. Extending the Active Directory schema is an option during SMS 2003 installation and can also be performed after the installation. When an Advanced Client roams outside of its site hierarchy branch to a grandparent site, the client may contact the management point at the new site to make content location requests. Content location requests come from Advanced Clients that are looking for distribution points so that they can download *content*. A resident management point provides content location responses to the Advanced Clients that contain a list of distribution points available within the current site. The Advanced Client can also contact its assigned management point if it is roaming into a subnet address range or Active Directory Site that is outside of its site boundary.

Distribution Points

With SMS roaming, an Advanced Client is able to access distribution points in the site to which it is connected. Be aware that the package source files must be available on the distribution point in the current site in order to be available. Plan your package creation and distribution according to where your clients will roam. Package IDs are used in SMS roaming operations. Therefore, packages should be created centrally in a site that is as far up the SMS infrastructure as possible.

Roaming boundaries can be used to protect a distribution point from client access across slow network links. For more about distribution points, see Chapter 4.

Active Directory

Active Directory integration provides two features that are used by SMS roaming clients. First, Active Directory sites can be used as roaming boundaries. Usually, an Active Directory site is a group of well-connected subnets. Second, the Active Directory schema can be extended to include SMS site data. This allows a client to roam outside its assigned site hierarchy while still being able to locate a management point. For more information on roaming clients, have a look at these resources:

- **SMS 2003 CONFIGURATION AND OPERATION OF ADVANCED CLIENT ROAMING** — `http://www.microsoft.com/downloads/details.aspx?FamilyID=37ac2246-453a-4418-b026-f7140a6fce3c&DisplayLang=en`

- **SMS ROAMING DEMO** — `http://www.microsoft.com/smserver/techinfo/productdoc/media/2596a_11_a05.swf`

Summary

This chapter described the second part of the SMS software distribution process. You learned software distribution "best practice" guidelines for creating advertisements and targeting collections. We covered the necessary steps to create collections and advertisements, and important considerations for distributing software to remote users and roaming clients. The flexibility of SMS roaming clients requires you to centrally plan the package creation and distribution process. You also learned how to quickly stop a distribution and resend an advertised program. The ability to quickly stop a program is important if the wrong group of machines is accidentally targeted. Finally, you learned the client-side advertisement process.

DID YOU KNOW?

There are many SMS queries, reports, MOF files and scripts available online for free that can save you a considerable amount of time. These downloads are made available from other SMS administrators in the myITforum community for you to use or modify according to your needs. To access them, go to `http://www.myITforum.com/downloads`.

The default view of this Web page only shows the most recently uploaded items. Click on the **List All** link to see all the items that are available or the **Sections** link to see all of the items for a specific section. Queries, reports, and MOF files can be downloaded and imported into your SMS site, saving you the time of creating them from scratch. Some scripts are designed to be distributed using SMS software distribution, while others are designed as utilities.

Delivering Windows Installer Packages

Windows Installer is an operating system service that is responsible for installing, repairing, and removing software. It has become extremely popular; the majority of off-the-shelf software packages utilize Windows Installer technology. It has become a software installation standard within the information technology industry. One of the reasons for its popularity rests on the Certified for Microsoft Windows Logo certification. Applications must utilize Windows Installer features in order to place the certification logo on their package. This certification logo appears on applications that meet certain standards designated by Microsoft. The logo indicates which Windows operating systems the application is certified to run on. Applications can be certified to be compatible with Windows Installer. For more information about the **Certified for Microsoft Windows Logo certification** program, visit `http://www.microsoft.com/windowsserver2003/partners/isvs/cfw.mspx`.

Consumers benefit from the certification program because they can be assured that the product is coded to properly interact with Windows Installer, based on certain minimum standards. Third-party vendors benefit because they will sell more products. Microsoft benefits because more vendors begin to get their applications certified so that consumers will buy them. Prior to Windows Installer, administrators had been requesting a standard installation technology from Microsoft for some time. Desktop support professionals became tired of trying to become proficient with multiple technologies, and most of all, tired of guessing what will happen when one them is uninstalled. This technology provides a standard, reliable method for installing software. When a standard technology became available, consumers readily embraced it, adding further to the popularity of Windows Installer. Having a standard is good for everyone. Vendors can code applications based on the standard and consumers know what they are buying if the application is certified by the vendor that created the technology,

Because of the popularity of this innovative technology, this book designates an entire chapter to Windows Installer architecture, features, command line syntax, and integration with SMS 2003. You will learn how to install and uninstall Windows Installer-based applications with SMS, and discover some helpful tips.

Benefits of Windows Installer

The benefits of Windows Installer over other software installation technologies include:

- **PROPER MANAGEMENT OF SHARED RESOURCES** — Windows Installer uses a reliable method of tracking resources that are shared between applications. *Resources* are those items that are delivered by Windows Installer:

  - **Files** are typically DLLs that contain program information.

  - **Registry keys** are locations in the system registry that contain information about programs.

  - **Keypaths** can be either files or registry keys that point to the location of components.

  - **Component Code** is a Globally Unique Identifier assigned to each component, feature, and product.

  This method is based on using Globally Unique Identifiers for application components and a tracking database.

- **IMPROVED METHODS FOR ENFORCEMENT OF INSTALLATION RULES** — Application installation rules determine how an application will track the resources that it installs and how it will use resources from existing applications. Prior to Windows Installer, each installation program used its own installation rules. Now, each application that uses Windows Installer uses a standard set of rules for installation.

- **ON-DEMAND INSTALLATION OF ENTIRE APPLICATIONS OR APPLICATION FEATURES** — This is done through administrative installation points (sometimes called administrative installations), which are source images of application installations placed at a network location. End-users then run their installation from the administrative installation point. On-demand applications work through the use of icons. The application isn't installed until the user attempts to use it. Application features can be set up to install when the user attempts to access them for the first time. This feature is sometimes called *install on first use*. This can be beneficial when trying to reduce the amount of disk space that an application requires, or when trying to speed up the initial installation time of an application if certain features are not commonly used within an organization.

- **REMOVAL OF SOFTWARE IS MUCH CLEANER** — Because Windows Installer has a more sophisticated method for tracking changes that an application installation makes to a PC, these changes can more easily be reversed when the application is uninstalled.

- **CONTAINS BETTER ROLLBACK SUPPORT FOR FAILED APPLICATIONS** — Rollback is the act of returning a PC to its original condition if an installation is canceled prior to its completion. Because of the more advanced tracking methods, rollback operations are more successful.

- **RUNTIME RESOURCE RESILIENCY** — This is also known as auto repair, dynamic repair, and self-healing; it allows applications to dynamically repair themselves if missing or corrupt components are discovered. Once the application determines it needs repairs, it accesses the administrative installation where it was installed and begins to copy only the necessary components.

- **PATCH SEQUENCING** — This allows patch authors to define the best order of patch installation within the MSI package. This feature drastically improves patch management of an application, allowing a much cleaner approach to installing and removing installation updates.

Windows Installer Architecture

Windows Installer consists of an operating system resident installation service, a standard format for component management (components are collections of resources), and a management Application Programming Interface (API) for application tools. Let's look at each section of the architecture.

Windows Operating System Installer Service

Prior to the Windows Installer technology, installation programs used their own setup executable or script. Each application vendor was responsible for obeying the proper installation rules, as *they* understood them. These rules were subjective because there was no qualified standard.

An analogy of what Windows Installer is to software installation standards can be seen in the way hardware drivers are written. Hardware vendors are responsible for writing drivers based on Windows API standards. In the same way, software vendors are responsible for writing software installation programs based on the Windows Installer standard. One central service is responsible for installing all software and keeping track of it.

Current versions of Windows Desktop Family and Server Family operating systems ship with Windows Installer integrated with the operating system. At present, the most recent release of Windows Installer is version 3.1. The installation download can be accessed at this location: `http://www.microsoft.com/downloads/details.aspx?FamilyID=889482fc-5f56-4a38-b838-de776fd4138c&displaylang=en`.

Requirements for this installation include Windows 2000 Service Pack 3, Windows 2000 Service Pack 4, Windows XP Service Pack 1, and Windows XP Service Pack 2. Windows Server 2003 ships with Windows Installer 3.1, but requires a hotfix offered by Microsoft (see Knowledge Base article KB898628).

A Management API for Application Tools

The management API exists to allow Windows Installer to manage all file paths for applications written to support Windows Installer. Because of this, other software features are supported, such as:

- **INSTALL ON DEMAND (FEATURE LEVEL)** — Allows application features to be installed from the administrative installation when needed, without the need to re-run the installation setup program.

- **INSTALL ON DEMAND (PRODUCT LEVEL)** — Allows programs to be installed when a program is executed from an icon run from the desktop, or from a Windows Programs group. It is supported by Windows 2000 and later operating systems only.

  From a Windows Group Policy Object standpoint, this Install on Demand feature is also said to be *advertised*. Advertisement is defined as the availability of a product or feature in the absence of installation files. The scope of advertising a product is limited to only installing the entry points to that product, such as desktop and **Start** menu shortcuts, file extension associations, and OLE registration. After an end-user runs the application shortcut, the installation files are pulled from an administrative installation.

  SMS advertisements are notifications with a range of options. The notifications can be visible or invisible to the users. Installation options can be mandatory or silent. Scheduling for the beginning and ending of advertisements is also an option.

- **RUNTIME RESOURCE RESILIENCY** — In the IT world, this feature has been referred to as self-healing and dynamic repair. It works in much the same way as the Install on Demand feature. Runtime Resource Resiliency performs two checks:

    ▪ It checks to see if the component and feature are installed. If not, an Install on Demand will be performed.

    ▪ Another check verifies that all components in the requested feature are properly installed. If problems with the install are found, or if the files are corrupt, they can be repaired without having to rerun the program's setup executable.

A Standard Format for Component Management

Other installation technologies use compiled or uncompiled scripts to deliver files, add, remove, or change registry key information, and install other resources. Windows Installer processes application information as a hierarchy of logical building blocks. These building blocks are as follows:

- Products are applications. An example of an application would be Microsoft Office. Products are contained in a single package file with the extension of .MSI. While products are at the top of the Windows Installer hierarchy, they do not have ownership over components or resources (described in the next two sections). In other words, components and resources may be installed with a particular application, such as Microsoft Office 2003, but they will be utilized by all applications on the system that require them to operate. When Microsoft Office 2003 is removed, the components and resources that are being used by other applications will remain on the system, but all unused components and resources will be removed. Like components, they have Globally Unique Identifiers (GUIDs). A list of product GUIDs is maintained by Windows Installer, in order to quickly check if a given application is already installed at installation time.

- Features are combinations of components of an application. Specifically, features are available to users when they select the custom installation option in an installation program. In the Windows Installer hierarchy, features don't have exclusive ownership of their components. In addition, features from multiple applications will share components—a concept that is not possible using older installer technologies.

- Components are collections of resources, which are those items that are delivered by Windows Installer.

Windows Installer defines the *component* as the lowest, most fundamental level of the application information hierarchy. Components are comprised of resources, such as files, registry keys, keypaths, and component code. Resources can only belong to one component; they are not shared among components. Components can be shared among applications. Resources are installed and removed together, as a component. Components "own" their resources.

A component's keypath can be a file or registry key that points the way to a component. When an application requests a path to a given component, Windows Installer returns the location of the keypath resource, which typically will be a file that has been designated as the keypath file. It is the responsibility of Windows Installer to manage the keypath information for each application that is installed, as long as the application supports Windows Installer. If keypath information is found to be invalid by Windows Installer, the Runtime Resource Resiliency feature engages.

The component code is *globally unique*. This means that a single component is guaranteed to have the same set of resources and the same Globally Unique Identifier (GUID). This concept is true regardless of what product it ships with. A given component's GUID is also known as its *component code*. Once a component is installed on a system, any future application feature that requires it will forgo the installation of the component and utilize the existing one.

Windows Installer manages applications at the component level. No two resources will ever be installed or uninstalled unless the component that owns them is installed or uninstalled. In addition, Windows Installer is able to effectively manage resources other than files. Older installation technologies could only manage at the file level and were unable to manage resources other than files. Shared files were managed by using the reference count (*refcount*) method. The operating systems would maintain a refcount of the applications that were using a given file. The refcount would be appended by one for each application that used a given file. Before the file would be removed, the refcount for that file would have to be zero. Unfortunately, there were no methods for keeping track of other resources, such as registry keys. Windows Installer, however, keeps a shared count at the component level. Because components "own" resources, all resources belonging to a given component have a proper shared count. As you can imagine, Windows Installer provides a much cleaner uninstall than former installer technologies.

Patch Sequencing

Beginning with version 3.0, Windows Installer provides the options for patch authors to group related patches into *patch families*. Then relationships can be defined between the patches in one patch family and between patch families. This feature will remove some of the burden from administrators in the field as they attempt to maintain applications that are standardized and updated to the latest version. Ultimately, patch sequencing will allow for patches to be applied or removed out of chronological order without leaving an application in an undesirable state.

Patch authors should begin taking advantage of this helpful set of properties within Windows Installer. For more information on this feature, see the "Patch Sequencing for Windows Installer 3.0" whitepaper for installation developers and setup authors at `http://www.microsoft.com/downloads/details.aspx?FamilyID=ad7ac91e-2493-4549-ae6f-bf5e007c12a3&displaylang=en`.

Locked Down Environments

It is becoming quite common to utilize the Windows group policy features to control the end-user's ability to perform certain activities at the desktop. How will Install on Demand and Runtime Resource Resiliency features operate in this environment? Windows Installer can run under the user context or the local system account. Administrators can set the group policy to run all configuration operations (including installation, repair, and uninstall features) for specified programs under local system accounts. Group policy will only work with workstations that have Windows 2000 or later installed and it does not provide any flexible scheduling or status messages.

The Windows Installer Package File

Windows Installer products are described by package files in a database format optimized for installation performance. The package file describes any necessary installation instructions. The Windows Installer service relies on Msiexec.exe to interpret the package file. The package file generally has an extension of .MSI and can contain all the files necessary for installing a product. Some packaging vendors provide a method of packing MSI installations with an .EXE extension, but in most cases the .MSI extension is used. An example of an MSI package comes with the Windows Server 2003 Administrative Tools Pack and is called Adminpak.msi. This is the only file necessary to install this product. All the supporting files are compressed inside this MSI package. As you run Adminpak.msi, Msiexec.exe on the local machine reads the MSI package and begins to install it. In order to make all of the Windows Installer features available to organization, an administrative installation is necessary. Features such as Install on Demand, Runtime Resource Resiliency, and Run from the Network all require an administrative installation. See the "Creating an Administrative Install" section later in this chapter.

Command Line Customization

Customization of Windows Installer installations is accomplished through the use of command line options. There are so many command line options that it can be rather confusing. There are Windows Installer options and User Interface (UI) options provided with versions previous to 3.0 and a new set of options released for version 3.0 and later. The first set of options affects how Windows Installer processes the MSI package. The second set of options controls the user interface.

Table 8.1 provides the syntax for each of the command line options. The following line is the Windows Installer command line syntax:

```
Msiexec /Option <Required Parameter> [Optional Parameter]
```

Option Type	Option Syntax	Description
Install Options	`</package | /i> <Product.msi >`	Installs or configures a product.
	`/j<u|m> <Product.msi> [/t <Transform List>] [/g <Language ID>]`	Advertises a product; - m to all users, u to current user
	`/a <Product.msi>`	Administrative install
	`</uninstall | /x> <Product.msi | ProductCode>`	Uninstalls the product.
Display Options	`/passive`	Unattended mode - progress bar only
	`/quiet`	Quiet mode, no user interaction
	`/q[n|b|r|f]`	Sets user interface level. n - No UI b - Basic UI r - Reduced UI f - Full UI (default)
	`/help`	Help information
Logging Options	`/l[i|w|e|a|r|u|c|m|o|p|v|x|!|+|*] <LogFile>`	i - Status messages w - Nonfatal warnings e - All error messages a - Start up of actions r - Action-specific records u - User requests c - Initial UI parameters m - Out-of-memory or fatal exit information o - Out-of-disk-space messages p - Terminal properties v - Verbose output x - Extra debugging information ! - Flush each line to the log. + - Append to existing log file. * - Log all information, except for v and x.
	`/log <LogFile>`	Equivalent of /l* <LogFile>

Table 8.1: Windows Installer Command Line Options Version 3.1.

Option Type	Option Syntax	Description
Restart Options	`/norestart`	Do not restart after the installation is complete.
	`/promptrestart`	Prompts the user for restart if necessary.
	`/forcerestart`	Always restart the computer after installation.
Update Options	`/update<Update1.msp>[;Update2.msp]`	Applies update(s).
	`/uninstall`	Remove update(s) for a product.
Repair Options	`/f[p|e|c|m|s|o|d| u| a|v] <Product.msi | ProductCode>`	Repairs a product. p - only if file is missing o - if file is missing or an older version is installed (default) e - if file is missing or an equal or older version is installed d - if file is missing or a different version is installed c - if file is missing or checksum does not match the calculated value u - all required user-specific registry entries (default) a - forces all files to be reinstalled m - all required computer-specific registry entries (default) s - all existing shortcuts (default) v - runs from source and recaches local package
Setting Public Properties	`[PROPERTY=PropertyValue ]`	Sets Public Properties.

Table 8.1: Windows Installer Command Line Options Version 3.1 (continued).

Advanced Customization

Basic customizations can be applied from the command line, while more advanced customizations are performed using *Transform files*. Transform files provide a variety of installation types from the same administrative installation; they can not be applied after the installation. They contain .MST extensions and are created with tools such as Wise for Windows Installer (`www.wise.com`) and Macrovison FLEXnet AdminStudio (`http://www.macrovision.com/products/flexnet_adminstudio/adminstudio/index.shtml`). Larger products, such as Microsoft Office, may include a custom installation tool to create Transform files. The following Windows Installer syntax places the Transform argument after the MSI package name:

```
Msiexec <Options> <Package>.msi
Transforms=<TransformPathAndName>.mst <BasicUIOptions>
```

Distributing a Windows Installer Service Update with SMS

To take advantage of the latest features available in Windows Installer, be sure to update to the latest version. There are several methods that can be used to upgrade the Windows Installer service using SMS.

First, you can distribute the Windows Installer service update as a stand-alone SMS advertisement. This is the preferred method, unless there are simple maintenance tasks that also need to be performed. Configurations such as registry edits, file copies, or file deletions would be considered simple maintenance. Windows Installer installations require a reboot.

Alternately, you could install the Windows Installer service update as a dependent program with another advertised program (see Figure 8.1). This option can be a bit trickier. End-users should not be provided with any options for canceling the Windows Installer installation. If they do cancel it, the second program will never be run.

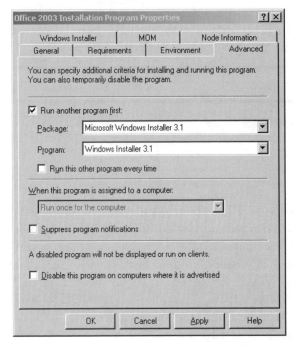

Figure 8.1: Updating the Windows Installer Service as an SMS Dependent Program.

You could also choose to call the installation with a script and include any other system maintenance tasks that may need to be performed. In this situation, the script would be called a *wrapper program*, or simply a wrapper. Wrapper programs contain commands that customize a software distribution while advertising a single SMS program. If other maintenance tasks need to be performed on the target systems, using a wrapper to include them with the upgrade of Windows Installer can reduce the number of times that end-users will be interrupted. Be sure to thoroughly test the script. As the script grows in complexity, the chance of installation problems becomes greater. For more information on wrappers, see Chapter 9.

Distributing Windows Installer Updates

Current versions of Windows Desktop Family and Server Family operating systems ship with Windows Installer, integrated with the operating system. At present, the most recent release of Windows Installer is version 3.1. To find the current version of Windows Installer, go to **Start**⇨ **Run** and type `msiexec` in the **Open** text box. A dialog box resembling Figure 8.2 will appear. The version is located after the **V** on the first line in the dialog box.

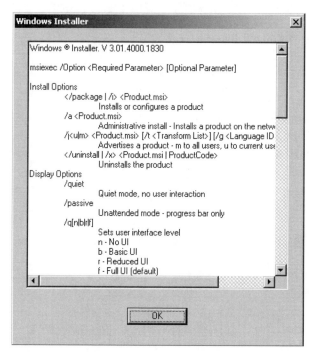

Figure 8.2: Viewing Windows Installer Command Line Options.

Download the proper upgrade for the versions that are installed in your environment. Currently, the installation download can be accessed at this location: `http://www.microsoft.com/downloads/details.aspx?FamilyID=889482fc-5f56-4a38-b838-de776fd4138c&displaylang=en`.

To find the latest version, try using Google.com to search for "Windows Installer download" and look for links to Microsoft.com. Also, monitor newsletters from online communities such as MyITForum.com to stay up to date with the latest releases.

For installation requirements, see the "Windows Operating System Installer Service" section earlier in this chapter.

The steps for updating Windows Installer are as follows:

1. Download the most current version of the Windows Installer installation. The file name is WindowsInstaller-KB893803-v2-x86.exe.

2. Determine the appropriate command line options to use by using the /? switch (see Figure 8.2).

3. Create the SMS package. Configure the source directory to point to the location of WindowsInstaller-KB893803-v2-x86.exe, or the filename for the latest version of Windows Installer.

4. Create a program using the proper command line syntax.

    *   On the **General** tab, configure the command line to use the syntax listed in Step 2 (For example: `WindowsInstaller-KB893803-v2-x86.exe /passive`).

    *   Select the **Run with administrative rights** option if the end-user does not have administrative rights on the local machine (see Figure 8.3). Make any additional program configurations.

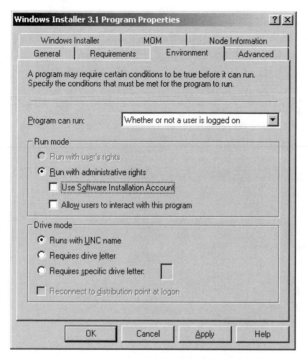

Figure 8.3: Configuring the Run with Administrative Rights Program Option.

5. Add distribution points.

6. Create and configure an advertisement.

Distributing MSI Packages with SMS

To distribute MSI files with SMS, follow these steps:

1. Update the Windows Installer service on the target machine (if not already updated).

2. If you wish, create the administrative installation of the MSI program. Use this command line installation syntax for creating an administrative installation: `Msiexec /a \\<ServerName>\<ShareName>\<Package>.msi`. Notice that a dialog box will appear, requesting the location of the administrative install.

3. Create an SMS package. Configure the source directory to be the administrative installation that you created in Step 2, if you chose to use the administrative installation option. Otherwise, use the share where you copied the original software files. This can be located on a distribution point. Note that a disadvantage of using an administrative

share for the SMS package source will cause the size of the package to be much larger, using more disk space on DPs and clients, and utilizing more network bandwidth. As a package creation alternative, use the Create Package from Definition wizard. To access this wizard, right-click the **Package** console tree and then select the **New⇨ Package from Definition** menu item. The **Welcome** page will appear. Click the **Next** button. The **Package Definition** page will appear (see Figure 8.4). Click the **Browse** button to select the MSI package file that you want to create a package from. Click the **Next** button and continue through the wizard.

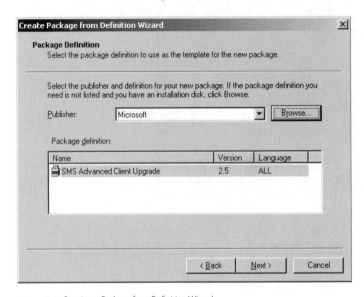

Figure 8.4: Creating a Package from Definition Wizard.

4. When using the **Run with administrative rights** option on the **Environment** tab, ensure that ALLUSERS=2 is set in the SMS program's command line options on the **General** tab, so that Windows Installer does a per-machine installation rather than a per-user installation. For example, if smstestprog.msi is an MSI application, run with this command line:

```
msiexec /I smstestprog.msi ALLUSERS=2
```

This will perform a per-machine installation. Otherwise, a per-user installation will occur for the local system account. This would result in only the local system account having access; anyone else using the machine would be denied.

5. Create and configure the advertisement. For best results, select the **Download from distribution point** option. This is especially true for MSI packages, because they require the Windows Installer to perform the installation. Since the Windows Installer is local to the client, the operation will be more successful if the MSI package is also local.

Planning for Resilient Sources

Resilient sources are installation share points that are available to systems with a particular MSI application installed, throughout the life of the application. Windows Installer advanced features such as application repair and install on demand require access to application files located on resilient sources. By default, Windows Installer adds a pointer in its database to the location from where it was installed. This pointer is called the *source list*. The source list can become inaccurate if the software sources move, which is likely to happen at some point.

Proper planning of resilient sources prior to deploying MSI packages is quite useful. Prior to the release of SMS 2003, it was critical to determine a stable location on the network for these source files that was unlikely to change. Planning an administrative installation was much easier than attempting to make changes to the Windows Installer database on each SMS client at a later time. Fortunately, Microsoft added integration for managing resilient resources into the SMS 2003 product.

Creating an Administrative Install

To create an administrative install with Windows Installer, follow these steps:

1. Access the CD from a CD-ROM drive or copy it to a network share.

2. Use the following syntax to create an administrative installation:

   ```
   Msiexec /a \\<Servername>\<ShareName>\<Package>.msi
   ```

   In this syntax, the **<Package>.msi** is the MSI file responsible for installing the product.

3. Enter the desired location for the administrative installation when prompted to do so. The dialog box may also ask for the CD Key, which is usually found on the CD jewel case.

4. Select an installation file from the administrative installation to use for distribution. The file will use the MSI or EXE format, depending on the product.

Product Source Update Management

SMS 2003 includes a component called Product Source Update Management that allows Advanced Client computers to dynamically update Windows Installer network locations, also referred to as source locations. Keep in mind these key points of Product Source Update Management:

- Even if SMS did not install the application, source network locations are updated for Windows Installer applications currently installed on the computer.

- Automatic Updates of source locations for each configured Windows Installer application occur from one central location.

- When an SMS Advanced Client computer roams around the network, source locations are automatically updated.

- Windows Installer per-machine and per-user installed applications are supported.

- Windows Installer applications that are installed with elevated or non-elevated privileges are supported.

There are several events that trigger a Windows Installer source locations update:

- Surpassing a 30-day interval.

- Running an SMS program that contains Windows Installer information.

- The client roams to a network location supported by a different management point.

- The client roams to a new network location for more than eight hours.

Components

There are two major components to Product Source Update Management. The Product Source Update Manager agent runs on the SMS Advanced Client. It is responsible for updating the list of network locations where Windows Installer can find the program source files. The Product Source Update Manager agent creates a log in the %Windows%\system32\ccm\logs directory in a file called SrcUpdateMgr.log.

The second component is the **Windows Installer** tab on the **Programs** property page of each SMS program. Within this tab, the administrator can specify the Windows Installer Product Code and Windows Installer (MSI) file name (see Figure 8.5). Creating an advertisement is not required for the Product Source Update Manager to begin providing source locations for the installed MSI application.

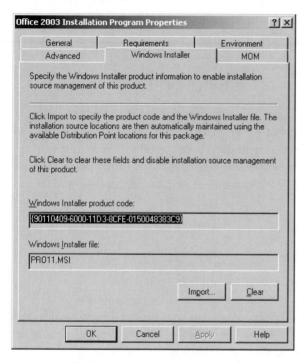

Figure 8.5: Configuring the Windows Installer Tab.

Dial-up Connections

Product Source Management is a great solution for well-connected clients. You will need to consider the results of dial-up users in your environment. Clients connected over dial-up will need a workaround for updates larger than 10 MB. The tips in this section will point you in the right direction:

- You can add multiple resilient sources to the source list during the initial installation of an application. This can be done by using a transform editor to modify the transform file or from the command line during the installation. Windows Installer begins at the top of the source list. The first location on the source list that it can access will be used. The command line syntax is as follows:

```
msiexec.exe /I \\<Server\share\msifile>.msi
SOURCELIST="\\<Server\share>;\\<Server\share>;\\<Server\share>
```

- Use special care with mobile or remote users to keep them from accessing resilient sources across slow networks. Pay close attention to the source list to ensure that it is not referencing a share that is across a slow link. CD drives can also be added to the source list. You may want to add the CD drive as the first location in the source list.

- To change the source list on your managed systems after MSI application deployment, see this reference for writing automation scripts, located on TechNet: `http://support.microsoft.com/default.aspx?scid=KB;EN-US;Q297168&`.

Installing MSI Packages from a Distribution Point

As mentioned in the "Distributing MSI Packages with SMS" section, MSI package installation works better in situations where the **Download program from distribution point** option is utilized, as opposed to the **Run program from distribution point** option. If you must run the package from a distribution point, it's best to not refer to Msiexec.exe in the command line of the program. Simply specify the MSI package with its required switches and options and let the operating system find Msiexec.exe.

Configuring System Restarts

Restarting systems is always an area of concern, because end-users could potentially receive an unwanted interruption and possibly lose their work. A reboot may be necessary after installing the Windows Installer update, or after installing an MSI-based application, if existing files that need to be replaced are in use. The only way to know if a reboot will be required is by properly testing the distribution. If so, you'll need to consider several issues.

For attended installations, it is better to provide a user dialog box to indicate that a reboot must occur, rather than just letting it happen. To do this, use either the **/quiet, /passive, /qb, /qr**, or **/qf** MSI command line options along with the **/promptrestart** option. You will also need to select the **Program restarts the computer** drop-down option on the **General** tab of the Program property sheet (see Figure 8.6).

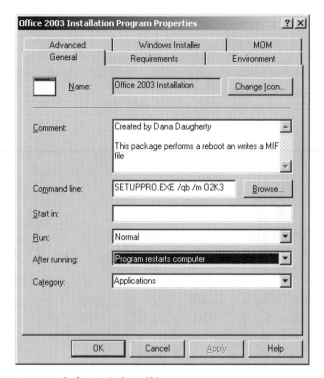

Figure 8.6: Configuring the General Tab.

For unattended installations, if that is your preference, use the **/quiet**, **/q** or **/qn** options. Then select either the **Only when a user is logged off** or **Whether or not a user is logged on** options from the **Program can run** option on the **Environment** tab. To configure the program to run when the workstations are not in use, be sure to select the **Only when a user is logged off** option, then remind users that they need to log off when they go home.

Generating Install Status MIFs

MIFs are Management Information Files. Clients send installation status MIFs to the SMS primary server where a package was created. The information contained in the MIF is then inserted into the database and can be viewed by administrators in the **System Status**⇨ **Advertisement Status** tree. Information about the success of the installation is contained in the file and displayed from the advertisement status messages. The installation status MIFs are generated for Windows Installer-based packages by using the **/m** command line option. An example of the proper syntax would look like this: `Msiexec /I setup.msi /m adacr7`. Note that the .MIF file extension must be left off.

To insert custom installation status MIF information into the database, the SMS package needs to know the name of the MIF. The other fields are required when there is more than one MIF file with the same name on the client. The text from the **Name**, **Version** and **Publisher** fields should be filled in with the data from the **General** tab of the same package. Add this information on the **Reporting** tab in the package property sheet (see Figure 8.7).

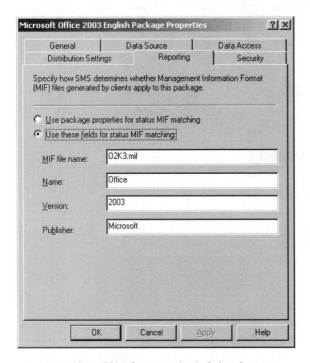

Figure 8.7: Adding MIF File Information within the Package Properties.

Automated Removal of MSI Installations

The standard msiexec.exe command line removal options, **/uninstall** or **/x**, will bring up an option dialog box similar to Figure 8.8, followed by another dialog box. In most situations, these dialog boxes will be undesirable, because users will be able to stop the removal process.

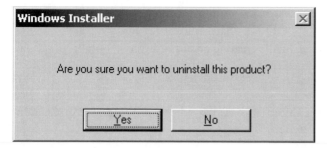

Figure 8.8: Result of Using the /uninstall Switch.

To perform a silent uninstall of an MSI-based application, use the following command line syntax:

```
Msiexec /uninstall <PackageCode> /quiet
```

In the syntax above, *PackageCode* is the code Globally Unique Identifier (GUID) given to a Windows Installer application. The GUID will exist in the following registry key: **HKEY_LOCAL_MACHINE\Software\Microsoft\Windows\CurrentVersion\Uninstall**.

For example, to uninstall the program Symantec PCAnywhere, retrieve the GUID for Symantec PCAnywhere. Create and distribute an uninstall program, using SMS, with this command line:

```
Msiexec /x {B05E8183-866A-11D3-97DF-0000F8D8F2E9} /q
```

Windows Installer Tips

Here are some helpful tips and cautions to keep in mind, as well as some descriptions of the Windows Installer Logging Options letter functions that will come in handy:

- To turn on Windows Installer logging, open Regedt32.exe and create the following key: **HKEY_LOCAL_MACHINE\Software\Policies\Microsoft\Windows\Installer**. Then add `Reg_SZ: Logging` with a value of `voicewarmup`. The name of the new log will begin with MSI, with random letters appended and an extension of .LOG. It will be located in the Temp folder. To quickly find the Temp folder, type `cd %temp%` at a command prompt.

- Letters placed in the registry entry value field will turn on different logging modes. They can be used in any order. The functions of each letter are described in the Table 8.1 earlier in this chapter. Logging should only be used for troubleshooting because it requires additional system overhead.

- Avoid distributing an MSI package that has a prompt that requests the CD key. Either use a Select agreement CD or use a CD key that is meant for multi-installs. Use the following command line parameters while creating an administrative install:

```
Msiexec /package <packagename.msi> PIDKEY=<"[CD-Key]">
```

- Standard Windows Installer error information is logged to the Windows Application Event log.

Summary

Using Windows Installer as a software installation technology requires some adaptations by administrators and end-users. These changes may be painful in some organizations, but the pain involved is well worth the benefits. Administrators must conform to a new syntax that must be used when issuing Windows Installer commands. There is a considerable learning curve associated with customizing MSI packages. Major customization may require special software packages that allow for editing and creating Transform files and MSI files. End-users must receive training if the Install on Demand feature will be used.

The benefits of Windows Installer are quite substantial, justifying the time that is necessary to learn how to use this service. Every software product that has the Certified for Microsoft Windows Logo certification uses Windows Installer for its installation technology. Because of this, administrators can rely on standard software installation and management process rules. Installing, uninstalling, and rolling back applications are more successful because of the new architecture. Installations finish sooner and take up less disk space, because application components are shared with other applications. New features such as Install on Demand, Runtime Resource Resiliency, and Run from the Network are now available for MSI packages. Also, distributing MSI packages to Windows 2000 and later machines can be done using Active Directory and Group Policy Object.

Part III

Advanced Topics

Customizing Installations

So far, we have focused on planning and configuring SMS to use the Software Distribution feature. We looked at the various processes that an administrator uses and the processes that SMS uses to delivery software packages. In Chapter 8, we discussed Windows Installer architecture, customization, and the process of delivering Windows Installer software packages with SMS. This chapter complements Chapter 8 by adding some information regarding software packaging and authoring for creating and modifying MSI packages. This chapter also focuses on the specifics of customizing the delivery of various types of software packages through the use of scripts, repackaging tools, and scripting tools. You will also learn how to use wrappers to customize SMS distributions. *Wrappers* are simple programs that call installation programs; they may also add customizations to the installation. The ability of SMS to distribute nearly any application that will install on a PC makes distribution of scripts, repackaged executables, MSI packages, and batch files easy.

In the software distribution process, SMS is responsible only for delivering an installation program. Contrary to what many think, SMS is only a vehicle for starting programs that install software. SMS is unable to edit a registry or even perform a simple file copy. Using repackaging and scripting technologies in the distribution process serves to perform these functions and to customize installations, in order to meet your organization's needs. These technologies can help to streamline the installation process and, when necessary, make them more user-friendly.

Windows Installer Package Customization

Windows Installer has become the most common software installation package format available. Windows Installer (MSI) packages can be customized at runtime by using a combination of the many command line options or by using a Transform file. Transform files can only be applied during an installation, but provide a variety of installation types from the same installation. They contain .MST extensions and are created by using special MSI customization tools. Larger products, such as Microsoft Office, may include a custom installation tool to create Transform files. These tools are specific to the application that they came with. More details about MSI Transform files and command line options are available in Chapter 8.

MSI Authoring Tools

There are several MSI authoring tools available. Some tools provide customization for the MSI file itself. These are called *MSI authoring tools* and require an in-depth understanding of MSI package concepts to use them. MSI authoring tools let you create MSI package files from scratch or edit existing ones. These tools are also quite costly, but there are less expensive tools that provide MST customization and require less skill. Wise for Windows Installer (www.wise.com) and Macrovison FLEXnet AdminStudio (http://www.macrovision.com/products/flexnet_adminstudio/adminstudio/index.shtml) are popular among administrators who author MSI packages. These tools provide many features, including:

- Capturing operating system configurations. OS configurations can be captured from a running machine at a specific moment in time. This is known as a *snapshot*. The snapshot can then be imported to determine potential conflicts between Windows Installer-based setups and an OS.

- Repackaging applications by analyzing an installation and then creating an MSI file based on the files and registry changes that were used for the installation.

- Windows Installer installation package development. This feature may be a bit beyond the scope of the typical administrator. It requires in-depth knowledge of Windows Installer development. One great resource for acquiring this skill set is Desktopengineer. com, a Web site is managed by Darwin Sanoy. There are plenty of articles, downloads, training information, and other links to get you started with Windows Installer development.

- Creating customized .MST files.

- Resolution of application conflicts by comparing the structure of the MSI package that you create with other MSI packages in a database. The database comes populated with many recent packages and you can add additional ones as well.

- Application isolation during development helps to prevent application conflicts. This is a feature of Windows Installer that allows an application to use dedicated copies of required DLLs rather than shared ones. Shared DLLs cause problems, because applications may be removed at different times, and this can cause a conflict with the remaining applications that share the DLL. These authoring tools take advantage of this feature, allowing developers to create applications with fewer conflicts.

FLEXnet AdminStudio 7 SMS Edition provides MST creation and editing along with repackaging, conversion of legacy package formats to MSI packages, and integration into SMS 2003. This product is offered for free. For these reasons, AdminStudio SMS Edition is becoming very popular among SMS administrators. It is available at the following location: `http://www.microsoft.com/smserver/downloads/2003/featurepacks/adminstudio/default.mspx`.

Repackaging

Packaging is developing an executable that performs all the necessary tasks to install an application onto a computer. The package contains all the files that the executable needs to run or copy onto the computer. *Repackaging* records all the changes that a packaging program makes to a computer. Here is an analogy: if you were to make some homemade soup, put it in a thermos, and place it in your lunch box, you would be packaging it. If, on the next day, you were to buy a ready-made sandwich from the store and bring it home, take it out of the bag, and put it in your lunch box, this would be repackaging. The repackaging process combines files, file operations, and registry settings into a single, self-extracting .EXE or .MSI file. The installation interface can then be customized. Additional actions can also be added to the installation to provide even more customization. In essence, repackaging tools change the process by which applications are installed on a PC. The repackaging tools track changes that occur on a resource machine after an installation and then compile all those changes into a self-extracting package file. The self-extracting package file is then distributed to many other PCs that use very similar hardware and software.

Prior to the popularity of Windows Installer, SMS administrators frequently repackaged applications as a way to customize software installations. Quite often, installation programs lacked the customizations necessary to allow them to be distributed to large numbers of systems—this created a need for repackaging. Today, the majority of program installations are Windows Installer-based, allowing administrators to customize installations while using standard installation options. The same set of command line options is available during any MSI installation. Even with the popularity of Windows Installer, there are some occasions where the repackaging process can be utilized. Reasons for repackaging applications may include:

- Providing alternate installation types that your organization needs, such as a *silent installation*. Silent installations require no interaction from the user.

- Packaging multiple applications into one package installation.

- Simplifying the self-extracting package process of copying files to a local machine, installing, and then deleting them. This is easier than copying files and directories from a standard installation source.

- Providing needed features not included in the original installation, such as:

  - Uninstall and rollback support

  - Installation logging

  - Multiple language support

- Customizing additional features needed, such as:

  - Custom dialog boxes

  - Custom graphics

  - Additional registry key editing

  - Additional file operations

All repackaging tools perform these basic steps:

1. An initial scan of the file system and registry.

2. The installation that will be repackaged is run on the reference machine.

3. A post-installation scan is completed. The repackaging tool records the registry and file structure changes that occurred.

4. Manual customization of the package and *compiling* can be performed at this point. Compiling is the process of converting the package into a .EXE or .MSI file format.

SMS Installer

SMS Installer is a repackaging tool that also includes a script editor. SMS Installer licensing is included with licensed versions of SMS 2003. At present, the newest version is v2.0.148.00, located at `http://www.microsoft.com/smsmgmt/downloads/installer.asp`. In the past, nearly every aspect of this product was useful. Unfortunately, this application hasn't received any development updates for several years and is nearing the end of its usefulness. This section provides details about features that continue to be helpful to SMS administrators.

Microsoft has built in an anti-piracy "feature" that requires the SMS Installer zip file to be located on an SMS site server in order for it to be extracted. Version 2.0.148.00 contains five tools:

- The Repackage Installation Wizard lets administrators repackage installation programs and compile them into self-extracting .EXE or .MSI package files.

- The Installation Expert Wizard allows you to customize the installation script, which is an .IPF file that is compiled into an .EXE or .MSI file.

- The Watch Application Wizard monitors DLL, OCX and VBX files, taking note of those being used by a specific application.

- Script Editor lets you use script commands when creating installation executables or Windows Installer programs.

- Windows Installer Support Tools provide support for compiling new packages and legacy packages into MSI format. This tool is rather old and lacks the features necessary for building robust MSI package files that take advantage of Windows Installer 3.1 features.

Repackage Installation Wizard

Repackage Installation Wizard allows administrators to repackage installation programs and compile them into self-extracting .EXE or .MSI package files. It is necessary to use a *clean* reference computer (without existing problems), with an OS and software configuration similar (if not identical) to the target machines. SMS Installer monitors and repackages any changes that occur on the reference machine. If the configuration of the target machine is different than the configuration of the reference machine, the .EXE or .MSI will apply the changes to the target machine incorrectly. This feature can come in handy for situations where you want to record configuration changes on a system and then distribute that change to multiple systems. Some configuration changes can be difficult to script, but can be captured by using the Repackaging Installation Wizard. See the SMS Installer product help for details.

Script Editor

The Script Editor Installation Expert tool lets you use script commands when creating installation executables or Windows Installer programs. These programs can be quite complex in nature, or they can be a simple wrapper program that calls another executable.

To access the Script Editor user interface, perform the following steps:

Choose the **Start**⇨ **Programs**⇨ **Microsoft SMS Installer**⇨ **SMS Installer 32** menu item. Then choose the **View**⇨ **Script Editor** menu item. If SMS Installer is opened in Installation Expert view (the default view), and the view is immediately changed to Script Editor by the user, multiple lines of code will be displayed (see Figure 9.1).

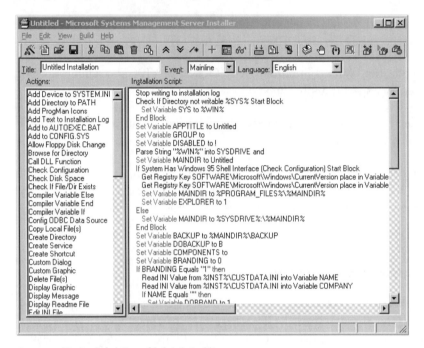

Figure 9.1: Viewing Default Lines of Code in Script Editor.

The code shown in Figure 9.1 is responsible for the default property selections in the Installation Expert view. This code can be edited or deleted if you desire. However, if you return to the Installation Expert and go back to the Script Editor, it will appear again. If you intend to use the Installation Expert, build the basic script using that tool. Later, you can add additional script actions from the Script Editor.

By default, when SMS Installer is closed, it retains the view in which it was closed. If SMS Installer is opened in Script Editor view, the Installation Script window will be blank. If script actions are then added, changing to the Installation Expert view can cause a loss of some script actions. The message shown in Figure 9.2 will also appear as a warning.

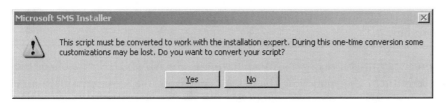

Figure 9.2: Viewing Loss of Script Actions Dialog Box.

Using Script Editor is pretty straightforward, and SMS Installer Help is thorough and easy to use. Script Editor is very handy for adding a few lines of code to call an additional program, or perform other script actions from a repackaged program.

Script Editor can also be used to create the entire program. To do this, follow these steps:

1. Save the script and then add any necessary variables and script actions. Saving first will help you avoid aggravation, because the interface can be a bit unpredictable.

2. Configure the Installation Properties by selecting the **Edit** menu. The third section down contains menu items that occur at runtime. Select the **Installation Properties** menu item and then the **Installation Properties** properties sheet will appear (see Figure 9.3).

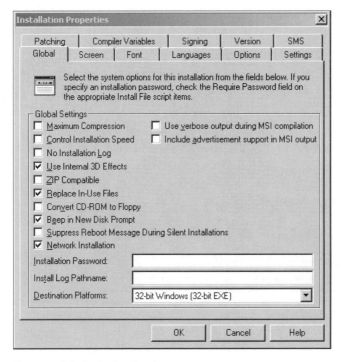

Figure 9.3: Selecting Runtime Menu Items.

3. When the script is complete, save it and then compile it from either the **Build** menu or the menu buttons.

When you create a new script, you may get errors referring to the **MAINDIR** variable or the **Check Disk Space** script item after removing the default code from the script editor window when you attempt to compile (See Figures 9.4 and 9.5).

Figure 9.4: Viewing the MAINDIR Error Message.

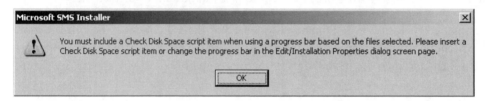

Figure 9.5: Viewing the Check Disk Space Error Message.

For the MAINDIR error, click the **Yes** button from the dialog box if asked whether you want to edit the Rollback.ipf script. Then remove the reference to the **MAINDIR** variable. The Check Disk Space error can be solved by selecting the **Screen** tab from the **Installation Properties** property sheet and then from the **Progress bar based on** drop-down box option, select the **Position in the EXE** item. If an error message indicates an invalid log pathname (see Figure 9.6), return to the **Installation Properties** property sheet and change the **Install Log Path Name** property.

Figure 9.6: Viewing the Invalid Log Pathname Error Message.

Installer Step-up Utility

Installer Step-up Utility (ISU) is a command line utility designed to take individual or multiple .EXEs generated by SMS Installer and migrate them to MSI format. ISU can only be run on Windows NT 4.0/2000 or Windows XP operating systems. By default, ISU completes the entire migration process for the specified setup package generated by SMS Installer. ISU can be run in batch mode by using wildcards and/or command line switches. See the SMS Installer online Help for more information.

Tips and Tricks for SMS Installer

The following information can save you some time and frustration while creating SMS Installer scripts.

- By default, SMS Installer automatically saves your changes upon exiting, without prompting. To elicit a Save prompt from the interface upon exiting, open the **Advanced Configuration** installation attribute, and select the **Options** tab. Select the **Prompt to Save** option.

- Script editor does not provide an undo command. This can be an unpleasant surprise if you make a mistake while modifying the script. As a workaround, be sure the **Prompt to Save** option is selected. If you save regularly, you can close the program when you make an undesired change. This will revert to the last time the script was saved.

- MSI compiling does not support some SMS Installer script actions, such as creating setup logs, support for 16-bit applications, or controlling the installation speed of the MSI.

- Script Editor Windows Installer tools do not work if Windows Installer (MSIExec.exe) is at an earlier version than v1.2. The tools will be grayed out.

- Script Editor Windows Installer tools do not work if Windows or Windows Installer is upgraded; the tools will be grayed out. This is a known issue with SMS Installer and ISU. The fix is to uninstall SMS Installer, remove the folders it leaves behind, then re-install it.

Resources for Repackaging Applications

For more information about using SMS Installer, Wise Package Studio, and InstallShield AdminStudio, see the following resources:

- The Web site `http://www.myITforum.com` contains forums dedicated to the SMS Installer, Package Studio, and AdminStudio products.

- The book *SMS Installer*, by Rod Trent, is very helpful. It was written prior to the Windows Installer tools features.

- Macrovision provides forums for its products, including Flexnet AdminStudio, at `http://community.installshield.com/forumdisplay.php?f=44`.

- Wise offers technical information and a knowledgebase at `http://www.wise.com/support.asp`.

Using Wrappers for Customizations

Wrappers are simple programs that call other programs, or contain additional customizations beyond those that are provided by the application that is being delivered. The goal of using a wrapper is to save time during SMS program and package development, or to add customizations to the application delivery process. Using a wrapper should complement an application that is being distributed by SMS. The wrapper is actually the program being called from the command line of the SMS program (see Figure 9.7).

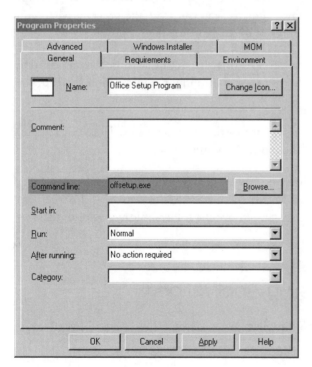

Figure 9.7: SMS Program Command Line.

In turn, the wrapper can call one or more applications, edit the registry, perform file operations, start or stop services, or perform a reboot. The knowledge of the administrator and the features of the scripting language limit the customization possibilities. Usually, the former causes a limitation before the latter. However, there are many great resources to solve this problem (see the end of this chapter). By becoming knowledgeable about the features and fundamentals of several languages, an administrator can also overcome the limitations of scripting languages, at least where software distribution is concerned.

Wrappers can be written in any scripting or programming language. Languages that are powerful, yet lightweight and simple, are good choices for wrapper scripting. SMS Installer is a popular scripting tool among SMS administrators. The reasons for its popularity include its flexibility, a Graphical User Interface (GUI), and the fact that it is free to organizations that have a valid SMS license. Other common scripting choices for creating wrappers are Visual Basic Scripting Edition (VBS), DOS batch scripting, Wise, and Macrovision. The use of variables and registry editing will save administrators from the need to create additional SMS programs and packages. It will also provide customizations that could not be obtained from other sources.

The following sections offer examples of useful customizations to add to a package via a wrapper. Language-specific syntax has been omitted.

Checking the OS Product Type

SMS advertised programs have no way to determine the difference between a Windows 2000 server and a Windows 2000 workstation. There are scenarios where administrators want to deploy an SMS package to one of these platforms but not to the other. A wrapper works well in this type of situation. To create the wrapper, OS product type information must be gathered from the following registry key: **HKLM\System\CurrentControlSet\Control\Product\Option\ProductType**.

Add the following logic to a wrapper:

- Place the data from the registry value: **HKLM\System\CurrentControlSet\Control\Product\Option\ProductType** into a variable, such as NTTYPE, if the system has Windows NT running.

- Create IF statements that check NTTYPE. This can be done by using the IF\While script item from the list of scripts in the left pane of the Script Editor interface.

- Determine if NTTYPE is a domain controller or member server; if it is, then exit the installation. If it is not, then call the program that installs the application.

Notice that workstation operating systems are specified as WinNT in the **HKLM\System\ CurrentControlSet\Control\Product\Option\ProductType** registry value, but server operating systems are differentiated.

Using a Predefined Variable

You can use a predefined variable that allows the wrapper to execute another program from the same directory. In other words, the wrapper is run from the \\<FileServer>\install\Adobe\ Acrobat\Reader directory. The wrapper calls Setup.exe from the same directory, rather than using the entire UNC path, such as \\<FileServer>\install\ Adobe\Acrobat\Reader\setup.exe. SMS Installer uses the predefined variable *%INST%* for this purpose; other scripting languages use other variables. This *%INST%* variable saves a tremendous amount of time in additional SMS program development and administration when using wrappers. This feature is extremely useful when using distribution points to distribute a package to multiple child sites. The example in the following section demonstrates the time that can be saved when using *%INST%* for SMS Installer wrappers.

Calling Programs from the Installation Folder

In this example, let's say that a silent installation of Adobe Acrobat Reader must be distributed to all desktops in an organization by the close of business tomorrow, because a new customer or client requires your company to use it when viewing some of their documents.

Here are the specifics:

- You have one primary site with 50 child sites reporting to it.

- You must deploy the package by using a silent install.

- You have Windows 2000 and Windows XP desktop operating systems.

- Due to IT policy, prior to attended installations, you must notify users with the SMS advertised programs dialog box, .

- You must use standard dialog boxes and backgrounds for attended installations.

- Due to the immediate deadline of this distribution, the program must be distributed using every available minute. Because of this, SMS advertised programs must be configured to run whether or not a user is logged on.

Here are the requirements necessary to complete this request:

1. Run a silent installation from the Adobe Acrobat Reader setup program. This is the best choice in this scenario, since it provides installations to all the OS platforms in the organization from one setup file.

2. Use a wrapper because the installation will be attended, at times. The wrapper must call the Acrobat Reader setup with the proper switch. It must also use the organization's standard background and dialog boxes.

3. Call the setup program from the wrapper. The best option is to place the wrapper script into the Adobe Acrobat Reader installation directory and use it as the source when configuring the package. Then use a predefined variable, such as *%INST%* from SMS Installer, to call the reader setup program from the same directory. *%INST%* is the directory of the compiled script executable at runtime. Using this variable will only require one SMS advertised program to be created for all 50 sites. Another option is to call the setup program from a file server share or a distribution point share using a UNC path. Unless some complicated programming techniques are used, this option would require 50 SMS advertised programs to be created. The program will need to call a setup program from a file server on its local LAN.

4. Create the wrapper. The script logic is listed below. SMS Installer and Wise Script Editor use the *%INST%* variable. Other scripting languages use different variables to perform the same functionality. Execute `%INST%\setup.exe /s` (see Figure 9.8). Use **Wait** to pause the script until the setup is complete. Configure the progress bar or dialog boxes to update users with the progress of the installation. Place the compiled script into the Adobe Acrobat Reader installation directory.

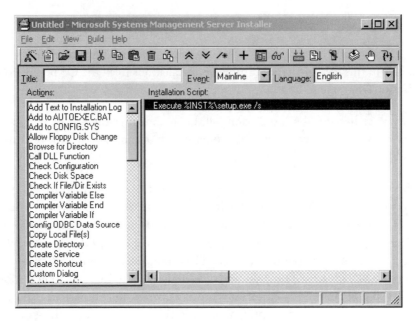

Figure 9.8: Using the %INST% Variable.

5. In the SMS Administrator Console, create the SMS package, configuring it to use the Adobe Acrobat Reader installation directory.

6. Create the SMS program for the SMS package. From the command line, select the wrapper. On the **Environment** tab, select the **Whether or not users are logged on** property and then select the **Run with administrative rights** property. Add distribution points.

7. Create the advertisement. Configure it to be mandatory. Select the proper target collection.

Using the methods recommended above, the application would be ready for testing within 30 minutes. When you are satisfied with the testing, the SMS package will be ready to distribute. Without using the *%INST%* variable, either the request could not have been completed, or the SMS administrator would have needed to work all night.

 NOTE

An alternative to using SMS Installer and the **%INST%** variable is to use Visual Basic Scripting Edition (VBS) to create a variable that contains the folder path where the wrapper is initiated, as in the following example:

```
ScriptPath = objFSO.GetParentFolderName(WScript.ScriptFullname) & "\"
```

Stopping and Starting Services

Windows services can be stopped or started using simple scripted commands. This customization can be quite useful for stopping and then restarting anti-virus scanning software prior to delivering a software installation. The logic is pretty simple:

1. Execute the **Net Stop** command to stop the Network Associates (NAI) anti-virus scanner.

2. Execute the installation setup.

3. Execute the **Net Stop** command to restart the NAI anti-virus scanner.

Perform File Operations

Wrappers can be handy to perform file operations, especially when files need to be edited or copied during the runtime of the installation setup program. For example, when distributing an older version of the Dell OpenManage Client, Autoexec.bat needs to be copied from its original location prior to the installation. It needs to be copied back after the installation completes because the installation program has a bug that corrupts Autoexec.bat. For this reason, the wrapper needs to retain the old version of Autoexec.bat. Follow these steps:

1. Copy <SystemDrive>\Autoexec.bat to the <WindowsDirectory>\temp\Autoexec.bat.

2. Run the installation, and pause the script action until the installation completes.

3. Copy Autoexec.bat from <WindowsDirectory>\temp\Autoexec.bat to <SystemDrive>\ Autoexec.bat.

4. Delete <WindowsDirectory>\temp\Autoexec.bat.

Call Multiple Programs

Administrators can save time by using an SMS advertised program to call a wrapper that calls multiple programs. Calling multiple programs with one wrapper works well, as long as reboots are not required between the programs that are called.

Here's how to call multiple programs with one wrapper:

1. Execute a program. Cause the wrapper script to wait until it completes.

2. Execute another program. Cause the wrapper script to wait until it completes.

3. Add additional customizations.

One negative aspect of using a wrapper is that SMS installation status messaging becomes trickier when the wrapper calls multiple programs. An SMS package can only be assigned one status MIF file, so the wrapper must include some logic to cause the MIF file to indicate a program error if one occurs. While SMS Installer does include the ability to create failure status MIFs, suppose the wrapper itself fails or that you are testing for a condition using the IF/While and Exit Installation script items. SMS Installer does not have the ability to determine if the program that it called has failed. It only knows that it finished. VBS Scripting can utilize a DLL called ISMif from the SMS 2003 SDK. Using a VBS script, a wrapper can be created with logic that is intelligent enough to determine if the call failed. The wrapper can then pass failure information to ISMif.dll to create a failure status message that contains information to help the SMS administrator troubleshoot the problem. This scenario works quite nicely. For more information on installation status MIFs, see Chapter 12. For information on delivering and registering ISMif.dll, see Appendix A. An example of a script that uses ISMif.dll is available as a free download when you register this book at www.agilitypress.com.

User Interface Customization for Attended Installations

Many installations provide either a full user interface, with lots of user input required, or they provide a completely silent installation. A full user interface will provide software that is installed in a variety of ways, because users can enter any values they want. This approach will yield a non-standard result and possibly failed installations. In most organizations, this is undesirable, because it makes supporting the application very difficult. However, in certain situations, neither will work effectively. Using a wrapper provides the ability to call a silent installation while adding user interface customizations, such as backgrounds, dialog boxes, or company logos. These options can be standardized to give a more professional presentation to end-users. Remember, one of the end-user's primary interfaces to SMS is the interaction with advertised programs.

Closing Programs before Calling another Program

Most programs must be closed before they can be upgraded. Wrappers can end currently running tasks, such as programs, by calling Taskkill.exe with the appropriate switches and syntax (see the following example). Taskkill.exe is available locally on Windows XP Professional systems and is an example of a utility that can be used to close a program.

As an example, let's use Taskkill.exe to close Word before calling an Office upgrade. Follow these steps:

1. Execute Taskkill with the syntax `Taskkill /f winword.exe`.

2. Pause the wrapper script until Taskkill completes.

3. Execute \\<FileServer>\Install\O2k3\admin\setuppro.exe.

4. Pause the wrapper script until Setuppro.exe completes.

5. Add additional customizations.

More Scripting Technologies

The applications that have been discussed thus far in this chapter offer repackaging features. Some of these applications also have scripting features. Let's review some other programs that are strictly scripting technologies.

AutoIT

AutoIT is a simple but very helpful scripting tool. It was designed to automate simple Windows tasks and fills the void that other scripting tools may miss. AutoIT reads a script file created by an administrator. The script can then be compiled into an executable. The functions that it performs include:

- Calling programs

- Sending keystrokes and mouse-clicks

- Minimizing, hiding, closing, restoring, or waiting for windows

- Editing the registry

- Using simple string and variable functions

There are many situations where this tool may come in handy. One example is installing software that requires user interaction. At this point, the IT support staff can only hope the right selection is made. By using AutoIT, you can select the correct option for the user.

AutoIT is free and so is the script compiler. The AutoIT home page is `http://www.hiddensoft.com`.

Windows Script Host and Visual Basic Scripting

Windows Script Host is a powerful Windows administration tool that exposes OS objects and services to various scripting languages. Visual Basic Scripting is a subset of Visual Basic for Applications and is the most popular scripting engine for use with Windows Script Host.

Windows Script Host (WSH)

WSH is a powerful Windows administration tool included with Windows operating systems. It is becoming very popular among IT support personnel because of its seamless integration with Windows operating systems. WSH provides access to OS objects and services and uses the proper scripting engine for the type of script that accesses it. WSH is not dependent on specific scripting languages, but it does require WSH-compliant scripting engines. WSH's niche is non-interactive scripting, such as login scripting and machine automation. WSH is an object-oriented technology. It uses Windows *objects*, which are groups of Application Programming Interfaces (APIs) that perform similar tasks.

Windows Scripting Host provides many valuable services for system administration. Your level of functionality can be as simple or complex as you need, or as your experience allows. WSH enables you to:

- Modify registry keys

- Modify and retrieve environment variables

- Map network drives

- Connect to printers

- Run CreateObject and GetObject functions

- Access Windows Management Instrumentation (WMI)

Windows 2000 Professional and Windows XP Professional ship with early versions of WSH. To update to version 5.6, go to http://msdn.microsoft.com/scripting.

WSH is comprised of two executables. Wscript.exe is initiated from the command line, but its output is sent to a GUI. Cscript.exe is also initiated from the command line, but its output appears in a DOS window. Many options are supported by both interfaces. Run Wscript /? from the command line to see the possible command line options (see Figure 9.9).

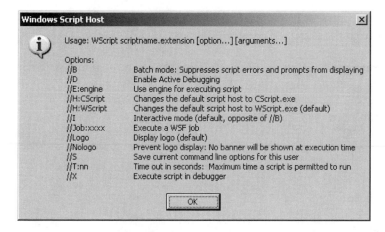

Figure 9.9: Wscript Command Line Options.

Visual Basic Scripting Edition (VBS)

Visual Basic Scripting Edition (VBS) is a scripting language used to create scripts that are hosted by WSH. VBS is an object-oriented scripting language that can be used to send code or messages to WSH. WSH recognizes VBS as a registered program and then runs the script.

Just like any other program, VBS scripts can be added to SMS packages and then distributed using advertised programs. However, there are a couple of limitations. Confirm that the version of WSH loaded on client machines supports the features you are trying to use. Depending on file and registry operations, end-users may need to have administrative rights to the local machine, as they would with any wrapper.

WSH and VBS Scripting Resources

For more information on WSH and VBS, see the following:

- *WMI Essentials for Automating Windows Management* by Marcin Policht

- http://www.msdn.microsoft.com/scripting

Batch Files

Batch scripting is the grandfather of all scripting technologies. Because of its lack of flexibility, it has become less popular than other scripting tools. DOS batch files can be distributed with SMS. Most likely, they will be used as wrapper files or called to perform simple file operations. To distribute a batch file with an SMS advertised program, follow these steps:

1. Verify that the batch file is present in the source directory that was configured on the **Data Source** tab, located in the Package Properties.

2. Open the **Program Properties** sheet for the SMS program that will be used to distribute the batch file.

3. Click the **Browse** button from the **General** tab.

4. Select the **All Files** (*.*) option from the **Files of type** drop-down box. The batch files will then appear.

Let's look at a few helpful batch tips:

Use the *%0\..* variable to perform operations within the same directory as the batch file. For example, Use %0\..\setup.exe to call Setup.exe from the same directory where the batch file is located.

Use the following commands to cause the black DOS screen to automatically close if required:

```
@echo off
Rem Add text here.
Cls
Exit
```

Remember that DOS allows the use of IF statements. Here is an example:

```
IF not exist "C:\program
files\Dell\OpenManage\client\actionagent.exe" goto oldlocat
REM
"C:\program files\Dell\OpenManage\client\actionagent.exe" /s:oldlocat
"c:\Dell OpenManage\client\actionagent.exe" /s
```

The code above tests two locations for the existence of Actionagent.exe. A command is then run based on the location of the .EXE.

For additional help, see `http://www.easydos.com/dosindex.html`.

Summary

Because SMS is only the vehicle for software delivery, you must become skilled at customizing application installations to your environment. Customization for application installations is performed through repackaging or scripting. This chapter provided you with an overview of the most popular tools for repackaging and scripting application installations. Repackaging solutions include Macrovision FlexeNet InstallShield, Wise Package Studio, and SMS Installer. Scripting tasks can be performed by using SMS Installer, WiseScript Editor, batch scripting, VBS/WSH scripting, and AutoIT. Windows Installer packages require some additional support from specialized applications for customizations. SMS Installer, Wise Package Studio and InstallShield each provide support for MSI applications.

DID YOU KNOW?

Microsoft recently released two new tools to allow SMS 2003 clients to scan for updates that are applicable to non-Microsoft applications and for configuration-related vulnerabilities. The Inventory Tool for Custom Updates (ITCU) and Scan Tool for Vulnerability Assessment (STVA) were released with SMS 2003 R2.

ITCU is designed to utilize catalogs created by vendors other than Microsoft and by corporate line-of-business software development teams. ITCU functions in a similar method to ITMU, a topic covered in this book.

STVA utilizes the Microsoft Baseline Security Analyzer (MBSA) 2.0 scan engine to scan SMS clients for known vulnerabilities caused by insecure configuration settings. SMS 2003 R2 is only free to Microsoft Software Assurance customers. Otherwise, there is a licensing fee.

Software Updates Management

Software updates management is considered to be a type of software distribution because it depends on the SMS software distribution feature to function. In broad terms, software updates management is concerned with detecting available software updates, also known as *patches*, releasing these updates into the enterprise, and then monitoring the enterprise to ensure that all systems are operating with the latest version of each update. Using SMS for software updates management requires an understanding of various workflow processes and SMS features. This chapter offers information about the change and configuration processes required to release a software update into the enterprise, the phases of delivering software updates, and the SMS 2003 Software Updates feature architecture. This chapter also covers the various SMS 2003 features used to deploy software updates, such as Inventory Tools for Microsoft Updates (ITMU), the Distribute Software Updates Wizard (DSUW), and various methods of viewing software updates information. Finally, you will learn how to troubleshoot problems with SMS 2003 software updates.

Change and Configuration Processes

Change and configuration processes help organizations release software updates into production with the least amount of disruption. Regardless of the software updates delivery mechanism, proper change and configuration processes should be in place to offer your customers the best possible service. The following steps should be utilized throughout any software updates delivery:

- **PLAN** — Prior to delivering software updates, plan for down time that is agreed upon by all parties who will be affected.

- **TEST** — To avoid disruption of production systems should something go wrong, apply the updates to test systems similar to those that will be targeted during the actual distribution. First, install the update without SMS to view the affects of the installation process. Later, use SMS to distribute the update to the test systems.

- **PILOT** — Select a small number of pilot systems that represent a cross section of the population that will be targeted with the final deployment. If the results are satisfactory, progress to a second and possibly a third phase, each with larger numbers of systems. Closely monitor the results. Make the necessary changes and re-pilot the changes before the final deployment.

- **DEPLOY** — If the first three steps were performed properly, this step should be pretty simple.

- **VERIFY** — Using accurate reporting mechanisms, ensure that the software updates are installing properly throughout the deployment step.

- **MONITOR** — This is an ongoing process. Reports should be in place and monitored regularly to ensure that all systems remain within the organization's standard baseline.

Delivering Software Updates with SMS

SMS 2003 utilizes multiple client and server processes and tools to deliver software updates. The Software Distribution Component is the one most heavily used because it is the delivery mechanism. The synchronization host is responsible for connecting to Microsoft.com and downloading the updated catalog file. The Distribute Software Updates Wizard (DSUW) is the administrator's user interface for authorizing updates and creating update packages. DSUW utilizes a catalog file to present available updates to the administrator. Currently, the catalog file name is wsusscan.cab and it contains a listing of the miscellaneous software updates that are available from Microsoft and various information about each update, such as the update ID. The **Software Updates** node located in the SMS Administrator Console contains a view of all software updates that have been approved. On the client, there is a scanning program that utilizes the catalog file to determine if the client requires any applicable updates and then sends the results back to the site server.

Phases

The following phases exist in the SMS software updates deployment process:

- **INVENTORY TOOL DEPLOYMENT** — This is a one time event. The most current software updates inventory scan tool is ITMU. See the "Installation of the Inventory Tool for Microsoft Updates (ITMU)" section later in this chapter for more information about installing ITMU.

- **PREPARATION** — The necessary processes to manage software updates should be performed at this phase. These processes will be different for each organization. Some examples include analyzing updates that are released by vendors, testing, piloting, development of release schedules, and communications with customers.

- **SYNCHRONIZATION** — This phase has two parts: synchronization host and Advanced Clients. The synchronization host connects to Microsoft.com and checks to see if there is a new version of the Windows Update catalog file (wsusscan.cab) available. If so, the synchronization host downloads the new file and copies it to the source folder for the Microsoft Updates Tool and updates the distribution points, if configured to do so. The synchronization host operation is initiated via a scheduled SMS advertised program that calls sync.exe. An SMS Advanced Client receives the updated wsusscan.cab file the next time it is scheduled to run the Microsoft Updates Tools.

- **SOFTWARE UPDATES INVENTORY COLLECTION** — After obtaining the newest version of the wsussscan.cab file, clients scan themselves to see if they are missing any available patches. The resulting data is converted to hardware inventory format and then sent along with a hardware inventory record up the site hierarchy.

- **AUTHORIZATION AND DISTRIBUTION** — The DSUW is the interface to use for this phase. Available updates can be viewed and authorized. Software updates packages, programs, and advertisements can be also created with DSUW.

Architecture

The most recent release for the SMS 2003 software updates components is called Inventory Tools for Microsoft Updates (ITMU). ITMU integrates a new scanning tool that utilizes the Windows Update Agent to inventory software updates released by Microsoft. It also installs an updated interface for the DSUW. Installation details are provided in the "Installation of the Inventory Tools for Microsoft Updates (ITMU)" section later in this chapter. In general terms, the ITMU requires an initial setup that installs components on a site server. These components include an SMS package that contains a scan tool to be distributed to each SMS Advanced Client. Once installed, the scan tool is initiated by a recurring SMS advertisement.

The SMS software updates architecture can be separated into three parts:

- Software Updates Components (server)

- Software Updates Components (client)

- Software Distribution Components

Let's look at each.

Software Updates Components (Server)

These include the following:

- **DSUW** — This is the interface for authorizing updates and creating update packages. To invoke the DSUW, right-click a collection, package, advertisement, or software update and select the **All Tasks** ⇨ **Distribute Software Updates** menu item. See the section "Using Distribute Software Updates Wizard (DSUW)" later in this chapter for more details regarding DSUW.

- **SYNCHRONIZATION HOST** — For security purposes, it is recommended to use a workstation with Internet access in this role rather than the site server. Using a workstation to access the Internet provides less risk to the site server, because many security attacks initiate from the Internet. The synchronization host is responsible for connecting to the Internet location that contains the Windows Update Catalog (wsusscan.cab). The synchronization host can be configured to download the catalog automatically when triggered by a scheduled SMS advertised program. Configuration for running in unattended mode and proxy authentication is also possible. See the *SMS ITMU Deployment Guide* for details.

- **SOFTWARE UPDATES NODE** — This is located in the SMS Administrator Console (see Figure 10.1) After ITMU is installed and functioning, software updates that are available with SMS are listed here. For the Microsoft Updates Tool, the list is generated from the wsusscan.cab file. A variety of information for each update is available in this view, such as the scan engine type, update name, language, machines requesting the update, machines that are compliant, update QNumber and update bulletin ID. If older versions of the scan tools have been installed, such as Microsoft Security Updates Inventory Tool or Microsoft Office Scan Tool, the **Type** column will display the other scan tool names.

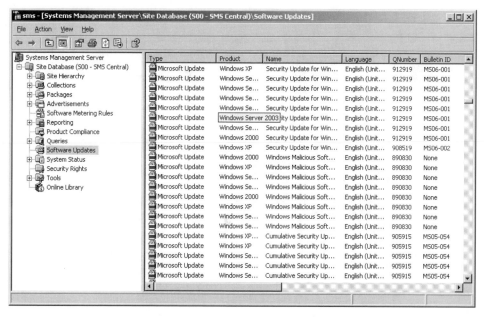

Figure 10.1: Viewing the Software Updates Node in the SMS Administration Console.

Software Updates Components (Client)

The following components are run on Advanced Clients:

- **SMS SOFTWARE UPDATES INSTALLATION AGENT** — Patchinstall.exe is the SMS Software Updates Installation Agent. The DSUW creates a software updates installation package specifically for this agent, using custom options. Patchinstall.exe is then included in the source folder of the patch package.

- **MICROSOFT UPDATE TOOL** — This includes various programs and XML files that are located in the Pkgsource folder of the ITMU installation. Figure 10.2 shows the folder once it is downloaded into the client cache. These are the files that comprise the Microsoft Update Tool. Notice the catalog file (wsusscan.cab) discussed earlier in this chapter.

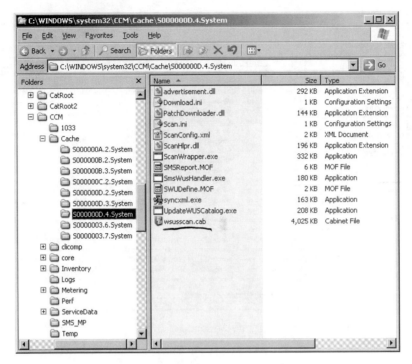

Figure 10.2: Contents of the Pkgsource Folder in the Advanced Client Cache.

Some files from the SMS client cache are then copied to the %System32%\VPCache\ <packagename> folder (see Figure 10.3). Not all files located in the initial download into the client cache are needed for scanning. Some are used by for other purposes, such as the synchronization host. Also Results.xml, which is the result of the software updates scan, is present in the VPCache folder because it is run from the VPCache folder.

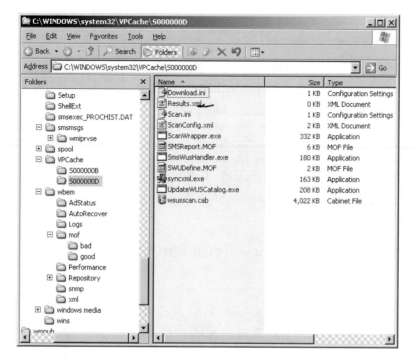

Figure 10.3: Viewing the Contents of the Pkgsource Folder in the Advanced Client VPCache.

- **WINDOWS UPDATE AGENT** — By default, Windows Update Agent runs on Microsoft operating systems and notifies end-users when a new update is available from Microsoft. The installation of ITMU provides an updated version of Windows Update Agent (2.0), which allows Microsoft Update Tool to integrate SMS 2003 and Windows Update Agent. During scanning operations, Windows Update Agent receives scan requests from scanwrapper.exe to perform local scans for the installation status of available software updates. The results are forwarded up the SMS hierarchy and inserted in each site server along the way. Systems with applicable updates can then be placed in a target collection to receive an advertised program from the applicable software updates package. Automatic Updates service allows Windows Update Agent to automatically download updates from Windows Update (http://windowsupdate.microsoft.com/). The service is not utilized by ITMU, but it must be enabled or else Windows Update Agent will fail.

Software Distribution Components

Understanding SMS package creation concepts is a requirement for distributing software updates. Another requirement is planning and implementing an SMS infrastructure that is designed with software distribution in mind. The configuration and use of Software Distribution Components have been described in detail in Chapters 1, 4, 6 and 7. Planning a software distribution infrastructure was covered in Chapter 2. This chapter focuses primarily on the software updates concepts and assumes an SMS 2003 software installation infrastructure is in place.

As with any software program that is deployed with SMS, software distribution objects must be created. The patch scanning package, program, collection, and advertisement are created when ITMU is installed. A patch installation package, program, and advertisement are created using the DSUW. The advertisement is then configured to target a collection. Initially, a package will be created that contains the source files for the Microsoft Updates Tools. This is the client portion of the ITMU. After the Microsoft Updates Tools are deployed, the DSUW can be used to create software updates packages, programs, and advertisements.

Installation of the Inventory Tool for Microsoft Updates (ITMU)

This section provides an overview of the installation process and guidelines for ITMU. Thorough documentation is provided from Microsoft in the SMS 2003 SP2 download located at `http://www.microsoft.com/downloads/details.aspx?familyid=37B20B4B-DFEC-464D-908B-5D78 3E2370D3&displaylang=en`.

Prerequisites

The latest version of ITMU must be installed on an SMS 2003 SP2 or later site server. The source files for the ITMU installation are included with the SMS 2003 SP2 upgrade files. After extracting the SMS 2003 SP2 source files, open the scantools folder. While it is not a requirement, Internet access from the site server is recommended. Install the ITMU as high as possible in the SMS hierarchy to provide a central point for distribution to all clients. To prepare your infrastructure for the ITMU installation, read the release notes and the help file named itmu_sp2.chm. The SMS Advanced Client with SP1 and hot fix KB901034 (or with SP2 or later) is also a requirement, as is Windows Installer version 3.1. To avoid possible client-side problems with Windows Update Agent (a dependent program), MSXML 3.0 SP7 is recommended.

Installation

To install ITMU, follow these steps:

1. Run SMSITMU.msi, located in the scantools folder. At the Welcome screen, click the **Next** button.

2. On the license agreement page, select the appropriate radio button and then click the **Next** button.

3. The **Destination Folder** panel appears. Be sure to direct the installation to your organization's standard package source location. This will be your source location for the ITMU scanning tools package.

4. At the **Automatically obtain latest Windows Update Catalog** screen, add the name of the synchronization host if you plan to use one. Otherwise, select the **I will download the catalog and synchronization host will copy it from a folder** radio button option. Then browse to the folder location.

5. The **Distribution Settings for the Inventory Tool** screen appears. Accepting the default information is recommended (see Figure 10.4). Click the **Next** button.

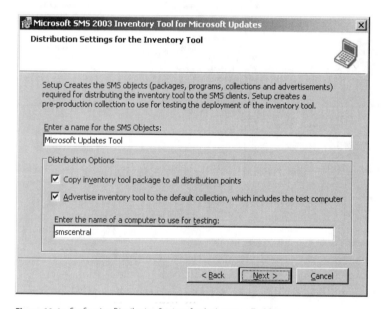

Figure 10.4: Configuring Distribution Settings for the Inventory Tool Page.

6. The **Distribution Settings for Windows Update Agent** screen appears. Typically, the defaults should be used here as well. Click the **Next** button and the Installation panel will appear. Click the **Next** button and the progress indicator will appear, followed by the **Setup Complete** screen. Once the installation is complete, view the various nodes in the SMS Administrator Console where changes will occur. These names are based on the installation defaults.

Packages and Programs

This section discusses the SMS packages and programs that are added to the site during the installation of the ITMU. These console objects will be used to install the ITMU on targeted SMS clients.

- The **Microsoft Updates Tool** package obtains source files from the Pkgsource folder within the ITMU installation folder (see Figure 10.5).

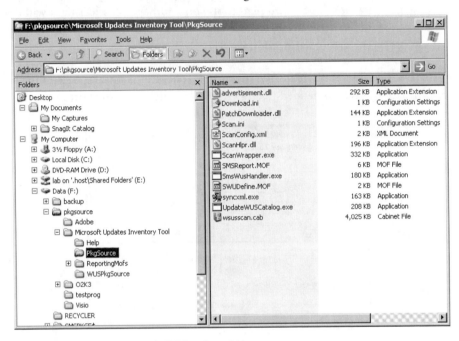

Figure 10.5: The Pkgsource Folder in the ITMU Installation Folder.

This SMS package contains three programs: Microsoft Updates Tool, Microsoft Updates Tool (expedited), and Microsoft Updates Tool sync. The Microsoft Updates Tool SMS programs initiate the scan tool on targeted Advanced Clients. These programs run the following command line: ScanWrapper.exe /Extended /cache. The expedited program also includes the **/kick** command line switch. This program initiates the scan tool and then immediately triggers a hardware inventory cycle to quickly send the scan data to the site server. In a large environment, this could cause a significant amount of traffic on networks and SMS servers, resulting in bottlenecks. The synch program runs on the synchronization host to perform a download of the catalog file from Microsoft. com if a new one is available. Here is an example of the command line:

```
syncxml.exe /s /site SMSCENTRAL /code S00 /package S000000D /target \\
SMSCENTRAL\PackageSrc
```

- The **Windows Update Agent** package contains one program, Windows Update Agent. This is configured as a dependent program on the Microsoft Updates Tool program properties (see Figure 10.6). Windows Update Agent runs as a dependent program only the first time the Microsoft Update Tool is run. The program silently installs the Windows Update agent by running the following command line:

```
WindowsUpdateAgent20-x86.exe /q
```

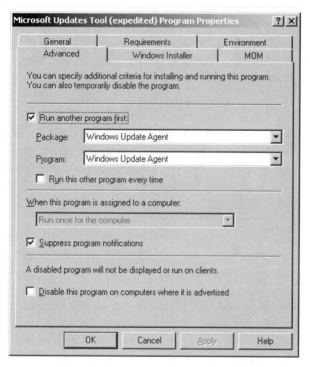

Figure 10.6: Microsoft Updates Tool Program Properties Advanced Tab.

Advertisements

- Microsoft Updates Tool delivers the scan tool to targeted clients. By default, the advertisement is configured with a recurring schedule. This is because the scan advertisements should be run regularly to allow you to continuously monitor your environment. This program is also configured to download and run from the distribution point, which is the most reliable way to configure an advertisement.

- Microsoft Updates Tool Synch targets the synchronization host and triggers the download of the most current wsusscan.cab file.

Collections

- Microsoft Updates Tool (pre-production) is a collection that is created for the purpose of piloting or testing. If the setup program creates the advertisement and the collections, you have the option to designate an Advanced Client to use as a test computer. The computer must have the SMS Advanced Client already installed, and it must belong to a collection that you can read with the account you are logged on with while running the setup program. The setup program adds the test computer to the Microsoft Updates Tool (pre-production) collection.

- Microsoft Updates Tool has one query-based membership rule to include all operating systems where the version is greater than or equal to 5.0.2195, which evaluates to all computers that are running Windows 2000, Windows XP, or Windows Server 2003. However, because the default query rule properties limit the Microsoft Updates Tool collection to the Microsoft Updates Tool (pre-production) collection, the effective membership after Setup completes includes only the single test computer. This ensures that the updates delivered with ITMU will run initially only on the known test computer. After you have completed your tests, you can remove the collection limiting option and the SMS 2003 Inventory Tool for Microsoft Updates will automatically be distributed to all computers that are capable of running it.

- The **Software Updates** node in the SMS Administrator Console is updated with new updates from the wsusscan.cab (see Figure 10.1. The new updates are preceded by the **Microsoft Updates** designation in the **Type** column.

One additional location to see changes from the ITMU installation is the SMS Web Reports. The ITMU setup wizard installs reports that allow you to examine the status of Microsoft Updates on the client computers. Setup installs new reports in the **Software Update** category. The data for these reports comes only from clients that have returned hardware inventory after running the inventory tool and immediately after a patch is installed with the installation status message. These are the reports, listed in the same order as they appear in the reports viewer Web interface:

- List of computers that have not scanned with latest synchronized catalog

- Compliance by Bulletin ID and QNumber

- All Computers with a specific update advertisement state

- Software update advertisement Status by software update ID

Using Distribute Software Updates Wizard (DSUW)

There are many different approaches for patch package strategies. It seems the most widely accepted strategy is to create two patch packages. The packages would include one huge package that contains all available updates that were released prior to the last patch cycle and one package that contains the patches that were released on the last patch cycle. Each month when new patches are released, the patches from the previous patch cycle should then be added to the huge patch package. The advertisements for the huge package should be configured to run the package from the DP. This method helps to simplify the process by consolidating all patches from previous patch cycles. It also frees the SMS Administrator console of the clutter associated with so many advertisements and packages that accumulate over time.

Other patch package strategies include creating one huge package and then adding newly released patches directly to the package. Another option is to create monthly packages. You could also create a patch package per operating system.

To distribute a software update with DSUW, perform these steps:

1. In the SMS Administrator Console tree, click the **Software Updates** node.

2. Select the **Action**⇨ **All Tasks**⇨ **Distribute Software Updates** menu item.

3. The **Distribute Software Updates Wizard** will appear. Click the **Next** button.

4. On the **Specify a Software Update Type** page, click the **Select an update type** radio button and then select **Microsoft Update** from the drop-down box (see Figure 10.7). Click the **Next** button.

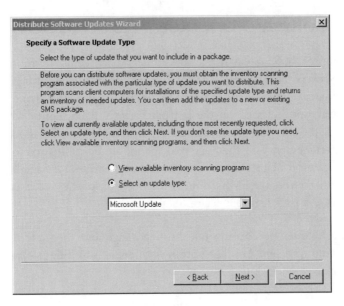

Figure 10.7: Configuring Software Update Type.

5. The **Create an SMS Package, or modify Packages and Updates** page will appear. The first time you use the wizard, ensure that **New** is selected from the box and then click the **Next** button.

6. The **Identify the SMS Package** page will appear. In the **Package name** box, type a name for the Microsoft Update package and click the **Next** button (see Figure 10.8).

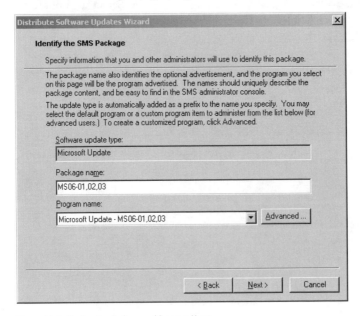

Figure 10.8: Configuring Package and Program Name.

7. The **Customize the Organization** page appears. In the **Organization** box, type the name of your organization. If you have created an .RTF file to provide details to end users, click the **Import** button and navigate to the location of the .RTF file. Select the file and then click the **Open** button and then the **OK** button to complete the import. Click the **Next** button.

8. On the **Select an Inventory Scanning Program** page, select the proper **Inventory Scan Tool** package (one of the Microsoft Updates Tool programs) and **Program name** options (see Figure 10.9) Click the **Next** button.

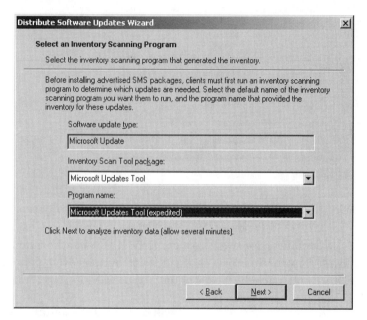

Figure 10.9: Selecting the Inventory Scan Tool.

9. The **Add and Remove Updates** page appears. It displays a list of updates that are applicable for the site. The page provides a handy filter to allow for customized sorting (see Figure 10.10). The filter can be used to remove the updates that do not interest you. For example, you could configure the filters to display only the patches that are related to Windows XP. Select an update where systems are showing as applicable. The **Requested** column indicates applicable systems. Click the **Next** button.

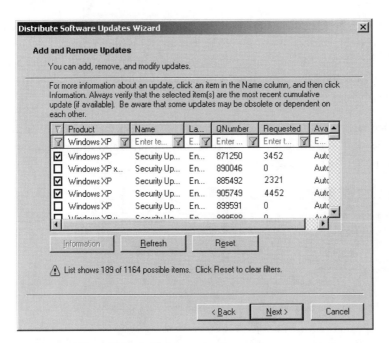

Figure 10.10: Adding and Removing Updates.

10. Typically the package source directory and package sending priority options should not be modified. See the "SMS Package Creation Overview" section in Chapter 6 for an explanation of the **Sending priority** package property. If you want to automatically download the update from the Internet, click the **Next** button. After the update is downloaded from Microsoft, click the **Next** button, and proceed to Step 17.

11. If you are going to use a local source, click the **I will download the source files myself** radio button and then click the **Next** button. You may want to use this option if the site server does not have Internet access.

12. If you are manually downloading the update, notice that under **Ready**, a value of **No** is listed. This indicates that the update file location has not been designated yet.

13. Click **Properties**. The **Binary path** displays the full path and name of the software update as it appears in the catalog (see Figure 10.11). Copy and paste this into a browser on a machine that has Internet access and manually download the file. Save the file to a location that can be accessed by DSUW. You will see that it has a very long file name, rather than the shorter file name listed in its associated security bulletin—for example, **windowsxp-kb871250-x86-enu_8a66a505679eadfbf9fe49c713fe68d3d8451a4c.exe** rather than **windowsxp-kb871250-x86-enu.exe**.

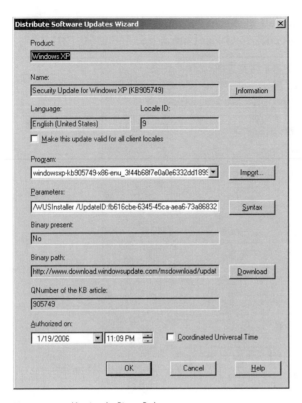

Figure 10.11: Viewing the Binary Path.

14. If you're manually downloading the update, click the **Import** button. In the **Open** dialog box, browse to the software update you manually downloaded and click the **Open** button.

15. The wizard attempts to verify the imported software update against the long file name listed in the catalog. If you downloaded the software update with its short file name (for example, by searching for the update in the Microsoft Download Center or following the links provided in the associated security bulletin), the check will fail. The wizard will warn you that it cannot verify the software update you imported. If you want the wizard to be able to verify it is the correct software update, click the **No** button and import the update with the long file name, using the URL displayed in the **Binary path** text box. If you are sure it is the correct software update, click the **Yes** button to continue.

16. Click the **OK** button, and you should now see your software update with a status of **Ready**. Click the **Next** button.

17. The **Update Distribution Points** page appears, prompting you to select the SMS distribution points to use for client access to the update. Select the desired distribution points and then click the **Next** button.

18. In the first **Configure Installation Agent Settings** page, select the agent settings to perform after installation and click the **Next** button (see Figure 10.12).

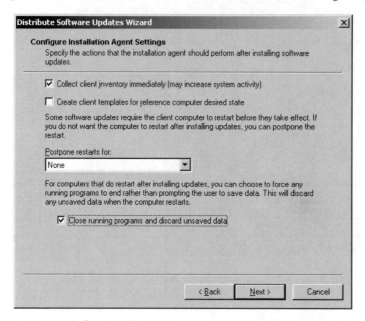

Figure 10.12: Configuring Installation Agent Settings.

19. In the second **Configure Installation Agent Settings** page, select the options you want to use and click the **Next** button (see Figure 10.13).

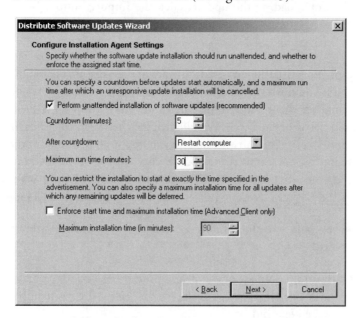

Figure 10.13: Configuring Installation Agent Settings.

20. In the third **Configure Installation Agent Settings** page, select the options you want to use and click the **Next** button (see Figure 10.14).

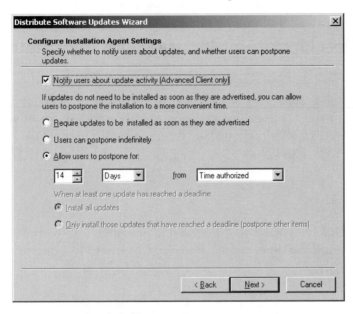

Figure 10.14: Notifying the End-User.

21. In the **Advertise Updates** page, select a recurrence interval for the update and click the **Next** button (see Figure 10.15).

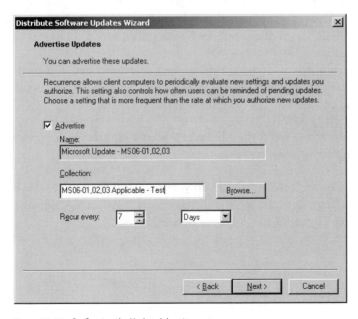

Figure 10.15: Configuring the Update Advertisement.

22. When the **Completing the Distribute Software Updates Wizard** page appears, click the **Finish** button.

Viewing Software Updates Management Information

Various members of an organization require software updates status information. This information helps information workers to identify and patch machines where updates are applicable. IT management wants to be sure that all the systems under their watch are safe from known vulnerabilities. The status of software updates can be viewed from multiple locations within SMS 2003, such as SMS Web Reports, Resource Explorer, and queries.

SMS Web Reports

SMS Web Reports is an especially good tool for viewing enterprise-wide software update statistics. Reports for individual machines are also available. Chapter 13 is dedicated to using and creating SMS Web Reports.

Resource Explorer

Resource Explorer is an SMS component for viewing software and hardware details including software updates status for a specific system. Resource Explorer displays the **Extended Software Updates** node when the inventory tool runs on an SMS client computer, and the hardware inventory cycle reports the status of the Microsoft Updates. Perform the following steps to see the software updates required on a specific computer by using Resource Explorer:

1. Open the SMS Administrator Console, expand the **Collections** tree, and then click the collection that contains computers where you want to view software updates details. In the right pane, you can view all the computers in this collection.

2. Right-click a computer and select the **All Tasks**⇨ **Start Resource Explorer** menu item. The **Resource Explorer** window opens.

3. Within Resource Explorer, expand the **Hardware** tree, and then select the **Extended Software Updates** item. You can see the details of the software updates of the SMS client computer (see Figure 10.16). Note the **Status** column.

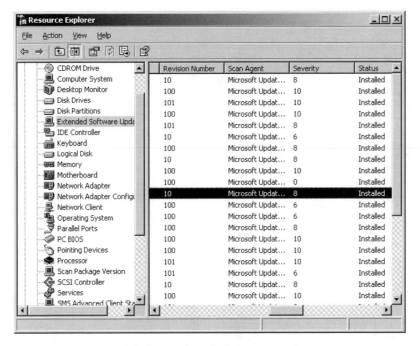

Figure 10.16: Viewing Extended Software Updates Information.

Queries

Queries can be used to list all the systems that have a specific status for a specific software update. The results can be exported into a Microsoft Excel spreadsheet. The query can also be imported into a collection to be used to target systems with a specific status for a specific software update. Figure 10.17 includes a query with the WQL language to include all systems that are applicable for a specific software update.

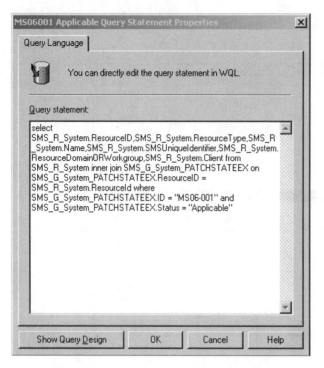

Figure 10.17: Configuring a Query for Applicable Software Updates.

Troubleshooting

As with any technology, the ITMU can have problems. To troubleshoot the ITMU, you must understand the scanning and software updates installation process. This requires a view of the "big picture." Let's examine the process in the following sections.

Software Updates Inventory Scanning Flow

Here is the process flow for software updates inventory scanning:

1. The Synchronization host downloads the latest wsusscan.cab and copies it to the Microsoft Updates Tool source folder (Pkgsource) and then updates the DPs.

2. The Microsoft Updates Tool advertised program runs on targeted clients. Clients verify that the newest version of wsusscan.cab is downloaded from the distribution point. The scan information is added to the hardware inventory data and returned to the SMS databases at the next hardware inventory scan cycle.

3. The next time the Microsoft Updates Tool runs on the client, new scan information becomes available on the client. The scan information is added to the hardware inventory data and returned to the SMS databases at the next hardware inventory scan cycle.

4. New software updates information from the client is available in the SMS database.

Installing Software Updates Flow

The following is a list of steps that occur during the software updates process:

1. The user creates a software updates package (including the SMS programs) through DSUW.

2. The administrator creates a target collection that contains all systems that are applicable for any updates included in the new package.

3. The targeted systems run advertised programs and install applicable updates.

4. Systems that have a status value of Applicable for a certain update can be targeted with the applicable update. DSUW is used to create and deploy the software update package. Alternately, you could target all machines and allow the evaluation occur at the client level. Using this option would depend on the control that you need over the distribution process. The advertised program is configured to call patchinstall.exe with a series of options corresponding to the commands entered in DSUW.

5. Advanced Clients install the update like any other SMS advertised program.

6. On the Advanced Client, SMS Execution Manager runs the update installation program and calls patchinstall.exe, which then installs the software update.

Grouping Components for Troubleshooting

Troubleshooting can begin at either end of the software update installation process.

Based on the architecture of the ITMU, troubleshooting should be broken into parts:

- Software Updates Components (server)

- Software Updates Components (client)

- Software Distribution Components

Software Updates Components (Server)

This troubleshooting part includes the synchronization host, DSUW, and the **Software Update** node within the SMS Administrator Console. There are many steps required to configure the synchronization host, such as security configuration with WMI, file folders, and the registry. Verify the configuration with the *Inventory Tool for Microsoft Updates Deployment Guide*, located in the ITMU download package. View the wsusscan.cab file date and version in the Microsoft Updates Tool package source folder to determine if a failure occurred during the downloading and copying of the .CAB file. There is a log file, WUSSyncXML.log, that can be viewed to verify that each step completed properly. The file is located in the %system32%\ccm\logs folder on the synchronization host.

DSUW and the **Software Updates** node both rely on the v_ApplicableUpdatesSummaryEx SQL Server view and its dependent tables and the wsusscan.cab file in order to display the proper available updates. If the data from this view and the .CAB file are both available, then DSUW and the **Software Updates** node will also work properly.

Software Updates Components (Client)

The log files for the client software updates clients components are located at %system32%\ CCM\logs. Each component will log its process details to the logs specified in this section. The Advanced Client scan process should follow this order:

1. Execution Manager (see execmgr.log for details) receives the instruction to run the Microsoft Updates Tool package.

2. Scanwrapper.exe (see scanwrapper.log for details) will initiate a request to Microsoft Updates Agent via SMS WUS Handler (see smswushandler.log for details). The process should complete, as noted by the following line in the smswushandler.log: `Execution is complete for program Microsoft Updates Tool`. The exit code is 0, and the execution status is Success.

3. The results are simultaneously written to the Win32_PatchState_Extended WMI class and to results.xml in the %system32%\VPCache\<Microsoft Updates tool package source folder> to be collected by the SMS client during the next hardware inventory cycle.

4. Execution Manager should report the finding of a success MIF if the program completes successfully.

5. The data will be retrieved seamlessly on the next hardware inventory cycle.

6. When Advanced Clients are targeted with an update using DSUW, patchinstall.exe (see patchinstall.log for details) is called to install the update, using the standard software distribution components. It runs with the parameters that were included in the SMS advertised program and looks for software installation status MIFs when it finishes. A follow up software updates scan is initiated and the results are sent to the site server with the installation status message and the status information received from the MIF.

Log files are a great place to begin looking for clues as to why a client software updates process may have failed. Client log files are located in the %system32%\ccm\logs folder. Start with execmgr.log to verify that the Microsoft Updates Tool program was initiated and completed successfully. If an error was reported, view the smswushandler.log file for more detailed results from the scan and to see if the newest catalog file is being used.

If error messages were listed in the Smswushandler.log file, see Table 10.1 to see if they match any of the errors listed there. Otherwise, search the Internet for more clues.

Error Code in Smswushandler.log	Cause	Solution
0x800705af	Page file is too small.	Create more free disk space.
0x8007000e	Out of memory exception	Windows Update Agent may be failing. The system may have memory errors.
0x80248011	The datastore folder has a CRC error when attempting to delete. Hard drive error.	Repair hard drive errors.
0x800800050x80070422	Automatic Updates service failure	Restart the system. Reinstall Automatic Updates.
0x80004002	MSXML parser update error	Ensure MSXML v 3.0 SP7 or later is installed.

Table 10.1: Errors in Smswushandler.log.

If the most recently released updates are listed in the Smswushandler.log file with a status value, then you know the most recent .CAB file is being used. If the newest .CAB file is not being used, check the Pkgsource folder on the distribution point. You can read LocationServices.log to determine the distribution point where the scan tools were accessed. If the newest .CAB file has not been used for scanning, look at the Pkgsource folder in the ITMU installation folder to see if the synchronization host downloaded it and copied it. If the newest .CAB file is missing from Pkgsource, look at the synchronization host log file for clues.

Problems with Anti-Virus Scanning Programs

There is a known issue with on-access anti-virus scanning programs that should concern you. Some files required by Windows Update Agent get locked by the anti-virus scanning program. If these files are locked, the ITMU will fail to function, leaving the SMS client host machine in a vulnerable state, as it will not be scanned and will not install new updates. To avoid problems, exclude the following files from being scanned by your anti-virus program:

- windir%\SoftwareDistribution\Datastore\Logs Edb*.log

- windir%\SoftwareDistribution\Datastore\Logs Res1.log

- windir%\SoftwareDistribution\Datastore\Logs Res2.log

- windir%\SoftwareDistribution\Datastore\Logs Edb.chk

- windir%\SoftwareDistribution\Datastore\Logs Tmp.edb

- %windir%\SoftwareDistribution\Datastore\Datastore.edb

Certain errors in the Smswushandler.log file on the client indicate that this problem is occurring (see Table 10.2).

Error Code in Smswushandler.log	Cause	Possible Solution
0xc80004080xc80001fe	A Windows Update Agent program file is locked.	Stop the Automatic Updates service. Delete the %win%\softwaredistribution folder.
0x80040154	Windows Update Agent program failure	Reregister Windows Update agent dlls with a batch file containing the following: • regsvr32 /s %systemroot%\system32\wuapi.dll • regsvr32 /s %systemroot%\system32\wuaueng.dll • regsvr32 /s %systemroot%\system32\wuaueng1.dll • regsvr32 /s %systemroot%\system32\wucltui.dll • regsvr32 /s %systemroot%\system32\wups.dll • regsvr32 /s %systemroot%\system32\wups2.dll • regsvr32 /s %systemroot%\system32\wuweb.dll • regsvr32 /s %systemroot%\system32\msxml3.dll Force WU Agent Reinstall using this command line: WindowsUpdateAgent20-x86.exe /q /f

Table 10.2: Errors Related to a Known Issue with Anti-virus Scanners and ITMU.

Figure 10.18 shows an example of an error being reported.

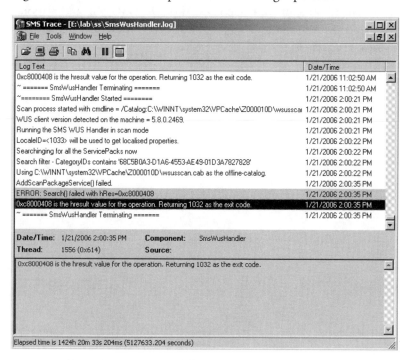

Figure 10.18: Viewing Errors in Smswushandler.log.

Software Distribution Components

The ITMU utilizes SMS Software Distribution Components to deliver and trigger the Microsoft Updates Tool on targeted Advanced Clients. The hardware inventory agent gathers the results from the Microsoft Updates Tool scans and sends them to the local management point to be forwarded to the site server and up the SMS hierarchy. If any of these processes breaks down, the results of the update scan will not arrive in the SMS databases. Therefore, the reporting for the client will be inaccurate. Chapters 14 and 15 are devoted to troubleshooting SMS Software Distribution Components.

Summary

In this chapter, you learned to use SMS for software updates management, including various workflow processes and SMS features. You discovered the change and configuration processes required to release a software update into the enterprise, the phases of delivering software updates, and the SMS 2003 Software Updates feature architecture. This chapter also covered the various SMS 2003 features used to deploy software updates, such as Inventory Tools for Microsoft Updates (ITMU), Distribute Software Updates Wizard (DSUW), and various methods of viewing software updates information. Finally, you learned how to troubleshoot problems with SMS 2003 software updates.

SMS 2003 Add-on Features from Microsoft

The focus of this chapter is the SMS 2003 add-on features offered by Microsoft that utilize the software distribution infrastructure. These add-ons include the SMS 2003 Operating System Deployment Feature Pack, the SMS 2003 Device Management Feature Pack, and SMS 2003 Desired Configuration Monitoring. This chapter gives you a general overview of the features, the installation requirements, and the installation process for each of these add-ons. After reading this chapter, you will be able to determine the feasibility of installing and operating each of these features within your environment. It is assumed that a fully functioning SMS 2003 SP1 or later infrastructure is in place in your environment and that only Advanced Clients are installed in the SMS hierarchy.

General Guidelines for Installing Add-on Features

As with any installation, system requirements must be in place, and proper testing and piloting must be planned and executed before the product is installed into a production environment. It is recommended to install the add-on features in a test lab that is similar to the planned production environment but contains fewer systems. Meaningful testing criterion and testing cases should be developed prior to testing. Piloting should affect non-critical systems and processes that are in the production environment, but only after the testing phase is successfully completed.

SMS 2003 Operating System Deployment Feature Pack (OSDFP)

Because the SMS 2003 Operating System Deployment Feature Pack depends on software distribution for the deployment of images, it seems fitting to provide an overview. An entire chapter could easily be devoted to this feature pack, but much of the material would be outside the scope of this book. The flexibility offered by the OSDFP also adds complexity that would require much explanation.

The OSDFP was released by Microsoft to offer an automated approach for deploying operating system images. An *image* is a file-based or sector-based replica of a system. File-based imaging copies the file structure and contents of a particular partition into a single file. Sector-based imaging takes a snapshot of a partition and places it into a file. File-based imaging is a much more efficient process. Most companies utilize imaging technology for two reasons: to save time and to maintain company-wide operating system configuration standards. Far less time is required to apply an image to a system than it takes to install an operating system (OS) on the same system. A technician will save hours per system by using an image versus installing the OS from scratch. OS configuration standards are a must for system management tasks in medium to large organizations. For example, attempting to create packages for automated deployment can quickly turn into a nightmare when multiple OS configurations exist in an organization. The OSDFP provides users with a centralized approach for deploying computer images, while offering the flexibility of performing custom actions before and after the image deployment.

Terms and Definitions

This section includes some terms that are useful to understand when discussing OSDFP:

- **DESTINATION COMPUTER** — The computer where a Microsoft Windows operating system is installed by the OSDFP.

- **IMAGE** — A collection of files and folders that duplicates the original file and folder structure of an existing computer, including the operating system. The image may also be a sector-based replica of a hard disk and may also contain other files added by the SMS administrator. The OS Deployment Feature Pack supports Windows Image format (WIM) images created with the Image Capture Wizard.

- **IMAGE CAPTURE WIZARD** — A Microsoft Windows disk imaging utility included in the OSDFP.

- **MICROSOFT IMAGING FILE (.WIM)** —The file format for an image captured by the OSDFP Image Capture Wizard. These files are compressed collections of files and folders.

- **ORIGINAL EQUIPMENT MANUFACTURER (OEM)** — A company that distributes computers to the public after purchasing computer components from other manufacturers, using the components to build computers and pre-installing the Windows operating system on the computers.

- **OS DEPLOYMENT PACKAGE** — An SMS package containing an operating system image created by the OSDFP. This package contains configuration files and, depending upon the type of image, the required image deployment environment and its associated tools.

- **REFERENCE COMPUTER** — A computer from which you generate the Microsoft Imaging file. The reference computer is configured in the same way as you want the destination computers to be configured.

- **SYSPREP** — A Windows system preparation tool used by the OSDFP during the creation of an image and during the preparation of an image for deployment to multiple destination computers.

- **USER STATE MIGRATION TOOL (USMT) 2.6** — A utility used by administrators to collect a user's documents and settings (called the *user state data*), prior to performing an OS deployment. The utility restores the user state data after the installation. It also captures desktop, network, and application settings, and then migrates them to a new Windows installation to improve and simplify the migration process. For more information about USMT 2.6, see the Windows XP Professional Deployment Web page at `http://www.microsoft.com/technet/prodtechnol/winxppro/deploy/`. You can download USMT 2.6 from the Microsoft Download Center at `http://www.microsoft.com/downloads`.

- **WINDOWS PREINSTALLATION ENVIRONMENT (WINDOWS PE) 1.5** — A Windows operating system with limited services, built on the Windows XP Professional Service Pack 2 (SP2) operating system platform. Windows PE is the primary image installation agent for the OS Deployment Feature Pack, and is used only in the preinstallation and deployment of Windows. You can find detailed documentation about Windows PE at `http://www.microsoft.com/whdc/system/winpreinst/`.

Creating and Distributing an Image

In simple terms, the process of creating an image and distributing it includes the following steps:

1. Capture the image.

2. Create the OS deployment package and program.

3. Deploy the Image.

Each of these steps is comprised of multiple tasks or phases. Let's have a closer look at each step for a better understanding.

Capture the Image

Use the Capture Image Wizard included in the OSDFP to create a replica based on the reference computer. The result is a single .WIM file that contains the entire image. The Capture Image Wizard must be copied to a bootable CD. This step is performed using the Create Image Capture CD Wizard from the SMS Administrator Console after the OSDFP is installed. To initiate the wizard, right-click on the **Images** node and then select the **All Tasks⇨ Create Operating System Image Capture CD** menu item. When the Welcome screen appears, click the **Next** button and supply the data requested by the wizard (see Figure 11.1). The reference computer is booted from the CD, where Sysprep is run and an image file of the active partition of the reference computer is created and placed at a designated network location.

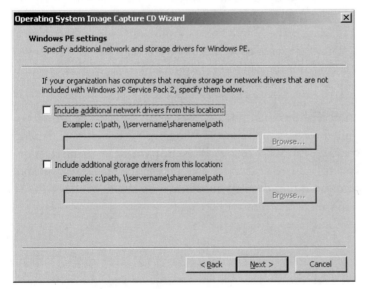

Figure 11.1: Initiating the Create Image Capture CD Wizard.

Create the OS Deployment Package and Program

The image that was created with the Image Capture Wizard is used to create OS Deployment packages that can be distributed to destination computers with SMS. The OS Deployment packages are managed from the **Image Packages** node in the SMS Administrator Console. An OS deployment package includes configuration information, a system image, the image deployment environment, and the tools for installing the image on destination computers. The OS deployment package also includes the SMS program used to install the image on the destination computer. Similar to any program source files, SMS software distribution can be used to deploy OS deployment packages to SMS 2003 Service Pack 1 (SP1) Advanced Client or Legacy Client computers. To initiate the New Operating System Wizard, right-click on the **Image Packages** node and select the **New⇨ Operating System Image Package** menu item. When the Welcome screen appears, click the **Next** button and supply the data requested by the wizard (see Figure 11.2).

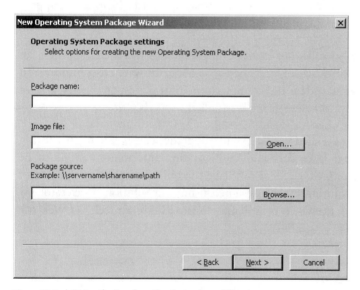

Figure 11.2: Initiating the New Operating System Image Wizard.

A bootable installation CD called "OS Image Installation CD" can be created that references the OS deployment package and contains configuration parameters for running the package. The bootable installation CD can also be hosted on a Remote Installation Server (RIS) server. To initiate the creation of the OS Image Installation CD, right-click on the **Image Packages** node and select the **All Tasks⇨ Create Operating System Image Installation CD** menu item. The Operating System Image CD Installation Wizard will commence.

Deploy the OS Image

There are three primary scenarios for deploying an image using an OS deployment package:

- **NEW COMPUTER INSTALLATION** — In this scenario, the computer is not being managed by SMS. The OS Image Installation CD can be used to boot the computer and install an OS deployment package from an SMS distribution point or from another network location. This CD can also be used with a Windows RIS server to utilize Pre-Boot Execution Environment (PXE) capabilities. PXE is an Ethernet technology that allows Windows Operations to occur prior to the full Windows OS initialization.PXE is an industry standard client/server interface that allows networked computers that are not yet loaded with an operating system to be configured and booted remotely by an administrator. For a TechNet article describing how to boot Windows PE from a RIS server, see `http://support.microsoft.com/default.aspx?scid=kb;en-us;304992&sd=tech`. Also, there is plenty of information in the Help and Support Center, located on the **Start** menu of any Windows 2003 Server.

- **REFRESH COMPUTER** — Also called an in-place upgrade, this is a scenario where an image is deployed to SMS 2003 SP1 or later clients via SMS Software Distribution. You can capture the current user state data and configuration information on the destination computer and reapply it after the new image is installed.

- **REPLACE COMPUTER** — Also called a side-by-side upgrade, this is where an existing computer is being replaced. User data and configuration information needs to be migrated to the new system. OSDFP does not have the built-in capability to perform these tasks, but a custom solution can be designed using the Solution Accelerator for Business Desktop Deployment, which is available on the Microsoft TechNet Web site and at `http://www.microsoft.com/downloads`.

Image Deployment Phases

There are six possible deployment phases that can be performed on destination computers. Each deployment scenario requires certain phases. The phases are as follows:

- **VALIDATION** — This phase is required for a refresh scenario. Custom actions can be performed to verify system requirements and provide end-users information about image specifics. This phase occurs prior to the OS deployment package notification message to end-users.

- **STATE CAPTURE** — This phase is required for a refresh scenario. Actions can be performed that capture the user's existing files and settings, such as the computer name, SMS site, and SMS identifier from the destination computer. These settings can be reapplied to the destination computer after running the OS deployment package. During this phase, you can configure any of the four actions available for this phase. The actions run in the order specified on the **Advanced** tab of the **Image Package Program Properties** dialog box.

  The four available actions are:

  - Custom

  - Capture user state

  - Connect to UNC path

  - Reboot System

- **PRE-INSTALL** — This phase is required for a new computer installation or computer refresh scenario. This phase allows you to configure and run actions that prepare the destination computer disk drive for the installation of the new operating system. The following actions can be run in this phase:

  - Custom

  - Connect to UNC path

  - Reboot system

- **INSTALL** — This phase begins after the preinstall phase completes successfully and reboots. Windows PE initializes on the destination computer. All files and folders other than those under the MININT folder are deleted, and the .WIM image of the new operating system is installed on the C: drive.

- **POST INSTALL** — This phase occurs during a new computer installation or a refresh computer scenario. This phase performs customized actions that further configure the new operating system image before installation completes.

- **STATE RESTORE** — This phase occurs when you run a refresh computer scenario. This phase performs customized actions that add optional applications and restore users' state.

The following actions can be run in this phase:

- Custom

- Connect to UNC path

- Restore user state

- Run SWD program

Installing the OSDFP

The primary system requirement for the OSDFP is that SMS 2003 with SP1 later must be installed on the primary SMS server where the OSDFP will be installed. Also, clients must be running SMS 2003 SP1. There are some additional requirements that depend on the features used and the OS of the reference and destination computers. These additional requirements, along with step-by-step directions, can be found in the *Microsoft Systems Management Server 2003 Operating System Deployment Feature Pack Users Guide* included with the OSDFP download at http://www.microsoft.com/smserver/downloads/2003/osdfp.mspx.

Additional Tools for OSDFP

Microsoft provides a free solution containing tools and best practice approaches for deploying desktops in a corporate environment. This solution is called Solution Accelerator for Business Desktop Deployment (BDD). BDD includes two desktop deployment methodologies: Zero Touch Installation (ZTI) and Lite Touch Installation (LTI). ZTI can be considered an extension of OSD and provides additional refinement and customization to the image deployment process. It utilizes most of the components of OSDFP. LTI utilizes third-party imaging tools such as Norton Ghost and does not require SMS. There is a considerable amount of documentation for BDD at http://www.microsoft.com/technet/desktopdeployment/bdd/enterprise/default.mspx.

Device Management Feature Pack (DMFP)

Mobile devices have become commonplace throughout organizations world-wide. While these devices offer enhanced productivity to employees, they can also be difficult to manage. The Device Management Feature Pack (DMFP) provides a solution for centralized management of mobile systems that run Windows CE (3.0 or later) or Windows Mobile software for Pocket PCs (2002 or later). DMFP offers the following features:

- Hardware inventory

- Software inventory

- File collection

- Software distribution

- Device settings management

- Password policy enforcement

Terms and Definitions

Let's review some terms related to the Device Management Feature Pack.

- **CABINET FILE FORMAT (CAB)** — This file format was designed to allow a single compressed file to contain multiple files for the purpose of distribution.

- **DEVICE** — Any information-processing tool, such as a handheld computing device. A device can also be referred to as a Personal Digital Assistant (PDA), or Pocket PC.

- **DEVICE CLIENT** — A device that hosts the Device Client Agent for SMS 2003.

- **DEVICE CLIENT AGENT** — A small software program that is hosted by Windows CE and Pocket PC-based devices and is used to configure settings for the Device Client, including software inventory, hardware inventory, software distribution, communication settings, and file collection.

- **DEVICE MANAGEMENT POINT** — SMS site system that communicates with Device Clients that are hosted on an SMS management point.

- **DEVICE SETTINGS PACKAGE** — Packages that can be deployed to apply configuration data to a mobile device.

- **DOCKED** — A device connected to a computer by an ActiveSync connection. For example, a device is docked when it is in the manufacturer's cradle.

- **MICROSOFT ACTIVESYNC** — Software that provides synchronization for Windows Mobile-based Pocket PCs. Information can be synchronized between mobile devices and computers with ActiveSync.

- **MICROSOFT WINDOWS CE** — An operating system that runs on devices. It is the platform on which Microsoft Windows Mobile 2003 software for Pocket PC is built.

- **MICROSOFT WINDOWS CE PLATFORM BUILDER** — A development environment in which a customized version of Windows CE can be built, based on the hardware of a specific device. Windows CE Platform Builder includes a Device Management Client.

- **MICROSOFT WINDOWS MOBILE 2003 SOFTWARE** — At the time of this writing, this is the latest version of operating system software for mobile devices, including Pocket PC.

- **PERSONAL DIGITAL ASSISTANT (PDA)** — Lightweight, handheld computers designed to provide specific functions such as personal organization and communications. A Pocket PC is a type of PDA.

SMS Site Changes During the DMFP Installation

This section describes the changes that occur within the SMS site hierarchy during the DMFP installation.

The **Use this site system as a device management point** option is added to the **Management Point** tab on the **Site System Properties** page (see Figure 11.3).

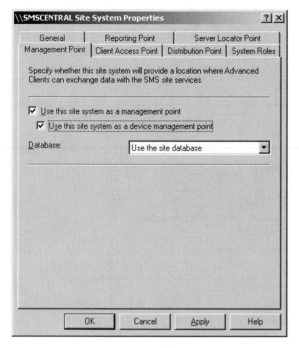

Figure 11.3: Viewing the Modification to the Management Point Tab.

The **Device Client Agent** property is added in the SMS Administrator Console under the Site Hierarchy **Client Agents** node (see Figure 11.4).

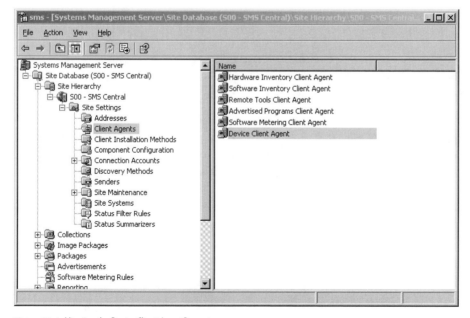

Figure 11.4: Viewing the Device Client Agent Property.

The Distribute Software to Devices Wizard is added to support software distribution to devices. To launch the wizard, right-click on the **Packages** node, then select the **Distribute Software to Devices** menu option. When the Welcome screen appears, click the **Next** button and supply the data requested by the wizard.

Four new collections are created by the wizard to target devices: **All Windows Mobile Devices**, **All Windows Mobile Pocket PC 2002 Devices**, **All Windows Mobile Pocket PC 2003 Devices**, and **All Desktops and Servers** (see Figure 11.5).

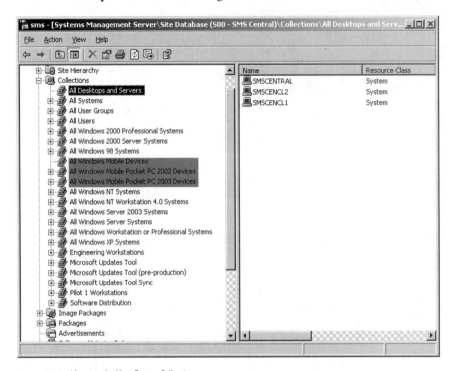

Figure 11.5: Viewing the New Device Collections.

Device-specific configuration property pages appear on advertisements property pages and on programs property pages. Right-click the **Programs** node within any package and select the **New⇨ Program for Device** menu option. The property sheet will appear (see Figure 11.6).

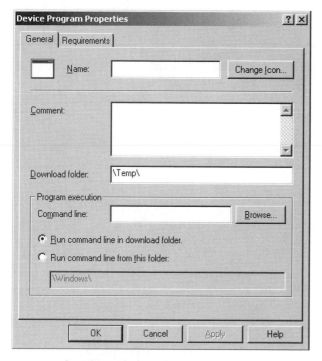

Figure 11.6: Device Program Properties Sheet.

The **Device Settings Manager** component is added under the **Tools** node (see Figure 11.7). It creates .CAB files that can be used with the Distribute Software to Devices Wizard to distribute configuration settings to devices, such as network, password, and security settings. Installation of this component is an option in the Device Management Feature Pack Setup Wizard.

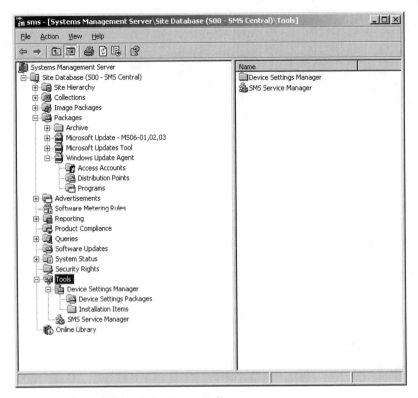

Figure 11.7: Viewing the Device Settings Manager Node.

The following additional changes to the SMS site occur after DMFP is installed:

- A device management component is added under the **Site Settings**⇨ **SMS Status Summarizers** node.

- The ActiveSync version on the desktop client is included with SMS 2003 computer hardware inventory.

- Hardware inventory details of ActiveSync-connected devices are now included with SMS 2003 computer hardware inventory.

SMS 2003 DMFP Architecture

Let's look at how the DMFP architecture works. Device Clients poll device management points using HTTP at an interval configured by the SMS administrator. At that time, any available policies are downloaded by the client. If the policy contains any advertised programs, the client schedules them. Based on a separate interval (also configured by the SMS administrator), hardware inventory and software inventory are sent to the device management point. When an advertised program begins to run, it utilizes a local distribution point to access source files via HTTP. While roaming, Device Clients take advantage of distribution points throughout the hierarchy. Device programs can be created and advertised to Device Clients. Device programs can be configured to run according to the network state of the Device Client, such as docked, on a fast network, or anytime.

The device management point is dependent on the SMS management point role. It is located on the same server as the management point and shares its Microsoft SQL Server connection configuration information. The device management point is the point of communication between the Device Client and the SMS site. The device management point forwards inventory data it receives from the Device Clients to the site management point. The management point forwards policies designated for Device Clients to the device management point.

Installing the DMFP

The installation procedure is covered in great detail in the *Microsoft Systems Management Server (SMS) Device Management Feature Pack Guide*, which is included in the DMFP download at `http://www.microsoft.com/smserver/downloads/2003/dmfp.mspx`. I won't rehash the installation steps here, but I will cover the prerequisites so that you can determine if installing this feature pack is feasible in your environment. Here are the prerequisites:

- Site servers must have SMS 2003 SP1 or later and .NET Framework 1.1 installed. SMS administrator consoles must also have .NET Framework 1.1 installed.

- Distribution points must be enabled for Background Intelligent Transfer Service (BITS) and must be running Microsoft Internet Information Server (IIS). Web Distributed Authoring and Versioning (WebDAV) extensions for IIS must be enabled on the distribution point.

- The Device Client can only be installed on Microsoft Windows CE 3.0 (or later), Windows Pocket PC 2002, and Windows Pocket PC 2003 (or later). Installation methods include distribution from SMS to SMS clients with ActiveSync-connected devices, manually running files on the device, and installing the Device Client from a connected desktop system.

- The SMS_Def.mof file must be edited to include the Device Client hardware inventory extensions. This is described in the *Microsoft Systems Management Server (SMS) Device Management Feature Pack Guide*.

Using the DMFP

This section explores using the DMFP for software distribution. Distributing software to devices with the DMFP is very similar to distributing software to Advanced Clients. The Distribute Software to Devices Wizard can be used or the software can be distributed manually. Before you can distribute software—either manually or with the wizard—you must first enable software distribution for Device Clients. To enable software distribution for Device Clients, do the following:

1. Under the Site Hierarchy, open the site where you want to enable software distribution to Device Clients.

2. Open the **Site Settings**⇨ **SMS Client Agents** node.

3. Open the **Device Client Agent** properties sheet. On the **Client Agent Software Distribution** tab, select the **Enable Software Distribution** check box.

Here's how to use the Distribute Software to Devices Wizard to create SMS programs and advertisements. To launch the wizard, right-click the **Package** node and select the **All Tasks**⇨ **Distribute Software to Devices** menu item. An SMS package and target collection that contains the devices where you want to install software must already exist before using the wizard. Alternatively, you can create the package, program, advertisement, and collection manually. For information on creating packages, programs, advertisements and collections, see Chapters 6 and 7.

SMS 2003 Desired Configuration Monitoring (DCM)

Another free add-on from Microsoft is Systems Management Server 2003 Desired Configuration Monitoring. It helps organizations to create and monitor standard configuration baselines. In the long run, this tool will help IT support staffs to provide higher availability for the Windows infrastructures they support. There is a strong correlation between configuration management and server availability, because server downtime is quite often the result of hardware and software configuration errors. An organization is usually unaware of the configuration state of its systems until the downtime occurs. DCM is designed to utilize SMS infrastructure components to deliver tools, gather data, and provide reporting in order to offer higher availability. Typically, configuration management is more of a concern for server environments, but DCM can be used for servers or workstations.

DCM allows configuration templates, also known as manifests, to be defined for each server role and then deployed along with the DCM engine as needed. The DCM engine utilizes the configuration manifest to determine if a server is within the limits set in the configuration manifest. Detailed reporting based on the manifest is provided, with along with the tools to create more reports. Administrators can be notified via MOM alerting (if MOM is installed in the enterprise) when servers fall outside the limits configured in the manifest. Also, advertised programs can be configured to automatically run if servers fall outside the limits set in the manifests, in order to quickly bring the server into compliance.

Installation Prerequisites

You may find that system requirements for DCM are a bit high, especially due to its dependency on SQL Server Reporting Services. Here are the details:

- The DCM engine and DCM Authoring Tool components require Microsoft .NET Framework 1.1, Microsoft Windows Server 2003, or Microsoft Windows XP.

- The DCM Reports component requires Microsoft Windows Server 2003, Microsoft SMS 2003, and Microsoft SQL Server Reporting Services.

NOTE

For SQL Server 2000, Reporting Services is only included in the Enterprise Edition. For SQL Server 2005, it is included in the Standard Edition. Going with Standard Edition will provide a considerable cost savings.

DCM Infrastructure and Knowledge

At a high level, Microsoft describes DCM as having two parts: infrastructure and knowledge. Let's look at each.

The DCM *infrastructure* includes the following components:

- **DCM DOCUMENTATION** — This is located in the download package (see the "Getting Started" section below for details). It consists of the following guides:

  - *Microsoft Systems Management Server 2003 Desired Configuration Monitoring Installation Guide*

  - *Microsoft Systems Management Server 2003 Desired Configuration Monitoring Deployment Guide*

  - *Microsoft Systems Management Server 2003 Desired Configuration Monitoring User Guide*

- **DCM SETUP** — These are the source files that install DCM. More information about the setup can be found in the *Microsoft Systems Management Server 2003 Desired Configuration Monitoring Installation Guide.*

- **DCM AUTHORING TOOL USER INTERFACE** — This component is used to gather data for DCM knowledge. The result is an XML manifest or document that contains the configurations that you want to monitor and rules on how to monitor them.

- **DCM ENGINE** — This is the component located on the client that determines if the machine is compliant, based on the XML manifest that it reads. Non-compliant machines are flagged accordingly.

- **REPORTS** — These are predefined configuration compliance reports. Compliance reports include DCM out-of-compliance and in-compliance reports. Additional reports can be created as well.

Manifests represent the *knowledge* because they contain the rules for specific configuration settings and their desired values. Rules are created based on "knowledge" that administrators have regarding the configuration settings on the targeted machines. The DCM engine gathers information about the configuration settings on the targeted machines by comparing rules in the manifests with configuration settings on the actual machine. The results are sent to the SMS database and then transferred to the DCM database.

Getting Started

DCM can be downloaded from `http://www.microsoft.com/downloads/details.aspx?FamilyId=93A72AB8-BF54-4607-B9BB-AC9739C6C292&displaylang=en`.

Perform the following activities in the order listed:

1. Download and Install DCM. You can install DCM by using the Microsoft Windows Installer package called DCMSolutionSetup.msi. The full installation details are included in the *Microsoft Systems Management Server 2003 Desired Configuration Monitoring Installation Guide.* DCM should be set up to use the top-most site in the SMS hierarchy for the systems that you intend to manage.

2. Create the DCM manifest. The DCM Authoring Tool creates the DCM manifest, also known as the configuration document. Use this tool to add, remove, or modify configuration settings and rules based on data from the registry, Active Directory, metabase, WMI, and file system.

3. Create the SMS 2003 package, program, and advertisement to deploy DCM. Once the DCM manifest is created, you can deploy it along with the DCM engine by using SMS 2003. See the *Microsoft Systems Management Server 2003 Desired Configuration Monitoring Deployment Guide* for details. Here are some high-level steps for doing this:

   ■ Create an SMS 2003 package containing the DCM engine and the knowledge.

   ■ Create an SMS 2003 program to schedule the DCM engine to run at a specified interval.

   ■ Create an SMS 2003 advertisement to targeted collection systems you intend to manage.

4. Advertise the SMS package to each managed node. Create a target collection and then deploy the advertised program to the collection.

5. Have SMS collect out-of-compliance data. This data is logged to WMI and the Windows NT Event Log on each managed node. Use the script included with the DCM installation source files to modify SMS_def.mof to allow SMS to collect out-of-compliance data during the hardware inventory process.

6. Run reports. After data is collected, run reports to determine machines that are out-of-compliance. Also, if MOM is installed in the environment, a MOM rule can be created to send an alert when machines are determined to be out-of-compliance based on rules located in the manifests.

Summary

This chapter focused on the SMS 2003 add-on features offered by Microsoft that utilize the software distribution infrastructure. These add-ons include the SMS 2003 Operating System Deployment Feature Pack, the SMS 2003 Device Management Feature Pack, and SMS 2003 Desired Configuration Monitoring. This chapter gave you a general overview of the features, installation requirements, and the installation process for each of these add-ons. This chapter discussed how to determine the feasibility of installing and operating each of these features within your environment.

DID YOU KNOW?

One preventive approach to verifying that SMS clients are functioning properly is to install the SMS Client Health Monitoring Tool, located at **www.microsoft.com/SMS/ downloads**.

One way to determine if an SMS client is functioning properly is to see if it is sending inventory and discovery data based on the configuration provided in the properties of heartbeat discovery and the hardware and software inventory agent. The Client Health Monitoring Tool compares the age of SMS client inventory and discovery data located in the SMS database against the age of each data item that you provide in the tool's configuration. The tool creates a list of clients suspected of having problems.

Next, the tool performs two tests: it pings the suspected clients and reads policy request logs from the management points of each site. Pinging the clients allows the tool to remove clients from the suspect list that are not online. Reading the policy request logs allows the tool to verify that the suspected clients requested a policy in a timely manner.

These two tests narrow the list of suspect clients down to those that are online, providing a true picture of SMS clients that are not functioning properly.

Part IV

Troubleshooting

Monitoring Remote Installation

If implemented properly, SMS can distribute software to hundreds of thousands of workstations. However, this still isn't good enough to be considered a successful enterprise-level system. Successful enterprise-level systems can monitor package distribution and advertisement processes in a timely manner. Knowing what is going on at the workstation end of a distribution is crucial to the success of that distribution. Software delivery systems can't simply be aimed at a group of machines with the administrator pulling the trigger on a distribution right before heading out the door. Properly monitoring remote distributions will enable you to catch problems before they are too widespread. Locating machines that failed to run packages and making adjustments to provide solutions for these failures will improve the reliability of your implementation of SMS software distribution. After reading this chapter, you will be able to view package and advertisement status summary information from the SMS Administrator Console, view and export status messages using SMS Status Message Viewer, understand the flow of custom advertised program status Management Information Format files (MIFs), and run status message queries. Chapter 13 covers reporting and will be helpful for displaying package and advertisement status summary information using a different format.

SMS Status Message Viewer

The SMS Status Message Viewer is used for viewing all status messages available in SMS. Because this book focuses on SMS software distribution features, you will learn about the Status Message Viewer from that point of view. The Status Message Viewer information available in this chapter is applicable to any SMS feature that provides status messaging.

Accessing Advertisement Status Messages

Advertisement error and warning messages allow the SMS administrator to be alerted about problems that may occur during a software deployment. Status messages also provide the general area in the advertisement process where troubleshooting needs to occur. To access the Advertisement status messages using the SMS Status Message Viewer, do the following:

1. Open the **System Status** tree in the SMS Administrator Console.

2. Select the **Advertisement Status** tree. The right pane provides a summary view of SMS clients that have run advertisements listed in the left pane. (see Figure 12.1). The next eleven bullets describe column headings viewable when selecting the **Advertisement Status** node from the SMS Administration Console.

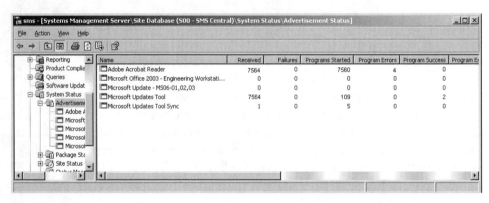

Figure 12.1: Viewing Advertisement Status Summary.

- **Received** is the number of workstations that have received the advertisement. This number will only be incremented once for each client that receives the advertisement.

- **Failures** are installation programs that failed to complete. A failure is based on a non-zero exit code from the program. SMS assumes that all programs will return a zero for a successful exit code. This is the case for most programs, so if the program fails, a number other than zero will be returned. However, some programs (InstallShield for example) return non-zero exit codes for successful program installations. Also, if a custom installation status MIF is created, SMS will base the success of the program on the custom MIF. In a situation where a legitimate failure occurs, the program is received and it starts, but it fails in the middle.

- **Programs Started** is incremented by one each time a machine starts the advertised program.

- **Program Errors** are caused when an installation program is never found or the program stops for a known cause, such as when the user cancels it or the network connection is lost.

- **Program Successes** occur either when a zero exit code is returned, or if a custom advertised program status MIF is used and the program completes properly.

- **Package** is the name of the SMS package where the advertised program is located.

- **Program** is the name of the SMS program that is currently being advertised.

- **Target Collection** is the collection that is receiving the advertisement.

- **Available After** is the date when the advertisment will begin to be available, as configured in the advertisement.

- **Expires after** is the date when the program will no longer be advertised.

- **Advertisement ID** is the number given to the advertisement. It begins with the site code. Each new advertisement is appended by one.

3. Select one of the advertisements from the list in the left pane. In the right pane, you will see the default summary view of status messages for the selected advertisement since it was first advertised (see Figure 12.2).

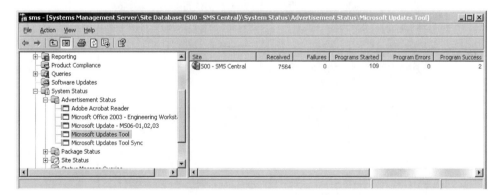

Figure 12.2: Viewing the Summary for an Advertisement.

To filter the advertisement status messages by a specific date interval, right-click the advertisement in the left pane, hover over the **Display Interval** menu option, and click one of the available sub-options that are displayed. The first six columns have the same interpretation as those listed in Step 2 above. **Summary Date** is the date and time the last software installation status message was received.

4. Right-click one of the sites in the right pane and select the **Show Messages**⇨ **All** menu item. The SMS Status Message Viewer appears (see Figure 12.3).

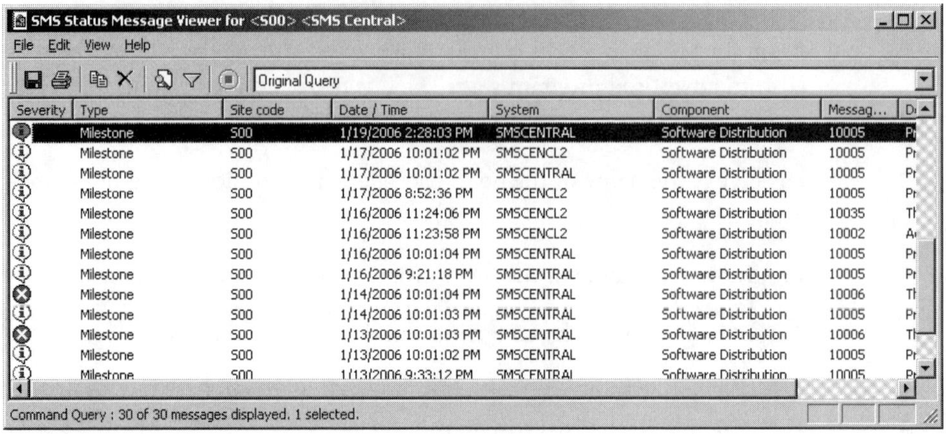

Figure 12.3: SMS Status Message Viewer.

By double-clicking on a message, it can be opened for easier viewing (see Figure 12.4).

Figure 12.4: Status Message Properties.

Table 12.1 describes the Status Message Viewer column headings.

Heading	Value	Description
Severity	Error	Error messages are either a Failure or Program Error. Read the description to find out.
Severity	Warning	Warning messages generally indicate issues that are less severe than error messages.
Severity	Informational	Informational messages describe the activities performed by the component listed in the **Component** column for the advertisement.
Type	Audit	Audit messages indicate actions made from an SMS Administrator Console that resulted in a change to the advertisement. This is a great way to track changes other administrators have made.
Type	Milestone	Milestone messages indicate successful or unsuccessful completion of one step of the advertisement process.
Site Code		The site where the advertisement was created.
Date/Time		The date and time the status message was generated.
System		The system where the client generated the status message.
Component		The SMS component responsible for carrying out the activities described in the **Description** column.
Message ID		Correlates to a specific description.
Description		Includes the details that surround the activity of the advertisement. Each description corresponds to a message ID.

Table 12.1: Advertisement Status Message Column Headings.

Successful Advertisement Status Messages

Advertised program client messages for successful installations are recognized by the informational **Severity** icon, as shown in the left column in Figure 12.5.

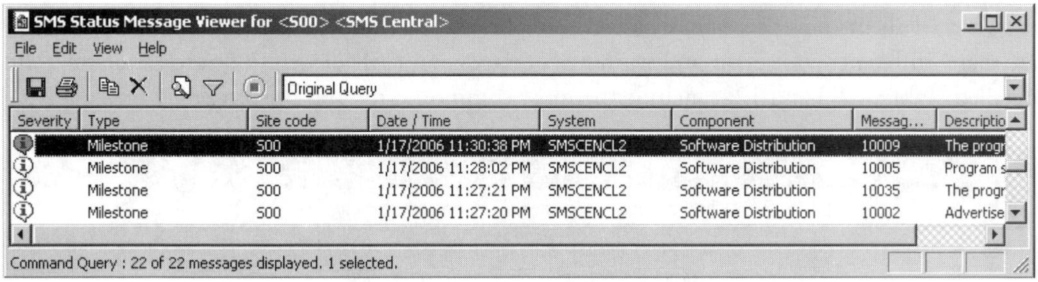

Figure 12.5: Viewing Advertisement Status Message Sending Order.

Successful advertisements messages are created and sent in a certain order. Table 12.2 shows the message IDs and descriptions in the order sent. Much more detail is included in the actual status message.

Message ID Number	Paraphrased Informational Message Description
10002	Advertisement was received.
10035	Download source files from the distribution point.
10005	Program ran.
10008 or 10009	Program completed successfully. 10008 is the default message created for programs that do not have a custom installation status MIF generated on the client. The description for message ID 10009 includes specific information from the MIF.

Table 12.2: Successful Advertisement Status Messages.

Unsuccessful Advertisement Status Messages

Advertised program client messages for unsuccessful installations replace successful status messages. They are easily recognized by the red severity icons (see Figure 12.6).

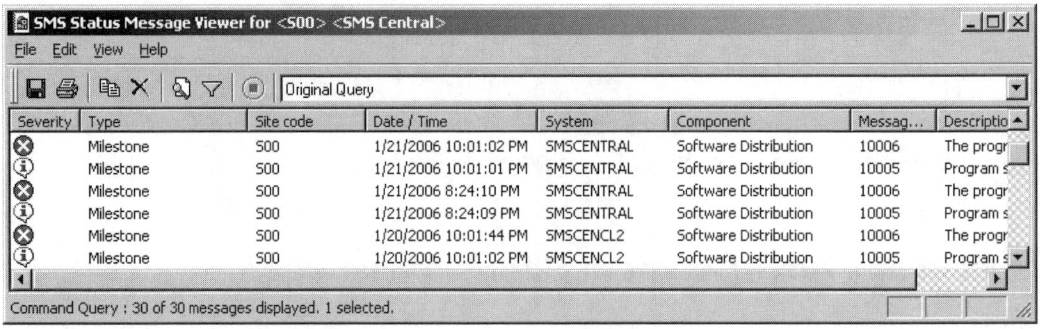

Figure 12.6: Unsuccessful Advertisement Status Messages.

However, if clients never receive the advertisement, there will be no status messages sent. There are many different status error and warning messages and their descriptions are generally quite detailed. Tables 12.3 and 12.4 include the most common error and warning messages.

Message ID Number	Paraphrased Error Message Description
10050	The total cache size is smaller than the size of the package content.
10030	Content download for the package has failed. The download failed because the content downloaded to the client does not match the content specified in the package source.
10051	The content for the package could not be located.
10070	The program for the advertisement exceeded the maximum allowed run time.

Table 12.3: Advertisement Status Messages with a Status of Error.

Message ID Number	Paraphrased Warning Message Description
10018	The advertisement was rejected because the client's platform is not supported.
10019	The advertisement was rejected because the advertisement has expired.
10055	An error occurred while preparing to run the program.
10056	The program could not be executed.

Table 12.4: Advertisement Status Messages with a Status of Warning.

Features of SMS Status Message Viewer

SMS Status Message Viewer is a tool in which to view, print, and export status message information. Status Message Viewer provides **File, Edit,** and **View** menu item features, as well as useful toolbar buttons. Let's look at each of these features.

File Menu Items

Status message information can be exported from the SMS system or printed. These menu options are quite useful for reporting purposes:

- The **Save** menu item allows the viewed information to be exported. To change the file format that the data will be saved in, go to the **View** menu and select the **Options** menu item, then select the **Export** tab.

- The **Print** menu item simply prints the information that is displayed.

Edit Menu Items

The **Edit** menu includes items to allow you to manipulate individual status messages. Operations can be executed on a block selection or on individual messages.

- **Copy** allows all the information from selected rows to be copied and pasted into a document. The **Status Viewer Options** dialog box will appear if **Force selection of export options for each export** is selected on the **Export** tab. The output to a document can be customized here.

- **Delete** removes the selected status message(s) from the database.

- **Select All** provides a block selection of all messages.

- **Find** provides advanced search capabilities (see Figure 12.7).

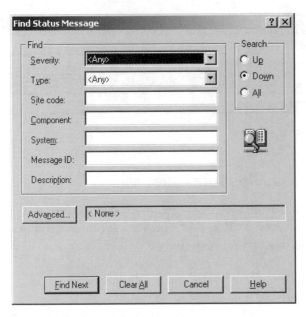

Figure 12.7: Searching with Status Message Viewer.

View Menu Items

SMS Status Message Viewer provides additional features that are not so obvious. The **View** menu contains these customizations. Here are some important Status Message Viewer features that are commonly overlooked:

- The **Detail** menu item displays the details of the selected status message.

- The **Filter** menu item allows administrators to display only messages for the criteria that are entered in the **Filter Status Message** dialog box (see Figure 12.8). There are more features available by clicking the **Advanced** button.

Figure 12.8: Using the Filter Status Dialog Box.

- **Query Information** provides the WBEM Query Language (WQL) code that is used to return the status messages that are being displayed. *WQL* is a subset of Structured Query Language (SQL) used in Microsoft SQL Server. This is quite helpful for learning to write custom queries to return other status information (see Figure 12.9).

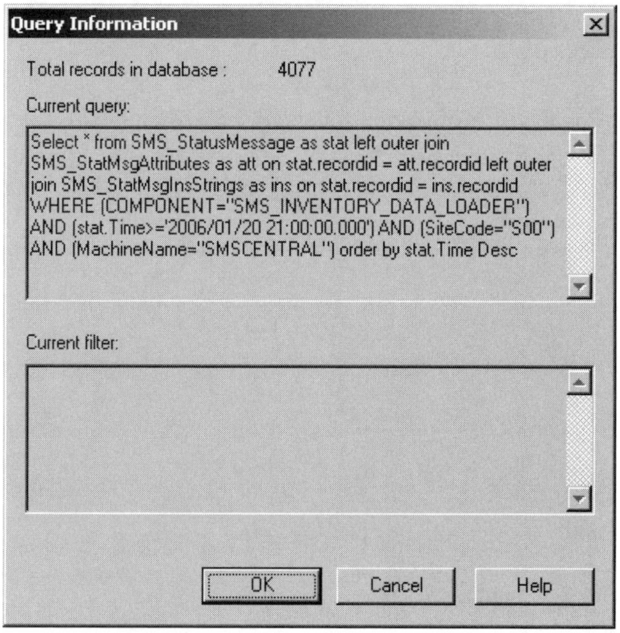

Figure 12.9: Viewing Query Information.

- The **Options** menu item provides customization for many other features, such as the following:

  - The **General** tab provides customization for auto-refresh frequency, number of messages returned, and time zone of messages displayed (see Figure 12.10).

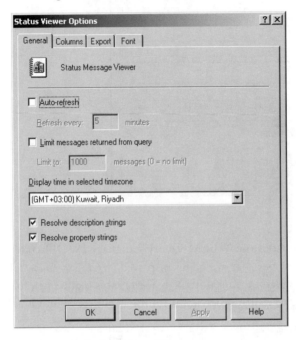

Figure 12.10: Configuring the General Tab.

  - The **Columns** tab provides customization for the displayed columns (see Figure 12.11).

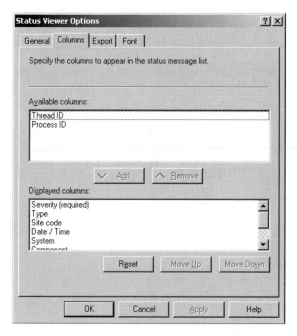

Figure 12.11: Configuring the Columns Tab.

- The **Export** tab provides customizations for exporting the data that is being viewed (see Figure 12.12).

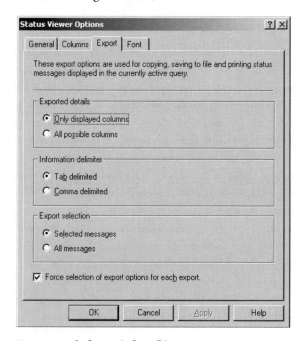

Figure 12.12: Configuring the Export Tab.

- The **Font** tab allows for the customization of the displayed and exported font (see Figure 12.13).

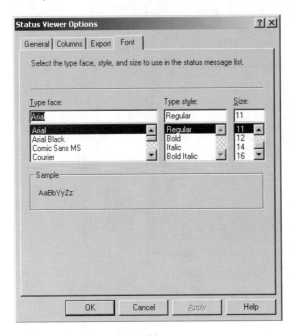

Figure 12.13: Configuring the Font Tab.

Tool Bar Buttons

The **Stop** button allows the user to stop the enumeration of the query that requests the status messages. This can be a very helpful tool. Because of the numbers of messages that are generated, status queries are one of the most resource-intensive requests that can be sent to SMS servers. Each user or system that receives an advertised program is likely to generate one of three status messages. If the installation goes properly, messages to indicate that the advertised program was received, run, and successfully completed will be sent. If the advertised program is received by clients, but has errors when attempting to run, these error messages will be sent in place of those messages intended to indicate running and successful completion. Client systems will never send messages if the advertised program is not received. While querying the SMS database for status messages is resource-intensive, no other enterprise software delivery application on the market provides this valuable feature.

The **Query** drop-down box allows for the selection of other queries.

Sorting can be performed by simply selecting a column header. The default sort order is **Date / Time**. When troubleshooting, it is helpful to sort by **System** or **Severity**.

An Introduction to Status MIFs

Installation status MIF files give SMS support personnel the ability to more accurately monitor installation progress at the workstation level. MIFs allow for true two-way communication between the workstation and the primary SMS server that sent the program.

Consider this analogy. You hire a carpenter to do some work for you. You ask him to keep you updated about the progress of the job, but unfortunately you only have a numeric pager for communication, which only allows the carpenter to send numbers. After a few hours, he sends you a page that only contains his phone number. Sending advertised programs *without using* installation status MIFs is like sending messages to a numeric pager. The details that can be received are limited to numbers only. Alternately, if you have an alphanumeric pager that allows letters and numbers, the carpenter can send the following message: "There is a problem with the job. I have to buy more wood. I'll be back tomorrow." Microsoft strongly recommends using MIFs to determine installation status, rather than relying on the default status messages described in the next section.

Default SMS Installation Status Messaging

Administrators not using MIFs have to rely on the default method that SMS employs to determine if a program completes successfully. This method reads the exit code of the program that is delivered. Compare Figure 12.14 with Figure 12.15.

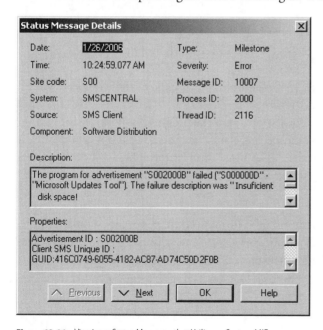

Figure 12.14: Viewing a Status Messages that Utilizes a Custom MIF.

Figure 12.15: Viewing the Default Status Message Details.

If the exit code is anything other than "0," it is considered a failed install. When a program fails, it can leave additional troubleshooting information in the MIF file. SMS can pick this up and present it to SMS administrators, as shown in Figure 12.14. Using the default SMS method for determining failed installations isn't as reliable as using custom status MIFs, for the following reasons:

- Some programs use exit codes other than "0," even when the installation is successful.

- If a wrapper is used to call the actual installation, the exit code of the wrapper is going to be read by the SMS client and returned to the primary server. In this case, the status messages will only provide information about the program responsible for calling the main program. The wrapper could be successful, but the actual application that is being distributed could fail. This causes inaccurate status information to be sent to the SMS database. The wrapper could be successful, but the actual application that is being distributed could fail.

- MIFs have more helpful troubleshooting information than do the standard SMS program error messages. The SMS client can't determine why the program may have failed. It just knows that something other than "0" was returned as the exit code. MIFs are written by the installation program, so it "knows" why the program failed.

Configuring Packages to Use MIFs

Creating installation status MIFs is really pretty simple. Unfortunately, there is very little documentation on the subject, and the text boxes provided in the SMS Package Properties are a bit confusing. Here is the process for configuring SMS to rely on status MIFs for installation status messages:

1. Create a MIF on a test machine. Find the commands within the installation program product documentation. Here is an example of command line syntax for creating MIFs using a Windows Installer program named setup.msi: `Setup.msi /m <MIF_FileName>`. Do not add an extension for the MIF filename. The MIFs will look similar to the MIF file example in Appendix B.

2. Open the Properties of the package that contains the program being advertised, and select the **Reporting** tab.

3. Add the proper information on this tab (see Figure 12.16). SMS uses a process called MIF matching, where it is critical to add the information properly; otherwise, the MIF will be ignored.

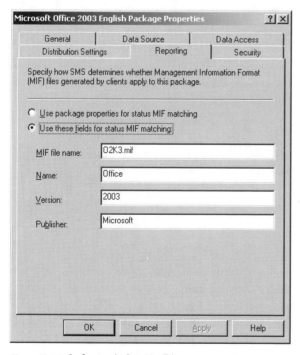

Figure 12.16: Configuring the Reporting Tab.

4. Enter the MIF file name. It must match the MIF file that is placed on the machine. Remember to include the .MIF extension.

5. Enter any desired information to the remaining fields; it must match the same fields on the **General** tab of the package. Compare Figure 12.16 with Figure 12.17. The fields can be left blank, but it is advantageous to use them. Otherwise, there is a chance that another MIF is present on the machine with the same name. The additional fields provide another layer of matching, in order to avoid passing information from the wrong MIF back to the primary server.

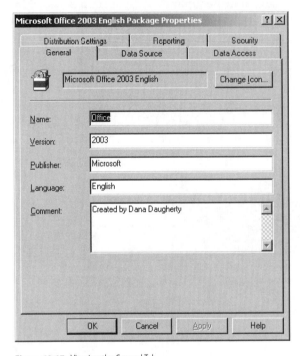

Figure 12.17: Viewing the General Tab.

Monitoring Packages

SMS provides information about package status in regards to the creation and installation process. The installation process includes copying source files to local distribution points and replicating them to other sites. Viewing package information is helpful when troubleshooting remote installation problems. From the SMS Administrator Console, packages can be monitored in much the same way that advertisements are monitored. See the "SMS Status Message Viewer" section in this chapter.

Accessing Package Status Information

Package status messages are useful to determine if a package successfully reached a targeted distribution point. There may be a delay of 30 minutes or so, depending on the location in the hierarchy where the target distribution point exists. To access package status information, follow these steps:

1. Open the **System Status** tree and select the **Package Status** tree. Summary information is available in the right pane (see Figure 12.18). Because the site in our example has only one DP, the values for the **Targeted, Installed** and **Retrying** columns can only be "1" or "0" depending on whether the DP has been targeted or not.

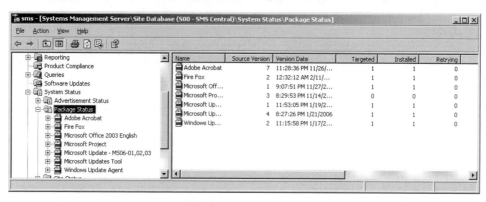

Figure 12.18: Viewing Summary Information for Packages.

2. Choose a package from the left pane; the right pane will be enumerated with SMS sites and summary information from the chosen package (see Figure 12.19).

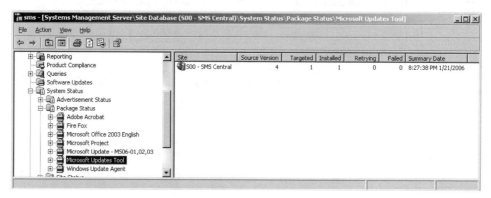

Figure 12.19: Viewing Summary Information for a Package.

The package status summary information headings are briefly explained in the following bullets:

- **Source Version** is the actual number of times the source files have been updated.

- **Targeted** indicates the number of distribution points that are targeted. The value for this column can be either "1" or "0" but it should match the value of the **Installed** column. A value of "0" indicates that no distribution points in the site are targeted.

- **Installed** indicates whether the source files were successfully installed. The value for this column can be either "1" or "0."

- **Retrying** indicates if the primary site is making additional attempts to copy source files to distribution points. The value for this column can be either "1" or "0."

- **Failed** indicates a failed attempt to copy source files to the distribution point.

- **Summary Date** is the last time that source files were successfully copied to the distribution point.

Viewing Package Status Messages

Package status messages are useful to monitor each phase of the package creation and distribution process. To view package status messages, do the following:

1. Open the **System Status** tree, then open the **Package Status** tree.

2. Right-click on a package and select the **Show Messages** menu item. Next, select an option from the contextual menu.

3. The **Status Messages: Set Viewing Period** dialog box appears (see Figure 12.20).

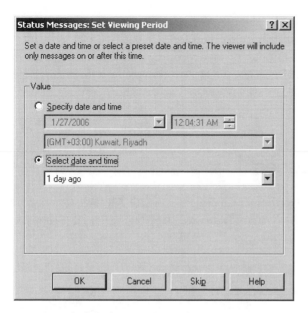

Figure 12.20: Configure the Set Viewing Period.

- **Specify date and time** allows user-defined information to be configured. All package messages after the date and time that you specify will appear.

- **Select date and time** displays all messages for the package, after a choice is made from the drop-down box.

4. Notice that, as with monitoring advertisements, package messages are read using the SMS Status Message Viewer (see Figure 12.21).

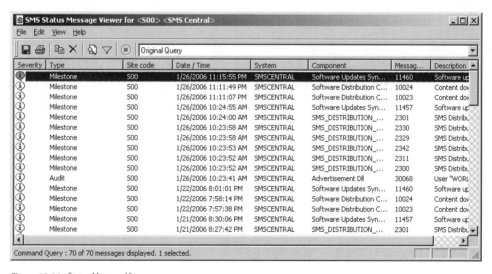

Figure 12.21: Status Message Viewer.

The columns that are displayed are the same as those that are displayed for advertisement messages. The package creation and distribution events for each package are clearly listed in this window. There may be a delay of 30 minutes or so, depending on the location in the hierarchy where the target distribution point exists. View the **Description** column for the message details. For more information, see the "SMS Status Message Viewer" and "Features of SMS Status Message Viewer" sections earlier in this chapter.

Status Message Queries

Another method of monitoring advertisement messages is Status Message Queries. These are predefined queries located under the **System Status** tree (see Figure 12.22). They can return information for packages and advertisements.

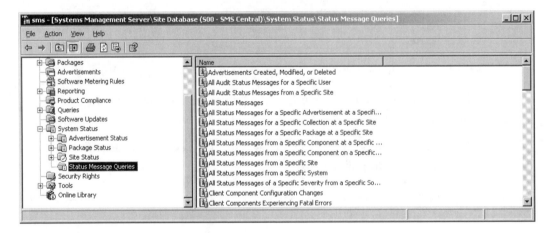

Figure 12.22: Navigating to Status Message Queries.

Helpful Queries for Monitoring Remote Installations

There are many queries that are helpful for monitoring remote installations. Here are a few of them:

- Advertisements Created, Modified, or Deleted

- Packages Created, Modified, or Deleted

- Programs Created, Modified, or Deleted

- All messages for a Specific Advertisement at a Specific Site

- All messages for a Specific Package at a Specific Site

- Clients that Failed to Start a Specific Advertised Program

- Clients that Started a Specific Advertised Program

- Clients that Ran a Specific Advertised Program Successfully

- Clients that Failed to Run a Specific Advertised Program Successfully

- Clients that Rejected a Specific Advertised Program

How to Run Status Message Queries

To run a query, follow these steps:

1. Right-click on a query from the right pane and select the **Show Messages** menu item.

2. Supply the requested information in the dialog box that appears (see Figure 12.23).

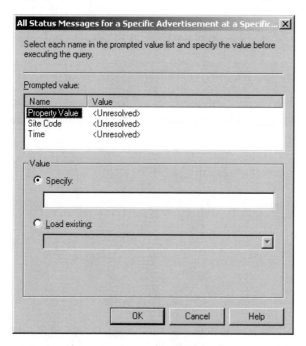

Figure 12.23: Status Message Queries Dialog.

The information requested from the user will vary, depending on the query that is selected. Click the **OK** button.

3. Notice that, once again, the SMS Status Viewer will appear, containing the status messages (see Figure 12.24).

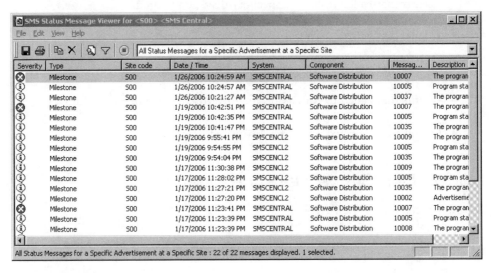

Figure 12.24: Viewing SMS Status Message Viewer.

Using SMS Web Reports to Monitor Advertisements and Packages

One additional interface can be used to access status messages for packages and advertisements. SMS Web Reports offers a Web-based approach to monitoring a distribution. There are useful reports under the following sections:

- Software Distribution – Advertisement Status

- Software Distribution – Packages

- Status Messages

Measuring Success

Based on the technology that is currently available, software distributions *should* be 100% accurate. However, the truth is that there are several more factors involved besides technology. Some items that can lower the percentage of successful installations include:

- Workstations in improper states. Advertised programs are configured to run depending on whether or not users are logged in. If a program is set to run only when a user is logged on, but the workstation has no one logging in to it for weeks after the deployment is completed, it will lower the average percentage for workstations that successfully installed the software. Wherever possible, SMS programs should be configured to run with the **Whether or not a user is logged on** program option, located on the **Environment** tab in the program's properties. Using this setting will allow the SMS program to be installed on more workstations more quickly, because the SMS program is not dependent on a user being logged on. Also, programs cannot run if systems are switched off. There are third-party products available from 1E to help with this issue. One product that accomplishes this task is called SMS Wakeup. See the 1E.com Web site for more details.

- Nonstandard desktop configurations. This problem can come from a lack of standard installation or imaging procedures. It can also be caused by end-users with Administrator or Power Users access on the local system. Desktop images should be created based on a company standard. The images should be versioned, so that those staff members who apply the image will be able to easily tell them apart. By limiting administrative and power user access to only the users who need it to perform their job tasks, you can reduce the amount of configuration changes that are made to workstations. Limiting the configuration changes that occur on the workstations will allow software packagers and SMS administrators to more accurately predict the configurations of the target workstations, thereby allowing them to create more effective software distributions with a higher percentage of successful software installations.

- Users canceling installations. Some wrappers or installation programs allow users to cancel them. To avoid this problem, use silent installations wherever possible. If this approach does not match your corporate culture, then configure passive user interfaces that do not allow end-users to stop the installation.

- Improper testing. Administrators who fail to properly test the delivery of advertised programs and the interaction of the delivered program with the existing programs are sure to experience failures. Proper testing in a lab environment is crucial. Following lab testing, there should be a phased deployment in the production environment. For more on this topic, see Chapter 5.

Phased distributions can be difficult to properly assess. The solution is to distribute the advertised program to only one collection. To do this, create the target collection and then simply add the computers or users in phases. This can be accomplished using the Direct Membership Rule wizard, or by using the Query Rule wizard to create multiple query rules. Another option is to use sub-select query rules that add the membership of other collections into the membership of the target collection. A final option is to use subcollections if the advertisement is configured to include subcollections.

Summary

This chapter gave you the necessary information to monitor software distributions. Monitoring distributions is really a matter of viewing status messages for the proper SMS object. SMS Status Message Viewer is the default message viewer that ships with SMS, and it is quite useful for displaying advertisement and package status messages. It can be evoked from any tree within the SMS Administrator Console that contains status messages for any SMS object. Also, status MIFs provide a way for vendors and administrators to customize the status messages that are reported. Customized status MIFs can give administrators more information for troubleshooting failed installations.

Monitoring Software Delivery with SMS Reporting

SMS reports allow you to easily monitor the software distribution process from beginning to end. As data is received by clients, it quickly becomes available as SMS reports content, allowing current data to be utilized for monitoring purposes. The Web-based report viewer interface allows administrators to easily provide Web links to staff members who may be interested in a specific report. This chapter shows report categories for various predefined software distribution-related reports. Predefined reports are those that are available for free from Microsoft after the SMS reporting installation is complete. This chapter also shows the steps for creating customized reports and *dashboards*. Dashboards contain several reports within a single SMS Report Viewer window, giving you an overview of various topics with a quick glance.

Installing SMS Reporting

There are three SMS reporting components:

- **SMS REPORTING POINT** — This component is installed on an SMS site system and requires Internet Information Server (IIS) to be installed and enabled. Installation details will follow later in this section. To use graphs in the reports, Office Web Components (Office 2000 SP2 or Office XP) must be installed. A reporting point can only communicate with the primary site server in the site where it is installed.

- **SMS ADMINISTRATOR CONSOLE REPORTING TREE** — This is visible in the top level of the console (see Figure 13.1).

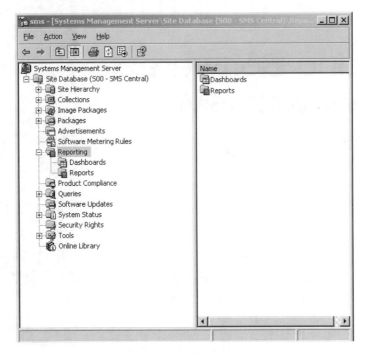

Figure 13.1: Viewing the Reporting Tree in the SMS Administrator Console.

- **SMS REPORTS VIEWER** — This is located on the reporting point and is accessed automatically through an Internet Explorer (version 5.01 SP2) or later window when clicking on a report link.

Generally, SMS reporting points are installed on the SMS central server (which is the top-most primary site server in the hierarchy), and on SMS sites where software advertisements are created. The reason for choosing the central site is that all SMS data (with the exception of advertisement status message data) flows upward to this point. Reports that are run from this site will reflect data from all sites in the hierarchy. Installing reporting points at other sites where advertisements are created may be a requirement if SMS administrators desire to see advertisement installation status reports. Advertisement status data does not flow past the site where the advertisement is created.

To install the reporting point, perform the following steps:

1. From the SMS Administrator Console, open the **Site Hierarchy** tree and then open the site tree where you plan to install a reporting point.

2. Select the **Site Settings**⇨ **Site Systems** node (see Figure 13.2) and then open the properties of the site server where you plan to install the reporting point.

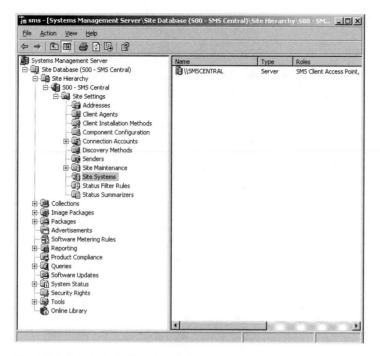

Figure 13.2: Browsing to the Site Systems Node.

3. Select the **Reporting Point** tab and then select the **Use this site system as a reporting point** check box (see Figure 13.3). Notice the URL field. This is the location to use to access the SMS Reporting Web page via Internet Explorer. By configuring IIS on the reporting point to use secure sockets (HTTPS), the **Use https** radio button becomes available for selection, as does the option to select a different port. Click the **OK** button to accept your selections.

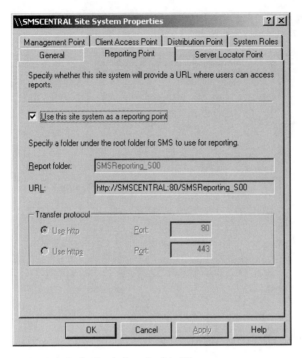

Figure 13.3: Configuring the Reporting Point Tab.

Using the SMS Report Viewer

Like other SMS objects, you must have the appropriate security credentials to view reports. See Chapter 3 for more specific information about configuring security for SMS objects. Using the SMS Report Viewer is pretty straightforward. To view reports and dashboards, perform the following steps:

1. Navigate to the reporting point Web page (see Figure 13.4). See Step 3 in the previous section to find the URL.

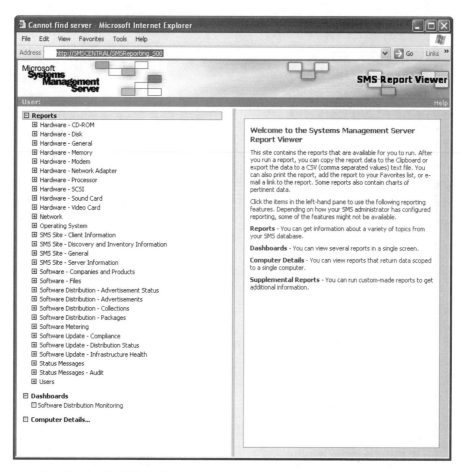

Figure 13.4: Accessing the SMS Report Viewer.

2. Notice a list of report categories and a list of dashboards. There are no predefined dashboards, so the list will be empty immediately after SMS Reporting is installed. From the SMS Report Viewer, open a category from the left pane and then select a report (see Figure 13.5). Notice the report description in the right pane.

Figure 13.5: Preparing to Run a Report.

3. Fill in the required text boxes in the right pane. Click the **Values** button if you want to select from a list rather than type the value in the box.

4. Click the **Display** button to view the results shown in Figure 13.6.

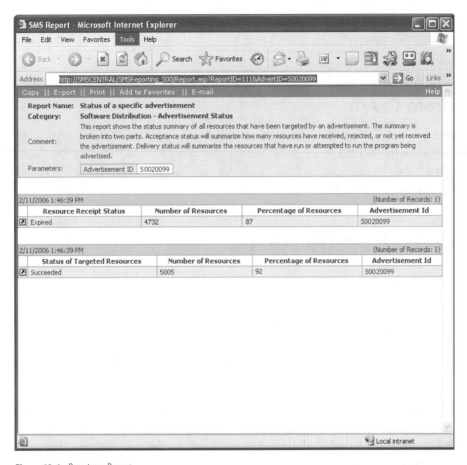

Figure 13.6: Running a Report.

5. Once the report is displayed, look for the white report links on the left. Click one of these links to open a target report with more detailed information.

The **Dashboards** section, shown back in Figure 13.4, lists any dashboards that have been created. The **Computer Details** link provides a special interface for viewing multiple details about a specific SMS client.

Launching SMS Report Viewer from the SMS Console

Alternatively, SMS Report Viewer can be launched by using the SMS console. To see a list of report categories, open the SMS Administrator Console and then open the **Reporting** tree. Right-click the **Reports** node and select the **All Tasks**⇨ **Run**⇨ **<reporting point server name>** menu item. The SMS Report Viewer will appear.

Individual reports can also be launched by right-clicking a report from within the SMS Administrator Console and then selecting the **All Tasks**➪ **Run**➪ **<reporting point server name>** menu item.

Export to CSV

Various commands exist to allow you to manipulate the report data. These commands exist in a menu bar at the top of each report (refer back to Figure 13.6). Most notably, the **Export** option allows report data to be exported into a CSV file, which allows you to use Microsoft Excel to format the data.

Predefined SMS Reports

Many predefined reports are available within SMS 2003 to monitor software distributions.

Viewing Report Categories

Various SMS reporting categories are available after the reporting point is installed. The categories that are particularly useful for monitoring software distribution include the following:

- **SOFTWARE DISTRIBUTION – ADVERTISEMENT STATUS** — This category provides reporting on installation status messages returned by clients for specific advertised programs. These reports are most useful for monitoring the delivery and installation status of a particular advertised program.

- **SOFTWARE DISTRIBUTION – ADVERTISEMENTS** — This category provides general reporting on advertisements that have been created at the site.

- **SOFTWARE DISTRIBUTION – COLLECTIONS** — This category provides general reporting on collections that have been created at the site.

- **SOFTWARE DISTRIBUTION – PACKAGES** — This category provides reporting on the status of copying software distribution packages from the site server to targeted distribution points. This data is useful for troubleshooting packages that fail to be processed.

- **SOFTWARE UPDATES – COMPLIANCE** — This category provides reporting on the status of software updates compliance on SMS clients throughout an organization. These reports help administrators to follow up on targeted clients that fail to install updates. The reports also help administrators to provide software updates compliance statistics to management.

- **SOFTWARE UPDATES – DISTRIBUTION STATUS** — This category provides reporting on the status of installing software updates on targeted SMS clients. These reports help administrators to follow up on targeted clients that fail to install updates.

- **SOFTWARE UPDATES – INFRASTRUCTURE HEALTH** — This category provides reporting on the status of Inventory Tools for Microsoft Updates (ITMU) scanning on SMS clients.

A Common Monitoring Scenario

SMS reports are useful to present data related to software distribution. The following scenario could occur in any organization. It depicts the use of predefined reports to monitor the common process of delivering software installations throughout an organization.

1. A software package is requested by an internal customer. An administrator creates and tests the software package. A pilot is designed. SMS packages, programs, advertisements and collections are created.

2. The following reports from the **Software Distribution – Packages** category are used to monitor the delivery of the package to the selected distribution points:

   - The Distribution status of a specific package

   - All distribution points

   - All status messages for a specific package on a specific distribution point

3. Pilot systems are targeted with the new advertised programs.

4. The following reports from the **Software Distribution - Advertisements** category are used to monitor the installation of the advertised program at the targeted SMS clients:

   - Chart - Hourly advertisement completion status

   - Status of a specific advertisement

5. An unacceptable number of program errors are reported during the pilot. Administrators become aware of the errors by monitoring the status of a specific advertisement report.

6. SMS administrators make modifications to the advertised program and re-pilot the software deployment.

7. Again, the reports listed in Step 4 of this scenario are used to monitor the installation of the advertised program at the targeted SMS clients.

8. All piloted systems run the program successfully.

9. The advertisement is configured to target the remaining production systems. SMS administrators continue to monitor the installations using SMS reports.

10. After the completion of the software deployment, reports from the **Software Updates – Compliance** category are used to produce statistics to management. Compliance reports are also used to monitor the organization for systems that become applicable for the software update in the future.

Creating Reports and Dashboards with SMS 2003

This section describes how to create reports and dashboards.

Creating SMS Reports

SMS reports are based on Microsoft SQL Server views, which are database objects. Views are defined using SQL SELECT statements and can reference one or more SQL tables. This is different than most objects within the SMS Administrator Console, which use WBEM Query Language (WQL). It is easier for administrators to work with views than to try and gather the data directly from the SQL Server tables. Views relieve the administrator from having to know all the details related to the SMS data and from having to be a skilled SQL DBA. With a working knowledge of SQL, you can create customized reports based on the requirements of your organization.

Like other SMS objects, you must have the appropriate security credentials to create reports. See Chapter 3 for more specific information about configuring security for SMS objects.

To create a new report or modify an existing report, open the SMS Administrator Console and then open the **Reporting** tree. Right-click the **Reports** node and select the **New⇨ Report** menu item. The **Report Properties** property sheet will appear (see Figure 13.7). Let's review the options available on each tab to configure the SMS report.

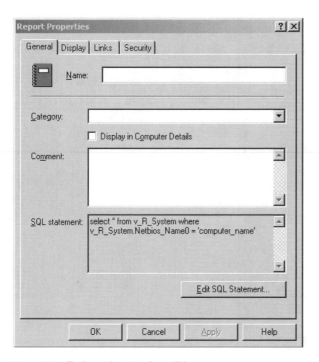

Figure 13.7: The Report Properties General Tab.

The General Tab

In the **General** tab, click the **Edit SQL Statement** button to modify the default SQL statement (see Figure 13.8).

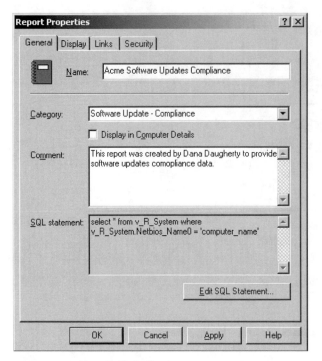

Figure 13.8: Modifying the SQL Statement.

The **Report SQL Statement** dialog box will appear, containing views that exist within the site database, along with the available column for each view (see Figure 13.9).

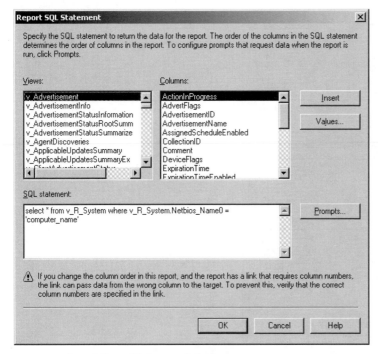

Figure 13.9: Using the Report SQL Statement Dialog Box.

Remember, this SQL statement is the core element of the report. Using the **Report SQL Statement** dialog box along with SQL statement examples from other reports can help you to create a new SQL statement for your report. The **Insert** button inserts the selected view or column value into the SQL statement. The **Values** button lists the available values for the column that is selected. The **Prompts** button allows the addition of prompts within the report interface. Prompts gather additional information from the end-user to provide more specific data within the report.

The Display Tab

Select the **Display** tab (shown in Figure 13.10) to configure the refresh interval chart properties of the report. Select a refresh interval only if you want to refresh the report automatically. This would be a rare occasion where end-users would require a report to remain open for an extended amount of time. It is best not to select this option unless you must, because network and server resources will be utilized on each refresh cycle—regardless of whether anyone is viewing the report. Choosing to provide a chart in the report will allow the user to select the chart or the default view.

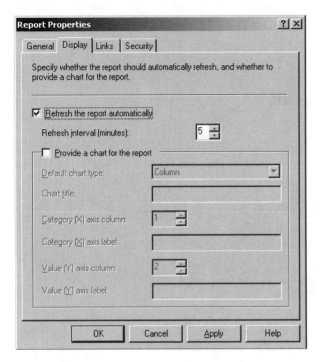

Figure 13.10: Configuring the Display Tab.

The Links Tab

Select the **Links** tab to configure the **Link type** property. This property allows report users to "drill down" to gather more details. Items such as another report, computer details, status message details, or a link to an external Web page can be linked to the report.

To link to another report, perform the following steps:

1. From the **Links** tab, select the **Link to another report** option from the **Link Type** drop-down box. After making this selection, additional options will appear on the **Link** tab.

2. Click the **Select** button and the **Select Report** dialog box will appear.

3. Select a report (or reports) from the list and then click the **OK** button. The report name(s) will appear in the **Reports** text box. The **Prompts** window contains the name and the prompt text of any prompts for the selected target report and displays the specified column of the source report that contains the data for each prompt. Prompts are fields that require input from the user. They appear when a report is selected, but prior to running.

4. Click the **OK** button to accept the selection and close the dialog box. View the report to verify that the link has been added.

The Security Tab

Select the **Security** tab to configure security for the Reporting class or for one report instance (see Figure 13.11). More details on security configuration are available in Chapter 3.

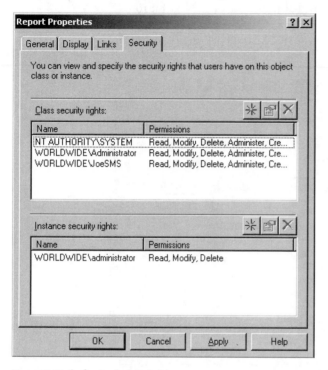

Figure 13.11: Configuring the Security Tab.

Viewing the Properties of an Existing Report

To view the properties of an existing report, simply select the **Reports** node within the SMS Administrator Console. Right-click on any report and select the **Properties** menu item. Click the **Edit SQL Statement** button (see Figure 13.10). View the SQL statement in the **SQL statement** window. From this point, you can edit the statement, or copy it and paste it into another report and then modify it.

Importing and Exporting Report Objects

Reports can be imported and exported using a wizard (described below). Only the *report definition* is imported or exported in the MOF file format, not the actual data. The report definition is the structure of the report. MOF file format is a standard type of text file. This feature can prove to be handy for sharing report definitions with the SMS administrators from other organizations.

Perform the following steps to export a report:

1. Open the SMS Administrator Console and then open the **Reporting** tree. Right-click the **Reports** node and select the **All Tasks**⇨ **Export Objects** menu item. The **Export Object Wizard** welcome screen will appear. Click the **Next** button.

2. Select a report to export (see Figure 13.12) and click the **Next** button.

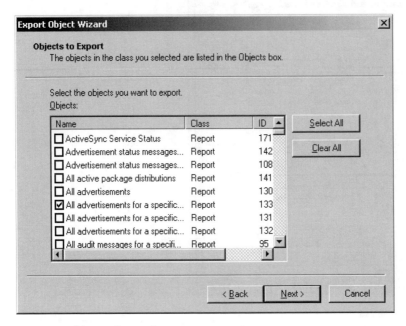

Figure 13.12: Selecting a Report to Export.

3. Provide the path and file name for the MOF file that will be created and enter comments (see Figure 13.13). Click the **Next** button, then click the **Finish** button to complete the export.

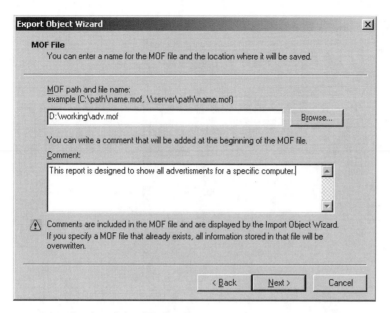

Figure 13.13: Providing a Path and File Name.

To import a report, open the SMS Administrator Console and then open the **Reporting** tree. Right-click the **Reports** node and select the **All Tasks⇨ Import Objects** menu item. The **Import Object Wizard** welcome screen will appear. Complete the wizard.

Creating Dashboards

A dashboard contains several reports within a single SMS Report Viewer window. Dashboards can be used to quickly obtain overview information about various topics. Unlike reports, dashboards cannot be imported or exported. Existing dashboards can be copied and modified to your specifications.

Perform the following steps to create a new dashboard:

1. Open the SMS Administrator Console and then open the **Reporting** tree. Right-click the **Dashboards** node and select the **New⇨ Dashboard** menu item. The **Dashboard Properties** property sheet appears (see Figure 13.14). Provide a name and comments for the new dashboard. Adjust the cell height as required.

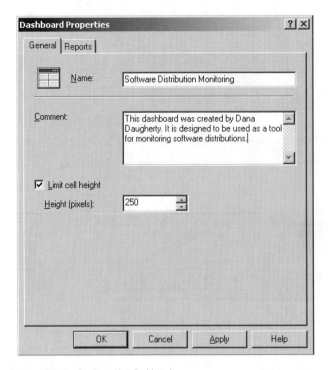

Figure 13.14: Creating a New Dashboard.

2. Select the **Reports** tab (see Figure 13.15). Configure the dashboard dimensions as required. The **Dashboard reports** section contains the list of reports that will be contained within the dashboard.

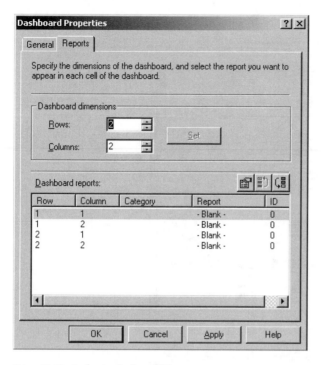

Figure 13.15: Configuring the Reports Tab.

3. Double-click on one of the reports that are listed to view the **Select Report** dialog box (shown in Figure 13.16).

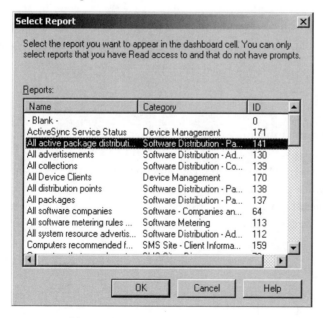

Figure 13.16: Selecting a Report.

4. Select a report and then click the **OK** button. The selected report will then appear in the list of Dashboard reports (see Figure 13.17).

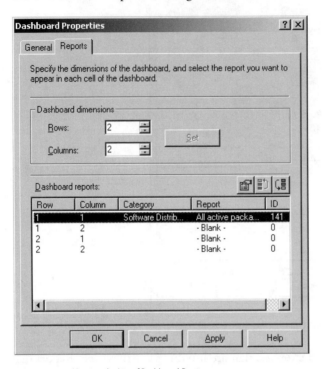

Figure 13.17: Viewing the List of Dashboard Reports.

5. Click the **OK** button to finish configuring the new dashboard. The new dashboard will automatically appear under the **Dashboards** section within the SMS Report Viewer.

Additional Support

Much more could be written on the topic of developing SMS reports, but it would be beyond the scope of this book. Additional sources exist that you will find useful. Chapter 11 in the *SMS Administrator Guide* provides more details on creating reports and using SQL statements. Also, the SMS administrator online community at myItforum.com provides an entire section of downloads for SMS reports. These reports could be used as they are, or they could be modified to the parameters of your organization. Here is the link: http://myitforum.com/downloads/default.asp?w=3&se=Reports.

Summary

After reading this chapter, you can see that SMS reporting provides a flexible method of reporting SMS data. Monitoring the software distribution process from beginning to end can easily be done with SMS reports. The data in SMS reports provides users with a great software distribution monitoring tool. The Web-based report viewer interface allows administrators to easily provide Web links to staff members who may be interested in a specific report. This chapter gave you a list of predefined report categories and descriptions. It also showed you the steps for creating customized reports and dashboards.

DID YOU KNOW?

System Center Configuration Manager (SCCM) will rely on Microsoft Visual Studio and Microsoft SQL Server Reporting Services for creating and displaying reports. It is wise to develop your skill with these products before the release of SCCM.

Troubleshooting Software Distribution: Server Side

Just like any software, SMS software distribution will occasionally pose administration challenges. The key to solving such challenges is to follow the software distribution process from beginning to end, or possibly from end to beginning. There are several SMS components that work together to form the software distribution feature. It is much easier to follow software distribution processes if you are familiar with the components that work together to complete each process. In this chapter, you will learn about the server-side components and processes that make up software distribution. When you finish this chapter, you will be able to follow each software distribution process, from beginning to end, by reading status messages and log files. You will learn to use log reading tools to aid you when troubleshooting.

Component Services and Component Threads

There are two types of SMS components:

- **Service Components** are Windows Server OS family services appearing in the Services applet.

- **Thread Components** are processes that run under the SMS Executive Service.

All SMS thread components and some SMS service components can be viewed by using SMS Service Manager, located under the **Tools** tree in the SMS Administrators Console (see Figure 14.1).

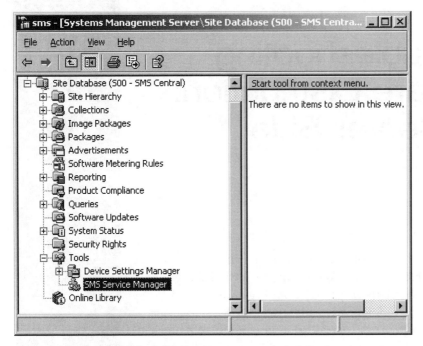

Figure 14.1: Navigating to SMS Service Manager.

Right-click the **SMS Service Manager** and then select the **All Tasks**⇨ **Start SMS Service Manager** menu item. You will see the tool automatically open (see Figure 14.2).

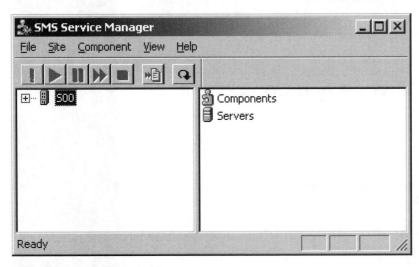

Figure 14.2: Launching SMS Service Manager.

SMS Service Manager can also connect to additional servers. To do this, select the **Site**⇨ **Connect** menu item. The **Connect to Site** applet will appear (see Figure 14.3). Provide the site server name where you want to make a connection and then click the **OK** button.

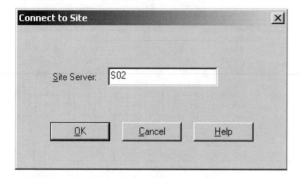

Figure 14.3: Connecting with SMS Service Manager.

After making a connection to a site server with SMS Service Manager, perform the following steps to view the state of the SMS components:

1. From the left pane, open the **<Site Code>** tree and then select the **Components** node.

2. From the top of the console, select the **Component**⇨ **Select all** menu item. All the components in the right pane should be selected.

3. Select the **Component**⇨ **Query** menu item. It may take several minutes to retrieve the information over slow or busy WAN links.

4. Notice that the right pane will display green status indicators for running components and red indicators for stopped components. There are some services that are supposed to be stopped because they are scheduled to occur, such as **SMS Network Discovery**, **SMS Site Backup**, and **SMS WINT Server Discovery Agent** (see Figure 14.4). The **Component Type** column will indicate service components and thread components.

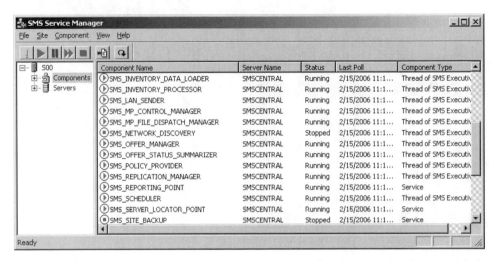

Figure 14.4: Querying Components with SMS Service Manager.

To configure the logging properties of a component, follow these steps:

1. Right-click on a component in the right pane and select the **Logging** menu item. The **SMS Component Logging Control Dialog – Single component** dialog box will appear (see Figure 14.5). Within this dialog box, you can enable or disable logging, modify the size of the log file, or modify the location of the log. If multiple logs are selected, they can be configured simultaneously. The option to use a single log file for all selected components is available, but will make reading the logs more confusing.

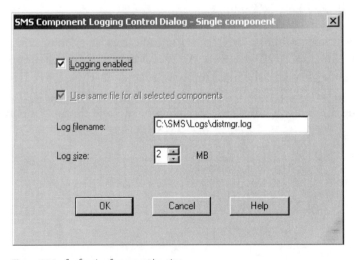

Figure 14.5: Configuring Component Logging.

2. After making changes in this dialog box, click the **OK** button.

3. Right-click the components that were modified and select the **Stop** menu item.

4. Right-click the components that were modified and select the **Query** menu item.

5. Right-click the components that were modified and select the **Start** menu item.

6. Right-click the components that were modified and select the **Query** menu item to verify that the component started again.

General Troubleshooting Principles

Let's look at several general principles that can be helpful during any troubleshooting scenario.

Develop an Understanding of the System

Before you can accomplish any measurable troubleshooting work, it is essential to develop an understanding of the system components that you are working with. The first place to start is the *Microsoft Systems Management Server 2003 Operations Guide*, available on the SMS 2003 product CD. Some of this same information is included in the SMS Administrator Console help file, accessible from the **Help⇨ Help Topics** menu item. Online links to SMS 2003 product documentation are located in the **SMS Online Library** menu item, which is installed in the **Systems Management Server** program group. The *Microsoft Systems Management Server 2003 Operations Guide* in particular builds a foundation for other more complex concepts. Check the online documentation link occasionally to see if there is an updated version of this guide. Here is the link: `http://www.microsoft.com/smserver/techinfo/productdoc/default.mspx`. There is a troubleshooting section at this link that contains several documents. One download worth looking at is the troubleshooting flowchart documentation, which can be helpful in some scenarios. Unfortunately, not all processes are thoroughly covered. This chapter provides a list of logs to search for each process and is a great resource for learning about the components responsible for SMS software distribution.

Define the Problem

Find out exactly what is occurring and the scope of the problem. Note all symptoms of the problem for future reference. The scope of the problem should include information about affected operating systems, SMS sites, applications, global location, network location, and so on. Try to find the things that the affected machines have in common and add this to your problem definition and scope.

Use a Strategy to Isolate the Problem

After obtaining a thorough understanding of SMS components, determine a troubleshooting strategy. Two good strategies are "divide and conquer" and "start at a known good state." *Divide and conquer* involves choosing a point in the middle of a broken process, determining what side of the process is not working properly, and then continuing to divide and conquer on the broken side of the process until the solution is found. Since SMS uses a client-server architecture, the dividing point is commonly the network.

Let's look at an example. Suppose an SMS Advanced Client will not install on a workstation. My initial response may be to begin looking at the server side of the *dividing point*. If the problem is not obvious, I must then begin dividing the server processes, such as communication and creation of the proper files. If I am unable to find a problem on the server side then I must try the computer on the other side of my initial dividing point—the client system.

Start at a known good state is another helpful troubleshooting strategy. First, find a point in a broken process where the problem began to occur. If you are certain that the process is working properly to the point where the problem occurs, start with the problem and continue through the process. Another angle for this strategy is to compare a properly functioning system with one that has no activity, which indicates there is a problem. Also, by becoming familiar with a system while it is working properly, an administrator may have an easier time troubleshooting when it isn't working. To get an idea of how the process is supposed to work, try using the troubleshooting flow chart located at the SMS 2003 product documentation site: http://www.microsoft.com/smserver/techinfo/productdoc/default.mspx. If you determine there are problems in the first part of the process, start at the beginning and move through the process. If you think the problem is towards the end of the process, start at the end and go backwards until you find it.

Usually, the best strategy for troubleshooting SMS issues involves breaking down the system into components. By understanding the responsibilities of each component, you can determine which components are most likely responsible for the problems you are seeing and begin focusing on these.

Additional Resources

If you need additional help defining or isolating the problem, you may need to utilize more resources. Here are a few ideas:

- Microsoft Tech Net contains knowledge base articles and information about known issues at http://support.microsoft.com/search/?adv=1.

- myITforum.com provides technical articles and forums where you can gather more information.

Using Component Logs to Troubleshoot SMS

Searching through SMS logs can sometimes make administrators feel like they are following an endless maze. It doesn't have to be that way. If you thoroughly understand the SMS components, have a good strategy, and use the proper tools, you will be more successful. In this section, you will learn how to troubleshoot SMS component logs. The skills that you learn here will lay the foundation for the remaining sections of this chapter. These troubleshooting approaches are not limited to software distribution components only—they can be transferred to all SMS components.

Modifying the Logging Properties

By default, most component log files are set to grow to 2.5 MB before being archived to a file with an extension of .LO_ in the same directory. Before reading the logs, you will need to verify that they are being processed. To do this, open the <SiteServerName>\SMS_<SiteCode>\Logs directory (see Figure 14.6). If the log you need to read is *not* present, you will need to activate it. If the log is present, verify that it has a recent modification date. In most sites, data is written to all logs at least daily.

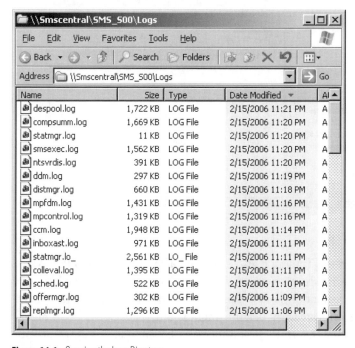

Figure 14.6: Opening the Logs Directory.

While there are several methods of activating component logs and modifying their properties, using SMS Service Manager is the safest. See the "Component Services and Component Threads" section earlier in this chapter for details on using SMS Service Manager to configure component logs.

SMS *logging* (also known as *tracing*) configuration information is stored in the registry of the site server. Another way to activate logging is to use Registry Editor to open **HKEY_LOCAL_ MACHINE\Software\Microsoft\SMS\Tracing** (see Figure 14.7). From the left pane, select the component where you want to activate logging. In the right pane, note the entry for the **Enabled** value: **0** = Off, and **1**= On.

To activate logging for the selected component, open the **Enabled** value and change the "0" to a "1." To deactivate logging for a component, change the "1" to a "0." After making the configuration, restart the component using SMS Service Manager, as described in the "Component Services and Component Threads" section earlier in this chapter. Unfortunately, there are no settings to allow all the logs to be activated or deactivated simultaneously.

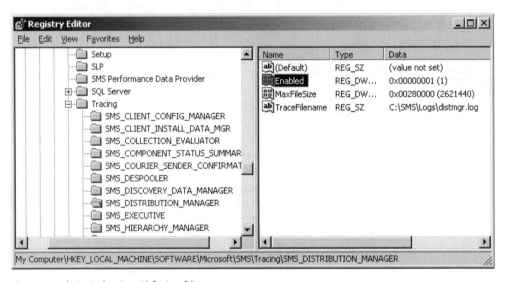

Figure 14.7: Activating Logging with Registry Editor.

Also, note the **MaxFileSize** value in the **Tracing** registry key; the default is 2621440 (2.5 MB). This value can be changed here to the size that you desire. It may be difficult to troubleshoot some components, because log information is lost due to the frequency of the components processing, causing the log to be truncated. By default, there is only between 1.5 MB and 5 MB of information in the .LOG and .LO_ files. If you increase the value significantly, be sure to lower it after troubleshooting is completed. The **TraceFileName** value, located in the **Tracing** registry key, is the location of the log file for the selected component.

Use the Proper Tools to Search the Logs

After determining the SMS components that are failing, the proper logs have been activated. Next, begin searching for logs that contain errors or failures; this will begin to narrow the problem down to specific components. Searching can be done using either of these two methods:

- Search the component log directory using the Windows search utility (see Figure 14.8), which can be launched from an Explorer window through a right-click menu. Use the **Containing Text** field to search for the following words: error, warning, and fail. Then consider the logs that are returned in your search. Generally, you want to focus on the logs that are related to the components suspected in your problem, but don't rule anything out.

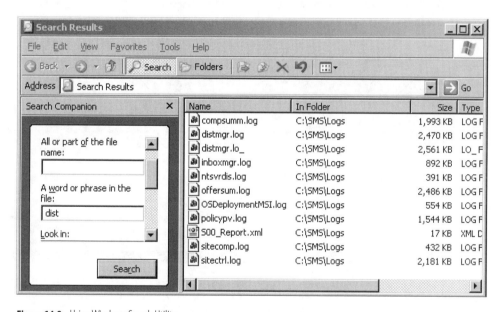

Figure 14.8: Using Windows Search Utility.

- Search the component log directory using a Global Regular Expression and Print (GREP) utility. GREP tools search for strings inside of one or more input files. Windows GREP tools are generally quite helpful for troubleshooting. They can search multiple SMS logs simultaneously and display the search output. This is one of the tools that Microsoft Product Support Services engineers use when helping administrators who open cases with them. GREP tools can save countless hours and possibly reduce the number of necessary support tickets that need to be opened.

Logs can be read using Notepad or by using log utilities. If you are viewing one or two logs, Notepad will serve the purpose. If you are troubleshooting multiple logs, use a log utility. SMS provides a tool called SMS Trace, especially designed for reading SMS logs (see Figure 14.9). The newest version is located in the Systems Management Server 2003 Toolkit 2, downloadable from `http://www.microsoft.com/smserver/downloads/2003/tools/toolkit.mspx`. This tool provides many helpful features that are not available from a simple text editor like Notepad.

- Logs can be read in real-time. SMS Trace supports updating the screen as a component writes to the log.

- Lines of text can be highlighted based on text strings.

- The **File⇨ Open on Server** menu item can be used to select an SMS server from a list, causing SMS Trace to open the Logs directory of the selected server.

- The displayed information can be filtered.

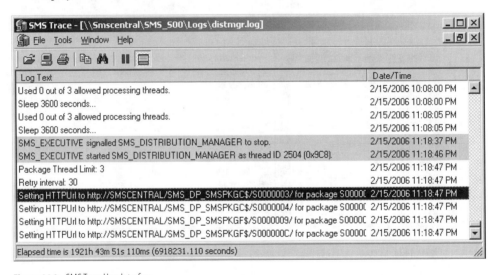

Figure 14.9: SMS Trace User Interface.

Once you feel confident about the source of the problem, go back to the flowcharts and walk through the process that was designed to occur. Compare it to what is actually occurring, based on the logs and activity that occurs on the Advanced Client or the site server. Some components and processes are set to occur at a specific time, or they are triggered by an event. Therefore, you will need to find the best way to restart the process in question while you are capturing the logs. This will ensure that the logged data will contain information about the process in question. After verifying the improper behavior of your SMS component, find possible solutions from one of these sources:

- The Systems Management Server Web page at Microsoft TechNet Online at `http://www.microsoft.com/technet/treeview/default.asp?url=/technet/prodtechnol/sms/default.asp`.

- Microsoft Support Knowledge Base at `http://support.microsoft.com/search/?adv=1`.

- News Groups and forums. The myITforum Web site provides both of these at `http://www.myitforum.com`.

SMS Software Distribution Server Processes and Components

SMS server software distribution processes and components can be grouped into four categories:

- **PACKAGE CREATION AND DISTRIBUTION** — This process utilizes several SMS components in order to complete administrator requests to package application source files and move them to the assigned distribution points. SMS Distribution Manager is an SMS thread component that plays a major role in software distribution processes. It is dedicated exclusively to software distribution processes and performs the "heavy lifting" required by the package creation and distribution process: compressing and decompressing package source files, placing packages on distribution points, sending package-related requests to Inbox Manager, and managing replication of package files to child sites.

- **ADVERTISEMENTS** — This process includes the tasks necessary to carry out administrator requests for advertisement creation. The tasks include preparing policies that contain program instructions for Advanced Clients, and placing policies on SMS management points.

- **STATUS MANAGEMENT** — This process is responsible for reporting the status of creating SMS packages and delivering them to DPs. A second status management task is to report the status of advertised programs as they are received, started, and completed by the SMS client.

- **COURIER SENDER** — While this thread component is dedicated to software distribution, it is not utilized unless the administrator chooses it. Courier Sender is responsible for writing package information and source files on physical media. This component provides a workaround for child sites located across slow, unreliable, or intermittent links. See the *SMS Operations Guide* for more information about this topic.

Inboxes and SMS Management Points

This section provides a foundation for understanding the more complex information contained in later sections of this chapter. Inboxes are the containers or directories that SMS uses to manage communications between SMS components. They are located under the \\<SiteServerName>\ SMS_<SiteCode>\inboxes share (see Figure 14.10).

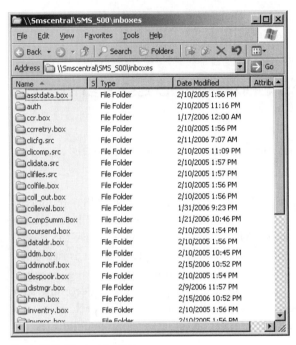

Figure 14.10: Viewing Inbox Folders.

When files are added to the inboxes directory, change notifications or polling cycles are used to trigger the appropriate SMS components. SMS components are notified of a change to the inbox and they respond according to a set of rules. These inboxes are used in a fashion similar to those in an employee's cubicle or office. Someone places information or requests in the inbox, and the employee responds to the request according to the organization's standard operating procedures. Likewise, SMS Inbox Manager is responsible for moving files in and out of inboxes, based on a set of rules for that file and inbox.

A management point is, in part, a set of directories located on an SMS site system that acts as an exchange between the site server and Advanced Clients assigned to the site. The MP outboxes folders are located under the \\<SMSSiteServerName>\SMS_<SiteCode>\MP share (see Figure 14.11). SMS Policy Provider creates a policy and a policy assignment based on the package, program, advertisement, and target collection. The policy is made available to the assigned Advanced Clients on the MP. Advanced Clients access the management point at `http://<managementpointservername>/SMS_MP` to access policies for download.

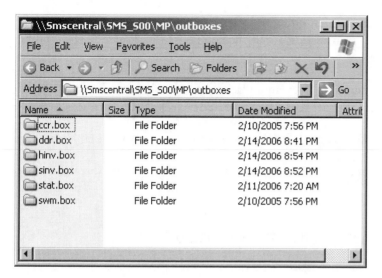

Figure 14.11: Viewing Management Point Folders.

Package Creation and Distribution Processes

This section focuses on the SMS components that are necessary for a package to be created and placed on distribution points, including child site distribution points. The following SMS components are required to create and distribute packages:

- **SMS Provider** writes package information to the site database, after an administrator enters information in the Package Properties sheet and clicks the **OK** button.

- **SMS SQL Monitor** places a package notification file (.PKN) in the Distmgr.box inbox.

- **Distribution Manager**:

    - Compresses the package, if it was configured that way in the **Package Properties**⇨ **Data Source** tab, or if the package will be sent to a child site. The compressed files are then stored in the SMSpkg share on the site server.

    - Copies the source files directly to the local distribution point.

    - Creates the package, distribution point list, and icon files at the site server. They are all placed in the Pkginfo.box inbox.

    - If Distribution Manager must replicate a package to a child site, it creates a package replication file in the Replmgr.box inbox. At the child site, it copies source files to its distribution points, updates the site database, and distributes objects to the appropriate inboxes.

- **Replication Manager** creates mini-jobs for Sender and places them in the Schedule.box inbox. The jobs contain information about the compressed package files that will be replicated to the child site.

- **Scheduler** packages replication files and places them in the Schedule.box\Tosend directory. It then creates a sender request in Schedule.box\Outboxes.

- **Sender** sends package files to the Despooler.box\Receive directory at the child site.

- **Despooler** decompresses the replication files at the child site and stores them at the site server.

Package Creation and Distribution Process Flow

The SMS server processes, described previously in this section, work together to create a package. The actual package creation and distribution process flow is listed in Chapter 1.

Troubleshooting the Package Creation and Distribution Processes

Let's look at an example of how you can troubleshoot a package creation or package distribution problem. We will look in detail at how to do the following:

- Describe the symptoms.

- Gather information.

- Decide how to approach the troubleshooting process.

- Draw appropriate conclusions from your observations.

For our scenario, here are the signs that will tip off the administrator that a package creation or distribution problem has occurred:

- Advertisements never appear to the users on Advanced Client machines.

- Advertisement status messages indicate that the advertisement was run, but the program source files could not be found.

- Error messages appear on the Site Server Console, or in the **System Status**⇨ **Site Status**⇨ **<SMS Site Name>**⇨ **Component Status** tree, for any of the components related to package creation and distribution.

- Error messages in the **System Status**⇨ **Package Status** tree indicate that a package could not be installed or could not be updated.

See Chapter 12 for more details about viewing package status messages.

 **NOTE**

A common distribution issue is caused by lack of disk space. Creating a package requires free space on the DP equal to 2.5 to 3 times the size of the package source files.

Symptoms

For this scenario, suppose that modifications that were performed to the wrapper script (located in the Microsoft Office 2003 source files) for a certain SMS package are not taking affect when the advertised program is run on some clients. Suppose that clients having the issue are running the program with the wrong parameters, causing the program to install without errors but with the wrong features.

Information Gathering

You should note any changes that may have been made to any of the package creation or distribution components. Using SMS Trace, view the SMS logs for the related components, listed earlier in this chapter in the "Package Creation and Distribution Processes" section. After looking through the execmgr.log file on a working client, you realize the package ID for Microsoft Office 2003 is S0000009. You also find that the first error occurred at 10:14 p.m. on 2/16/06 as seen in the **Package Status** node of the SMS Administrator Console. The package originated at the central site server with a site code of S00. There are multiple SMS sites containing multiple distribution points.

When troubleshooting a package distribution problem, gather important information in the following ways:

- **Review Advertisement status messages.** Open the SMS Administrator Console under the **Site Status**⇨ **System Status**⇨ **Advertisement Status** node.

- **Review Site status.** Open the SMS Administrator Console under the **Site Status**⇨ **System Status**⇨ **S00 – SMS Central** tree and select the **Component Status** node.

- **Review Package status messages.** Open the SMS Administrator Console under the **Site Status**⇨ **System Status**⇨ **S00 – SMS Central** tree and select the **Package Status** node.

- **Browse the package share on the DP to check the source files.** If this had been attempted in our scenario, the administrator would have realized that the package share was inaccessible.

- **View the Package Properties.** Look for any configuration settings that are non-standard. For our scenario, let's suppose that none were found.

- **Contact end-users.** For our scenario, suppose that the end-users tell you they are missing program features that they were expecting to be installed.

- **Contact other SMS administrators.** For our example, let's assume that no new information was provided.

Approach

The best approach for this troubleshooting scenario is to follow the broken process from beginning to end, looking for abnormalities. Follow the software distribution, using the process flow listed in Chapter 1. The most effective way to do this is by viewing log files. The following tables provide a mapping of SMS components to the proper log file names. Table 14.1 shows package creation and distribution-related server components and associated logs at the server where package creation originated. Table 14.2 shows package creation and distribution-related server components and associated logs at a child site.

Server Component	Log Files
SMS Provider	SMS\Logs\SMSprov.log
SMS SQL Monitor	SMS\Logs\SMSdbmon.log
Distribution Manager	SMS\Logs\Distmgr.log
Inbox Manager	SMS\Logs\Inboxmgr.log
Replication Manager	SMS\Logs\Replmgr.log
Scheduler	SMS\Logs\Sched.log
Sender	SMS\Logs\Sender.log

Table 14.1: Components and Associated Logs at the Server.

Server Component	Log Files
Despooler	SMS\Logs\Despool.log
Distribution Manager	SMS\Logs\Distmgr.log
Replication Manager	SMS\Logs\Replmgr.log
Inbox Manager	SMS\Logs\Inboxmgr.log

Table 14.2: Components and Associated Logs at a Child Site.

Based on the information listed in the "Symptoms" and "Information Gathering" sections above, we know that, in our scenario, clients are not receiving the updated Microsoft Office 2003 program installation. We also note that Distribution Manager at site S00 (the site where the package is created) is reporting an error. Clients at all sites in the SMS hierarchy seem to be affected by the problem. Based on this information, we should begin troubleshooting at the beginning of the package distribution process.

To verify the success of the package creation and distribution process, you can view the following logs:

- **SMSDBMON.LOG** — View this log at the site where the package is created. Search for <PackageID>.pkn (S0000009 in our example) and verify that the notification was created by SMS SQL Monitor in Inboxes\Distmgr.box (see Figure 14.12).

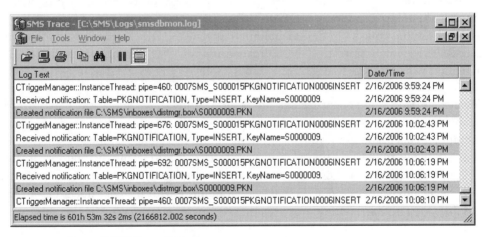

Figure 14.12: Viewing SMS SQL Monitor Notification.

- **DISTMGR.LOG** — This log can be viewed at each site server that contains DPs that are selected to host the package (see Figure 14.13). In our example, we will begin with the site where the package is created. We can see the errors that indicate an access issue with the package source folder.

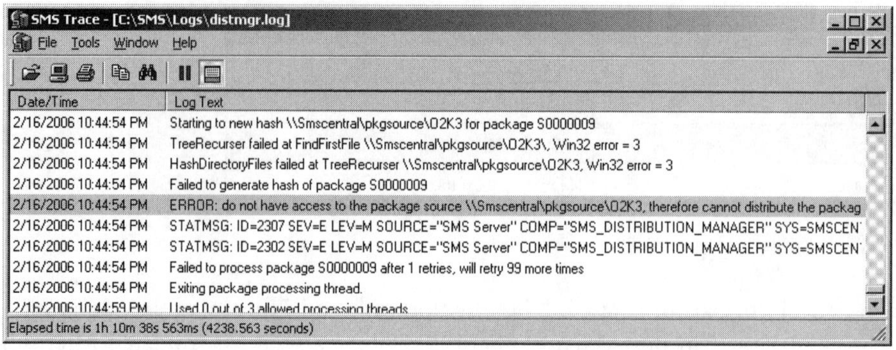

Figure 14.13: Distribution Manager Log Example.

Using the log information, we can deduce that the package notification in our scenario was created by SQL Monitor. We also see that Distribution Manager does not have access to the package source folder at \\Smscentral\pkgsource\O2K3, which causes it to fail when attempting to update distribution points.

Conclusion

Using the information from the Distribution Manager log, we can finish up our troubleshooting scenario by verifying the security settings at the package source folder. In this case, we find out that the folder is no longer shared. The package share must be enabled and the security settings must be verified. On its next attempt to update the DP, Distribution Manager succeeds. Eventually, we might learn that the ultimate cause was that someone from the security team thought it would be wise to disable the package source share to avoid security risks.

Solving all SMS component-related problems requires the same basic steps: describe the symptoms, gather information, decide how to approach the troubleshooting process, and draw appropriate conclusions from your observations. In the preceding example, these basic steps were illustrated while troubleshooting a "real-world" package creation and distribution problem. You will improve your troubleshooting effectiveness by continuing to use these steps to solve SMS component problems. Speed and accuracy will improve with the continued use of these steps and the varied troubleshooting situations that you experience.

Advertisement Processes

Let's look at the process of advertisement creation from the SMS Administrator Console. The process can only be initiated on an SMS primary server. There are five components involved:

- **SMS Provider** — After an administrator enters information in the **Advertisement Properties** sheet and clicks the **OK** button, this component writes advertisement information to the site database.

- **Offer Manager** – This component processes advertisement requests, and evaluates the membership for the target collection. Offer Manager also creates advertisement files and copies them to the Client Access Point (CAP). CAPs are only used by the SMS Legacy Client, which is a topic not covered by this book. If there is a child site configured to receive the advertisement, this component creates the outbound advertisement.

- **SMS SQL Monitor** — If package files for the advertised program are not ready, this component continues to monitor them and will notify Offer Manager of their status by sending notification files to Inboxes\OfferMgr.box.

- **Inbox Manager** — At the site where the advertisement originated, and at the child site, this component copies to the CAP all advertisement, lookup, and installation files. These files are created by Offer Manager for SMS Legacy Clients.

- **SMS Policy Provider** — This component creates a policy and a policy assignment based on the package, program, advertisement, and target collection. The policy is made available to the assigned Advanced Clients on the MP.

 NOTE

Offer is a term that was carried over from SMS 1.2; it can be used synonymously with *advertisement*.

You can view the advertisement process flow in Chapter 1, in the section "Creating an Advertisement: Behind the Scenes."

Troubleshooting Advertisement Processes

Let's look at an advertisement troubleshooting scenario, designed to illustrate the use of logs and status messages. Again, you need to follow these general steps:

- Describe the symptoms.

- Gather information.

- Decide how to approach the troubleshooting process.

- Draw appropriate conclusions from your observations.

In our scenario, the following signs tip off the administrator that an advertisement problem has occurred:

- Advertisements never appear on Advanced Client machines.

- Installation status messages for an advertisement do not appear at the site server.

Symptoms

The problem in our scenario is that none of the targeted workstations ever receive the advertisement for Microsoft Office 2003.

Information Gathering

For this example, let's start gathering information by viewing the status messages for the advertisement in question, noting any changes that may have been made to any of the advertisement components. You would view the related components listed previously in this chapter in the "Advertisement Processes" section. For our example, suppose that the package and advertisement originated at Site S00, and the advertisement ID for Microsoft Office 2003 is S002000F. The target collection for the advertisement has a collection ID of S0000012. Also, let's say that the advertisement was scheduled to be installed at 5:30 p.m. on 1/17/06 and that there are no child sites configured to receive this distribution. This information will be used when viewing status messages and log files. Perform the following steps:

- **Review Status Messages.** For our scenario, there were no warning or error status messages for any of the components or site systems for Site S00, nor for advertisement ID S002000F.

- **View the Advertisement Properties.** Look for any settings that may have been improperly configured. Verify that the proper start time was entered. In our scensario, all the settings look correct.

- **Contact other SMS administrators.** Ask them about any changes that may have been applied to the advertisement or dependent component. In the case of the Microsoft Office 2003 advertisement, no changes were made to the package, advertisement, or any of the dependent components.

Approach

When troubleshooting SMS problems, the best approach is to follow the broken process from beginning to end, looking for abnormalities. Our approach to this problem is to follow the advertisement through the SMS system, using the process flow listed in Chapter 1, in the "Creating an Advertisement: Behind the Scenes" section. Table 14.3 shows a mapping of SMS components to the proper log file names.

Server Component	Log Files
SMS Provider	SMS\Logs\SMSprov.log
Offer Manager	SMS\Logs\Offermgr.log
SMS SQL Monitor	SMS\Logs\SMSdbmon.log.
Inbox Manager	SMS\Logs\Inboxmgr.log
SMS Policy Provider	SMS\Logs\Policypv.log

Table 14.3: SMS Advertisement Component Logs.

In our troubleshooting scenario, Offer Manager added an offer file into SMS\Inboxes\Offerinf. box on the SMS site server and added an offer to the policy that targets the resources in collection S0000012 for advertisement ID S002000F. Figure 14.14 shows the processing performed by Offer Manager .

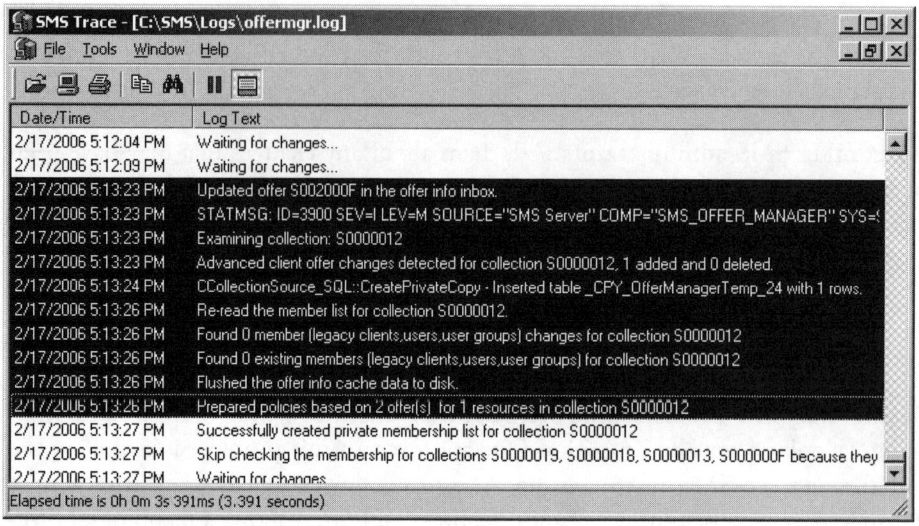

Figure 14.14: Viewing Offermgr.log.

Figure 14.15 shows the new offer file that was created in Offerinf.box.

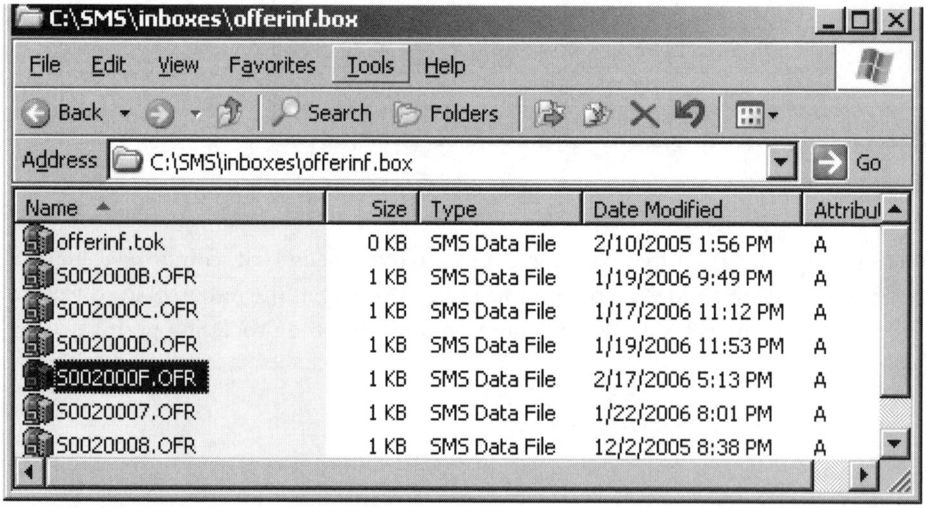

Figure 14.15: Viewing Offerinf.box with Microsoft Explorer.

Figure 14.16 shows the text in the new offer file, S002000F.ofr.

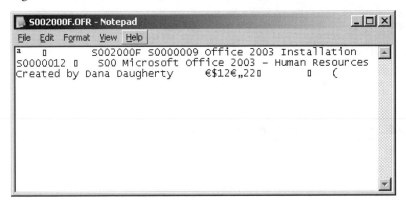

Figure 14.16: Text of the Offer File.

Even though this book deals with Advanced Clients which do not use offers from Offer Manager, it is still useful to review the offermg.log file, because it tells where problems began to occur in the overall process.

Next, we verify that SMS Policy Provider has created the new policy and policy assignments, by viewing the Policypv.log file (see Figure 14.17).

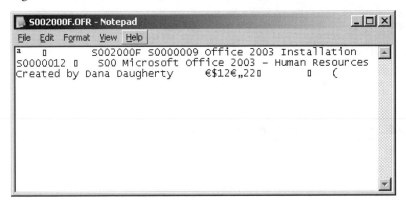

Figure 14.17: Viewing Policypv.log.

After verifying that the advertisement creation process completed successfully, we have only one more server component to investigate: the management point. Site status messages indicate that the MP Control Manager thread component has been stopped, as shown in Figure 14.18. In this scenario, SMS Advanced Clients were unable to access the MP in order to download its assigned policies.

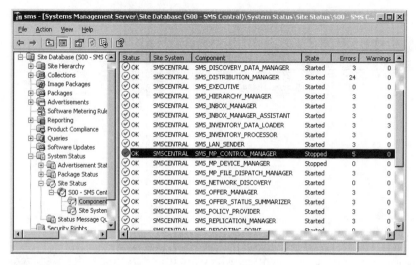

Figure 14.18: Viewing MP Control Manager Thread in a Stopped State.

Conclusion

The problem in our scenario was that the Advanced Clients were to be unable to access the new policy, because the MP was stopped. In the last step of the advertisement process, Policy Provider creates a policy and a policy assignment based on the package, program, advertisement, and target collection. The policy and its associated assignment are copied to the MP so that the targeted Advanced Clients can access it.

Summary

Because of the complexity of SMS, troubleshooting problems tend to be overwhelming. In this chapter, you learned that the SMS software distribution feature is actually several processes that are each comprised of certain components. You also learned how each of these components is designed to function. One way to determine if a component is working properly is to compare the way it is functioning to the way it is supposed to function. The actual functioning of a software distribution process can be determined by reading the log files and viewing status messages for the components that comprise that process. You also learned how to use some common logging tools to facilitate this. Another way to determine if a component is working properly is to monitor status messages, looking for any errors that may occur. A third way is to monitor the expected result of the software distribution process, which includes packages that are successfully delivered to DPs and advertised programs that are successfully installed on targeted clients.

Troubleshooting Software Distribution: Client Side

The SMS Advanced Client contains many sub-processes that work together to form the SMS Software Distribution Agent. These sub-processes are responsible for connecting to the management point (MP), downloading policies, processing advertisement requests, finding and accessing content, downloading content, scheduling and running the program and finally sending the results to the MP in the form of status messages. Because there are so many sub-processes involved with running an advertised program, it is easy to imagine how the process can break down. If you understand the process, it will be much easier to troubleshoot problems that may occur. This chapter guides you through the Advanced Client aspect of the software distribution process flow. You will learn how to use the available component log files for troubleshooting common scenarios from the real world. Finally, this chapter contains several troubleshooting tips to help you get started.

Software Distribution Client Processes and Components

Administrators are responsible for creating packages, programs, and advertisements from within the SMS Administrator Console. They must also enable the SMS Advertised Programs Client Agent, located in the SMS Administrator Console under the Site Hierarchy tree. Any additional configuration of the Advertised Programs Client Agent must also be performed from within the SMS Administrator Console. At the Advanced Client, the component that carries out software distribution tasks is called SMS Software Distribution Agent. It can be viewed in the **Start**⇨ **Programs**⇨ **Control Panel**⇨ **Systems Management** applet (see Figure 15.1). Many sub-processes work together on the Advanced

Client to obtain and run advertised programs created at a primary site server and transferred to distribution points. The SMS Advanced Client Software Distribution Agent has sub-processes and dependent processes that perform the following tasks:

- Processing program requests that are contained by policies

- Checking for content availability

- Executing programs

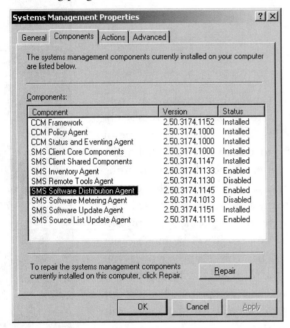

Figure 15.1: Viewing the Advanced Client Software Distribution Component.

There are additional SMS Advanced Client components that the Software Distribution Agent depends on for the following tasks within the software distribution process:

- Checking management points (MP) for policies that contain advertisements being offered to the system or the logged-on user

- Processing policies and forwarding advertisements to the SMS Software Distribution Component

- Scheduling jobs

- Transferring Data, including policies and advertised program content

- Sending advertised program status messages

For complete details about each of the Advanced Client processes that are required to obtain and run SMS advertised programs, see the "Client Processes" section in Chapter 1.

Troubleshooting Software Distribution Client Processes

This section shows an example of troubleshooting client components through the use of logs and status messages. You need to describe the symptoms, gather information, decide how to approach the troubleshooting process, and draw appropriate conclusions from your observations. SMS Advanced Client process problems that cause failed distributions will present themselves in the same way: clients never run the program. There are a variety of causes for the problem:

- The Software Distribution Client Agent could be corrupt or missing.

- There could be network issues on the client machine or between the client and SMS site systems.

- The client could be on a subnet that is excluded from accessing a protected distribution point. Protected distribution points provide access to Advanced Clients on specific subnets or Active Directory Sites.

- The SMS Software Distribution Agent dependency components could be experiencing problems.

- SMS site server components have failed.

Symptoms

A typical symptom might be that after targeting clients with the Microsoft Office 2003 program, the program never starts.

Information Gathering

Gather as much pertinent information as possible. For our example, suppose that the advertisement ID for Microsoft Office 2003 is S0020010. A workstation, named smscencl2, is having the problem and is available for us to use for troubleshooting. This information will be used when viewing status messages and log files. Here are some sources where information can be gathered about the problem:

- **Review Advertisement Status Messages.** For our example, let's assume that there were failure status messages sent from the workstations that attempted to run this advertised program.

- **Contact other SMS administrators.** In this example, they have not made any changes that should affect our distribution.

- **Turn on Debug or Verbose Logging on a client.** Debug logging provides additional logging information about broken processes specifically for troubleshooting purposes. As a last resort, this option will provide more detailed information in all the log files. Verbose logging provides additional details for each of the client processes that occur. These details are not provided by the default logging mode. Restart the SMS Agent Host service after making either of the following registry changes.

  To enable debug logging, create the following registry key:
  HKLM\SOFTWARE\Microsoft\CCM\Logging\debuglogging

  To enable verbose logging after installation, change the following value to
  0: **HKLM\Software\Microsoft\CCM\Logging\@Global\Loglevel**

  You might need to change the registry permissions on this key to change these values.

 CAUTION

When editing the registry, be careful to only make the specified changes, otherwise the system could become unusable.

Approach

The best approach to take when troubleshooting SMS client problems is to follow the broken process from beginning to end, looking for abnormalities. The best way to follow the client-side software distribution process is to start with the client component log files. Our approach to the problem in our example is to follow the client software distribution processes, described in the process flow listed in the "Client Processes" section in Chapter 1. Table 15.1 shows a mapping of SMS components to the proper log file names.

Client Component	Log Files Name
Content Access Services	CAS.log
SMS Agent Host Service	CCMExec.log
Content Transfer Manager	ContentTransferManager.log
Data Transfer Services	DataTransferServices.log
Execution Manager	execmgr.log
Location Services	LocationServices.log
Policy Agent	PolicyAgent.log
Policy Agent Provider	PolicyAgentProvider.log
Policy Evaluator	PolicyEvaluator.log
Status Agent	StatusAgent.log

Table 15.1: Component to Component Log Mappings.

Client logs are located in the %system32%\CCM\Logs folder (see Figure 15.2).

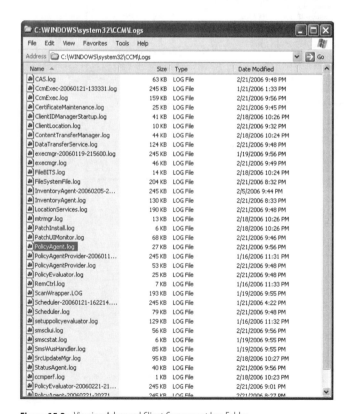

Figure 15.2: Viewing Advanced Client Component Log Folder.

Let's follow the client software distribution processes through our troubleshooting example:

1. View the Execution Manager log first (execmgr.log). Execution Manager is responsible for processing advertisement policies and initiating advertised programs (see Figure 15.3). When we began viewing logs, it was clear that at 10:46 pm. on 2/22/06, Execution Manager had no trouble accessing the MP to download the policy and process the advertisement request; otherwise, the request would not be present in execmgr.log. This can be verified by viewing policyagent.log (see Figure 15.4). We can safely say that all processes up to this point have been completed successfully.

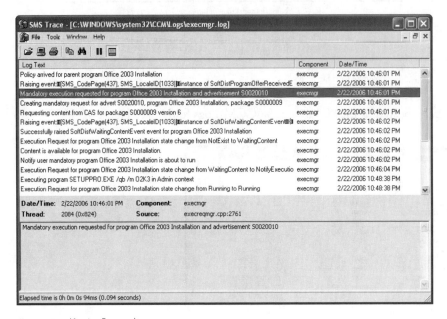

Figure 15.3: Viewing Execmgr.log.

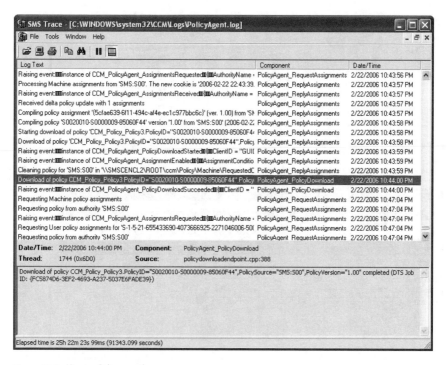

Figure 15.4: Viewing Policyagent.log

2. Let's follow the status of the remaining processes available in execmgr.log (see Figure 15.5). Here, we see Content Access Manager attempting to access the distribution point and eventually failing with error 0x00000003, which is translated to "The system cannot find the path specified." The translation is made by placing the error code into the **Error Code** text box and selecting the **Lookup** button within the **Tools⇨ Error Lookup** menu item. Execution Manager then attempts to try the Advanced Client Network Access Account and fails again. Eventually, a fatal error is returned and the Execution Manager stops attempting to run the program.

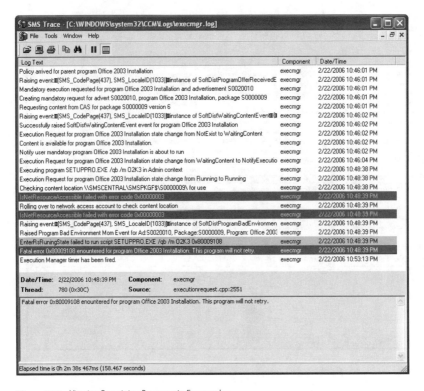

Figure 15.5: Viewing Remaining Processes in Execmgr.log.

3. View the Content Access Service log (CAS.log) to see any additional details that may be available (see Figure 15.6). We see that Content Access Service finds the source content, but simply cancels the job when it cannot get access.

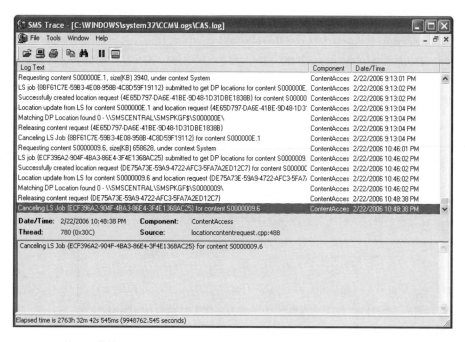

Figure 15.6: Viewing CAS.log.

4. Try connecting from the client to the package share (\\smscentral\smspkgf$) over the network. In our example, attempting to contact the package share from a run line results in the error displayed in Figure 15.7.

Figure 15.7: Viewing Run line Errors when Accessing the Package Share.

5. Log on locally to SMSCentral and view the Smspkgf$ folder using Windows Explorer. As shown in Figure 15.8, the sharing folder icon is missing, indicating the folder is not shared. If the folder isn't shared, there is no way for clients to run the program.

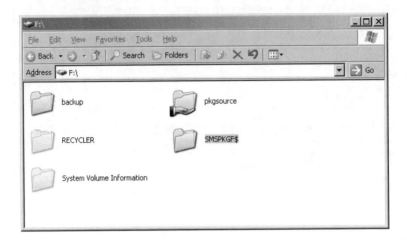

Figure 15.8: Viewing the Local Package Share from the Server.

Conclusion

In our scenario, the clients were accessing the MP with no problems. This allowed SMS Policy Agent to download the policy containing the Microsoft Office 2003 advertisement request from the MP. Execution Manager could then process the request and trigger Content Access Manager to look for the program content. The client was processing the advertisements properly, but was unable to find the source files. In this example, the process failed, as indicated by execmgr.log. We tried to access the package share from the workstation and found that it was inaccessible. Somehow the package source folder share had become disabled, causing SMS clients to be unable to access the source files required to run the advertised program. The problem was solved by sharing the package source folder.

Policy Retrieval Problems

Issues sometimes occur that prevent the Advanced Client from downloading the policy and extracting the execution request. We can determine this issue by viewing the execmgr.log file. If an execution request for a specific program never appears, then we can determine that the problem occurred during the policy download and evaluation phase. If we replay the approach listed in the troubleshooting scenario earlier in the chapter, but find that we still have a policy download and evaluation problem, our troubleshooting procedure might look like this:

1. View the Execution Manager log first (execmgr.log). Execution Manager is responsible for processing advertisement policies and initiating advertised programs (see Figure 15.9).

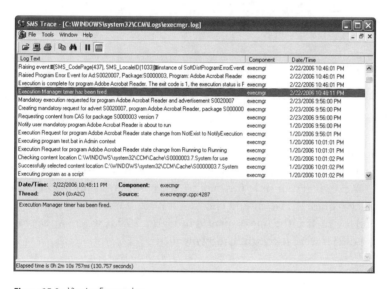

Figure 15.9: Viewing Execmgr.log.

We can see that Execution Manager never received the advertisement request for Microsoft Office 2003. We can safely say that the issue occurred prior to the program execution phase in the client-side software distribution process. This discovery indicates that we need to go backward in the process.

2. We need to verify that the policy containing the execution request was successfully downloaded and evaluated. This is done by viewing the policyagent.log file (see Figure 15.10).

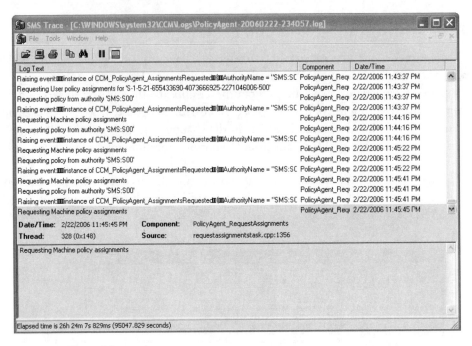

Figure 15.10: Viewing Policyagent.log.

3. Policyagent.log indicates that several attempts were made to retrieve a new policy from the MP, but there is no indication that policies were returned. The SMS Agent Host service (Ccmexec.exe) is responsible for making the connection prior to Policy Agent making the policy request, so we should check that next. We can now compare this log to a known good log such at the one displayed in Figure 15.11, where we see log entries indicating that policies were successfully downloaded.

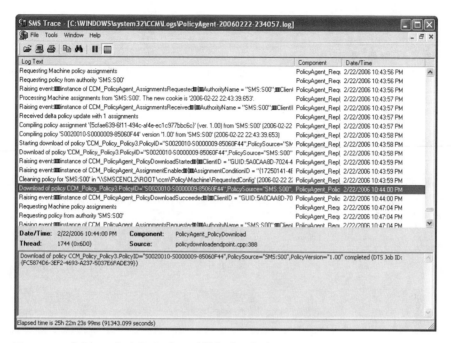

Figure 15.11: Policyagent.log Indicating Successful Policy Downloads.

4. View ccmexec.log to see if there is any additional information (see Figure 15.12). Ccmexec.log indicates that the SMS Agent Host service could not connect to the management point. This is the source of our problem. Through more troubleshooting, we would find out that the IIS service was stopped on the server that hosts the MP.

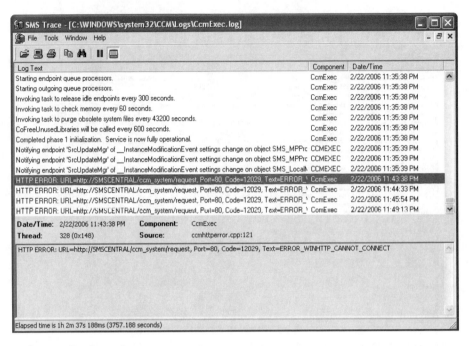

Figure 15.12: View Ccmexec.log.

Additional Troubleshooting Tips

Here are some useful tips, pointers and resources to help guide you during the troubleshooting process.

- Collect the component logs as soon as you think there may be a problem. This can help to avoid the log information being overwritten.

- If you get stuck on a problem, ask for advice from SMS newsgroups/forums. Though you may never have seen it before, someone else probably has. See http://myITforum.com.

- If no clues seem to turn up in the logs, re-run the process that is failing. This will provide new log information.

- Compare the component logs from a client that is displaying a problem with a client that is not having the problem.

- Before applying a solution to a production system, try it in a lab environment.

- Start a troubleshooting log. Document details regarding the symptoms and solutions. This will help save time if the problem reoccurs.

- If you can't seem to find errors in log files of components related to a process that is displaying problems, search the entire log folder. Use a Windows GREP tool, or the built-in Windows search utility, to search for a text string. Search for "Error," "Warning," or "Fail."

- Keep a *Change Control document*. This will document all changes that have been made to the entire SMS implementation. In the information gathering process, administrators can check this document for recent changes that may affect the problem they are troubleshooting.

Client Troubleshooting Tools

Microsoft released two client troubleshooting tools that may prove useful in some software distribution troubleshooting scenarios, especially where the approaches described previously in this chapter are not successful. The SMS 2003 Toolkit 2 contains Advanced Client Spy and Policy Spy—tools that can be useful for following the flow of policies and advertisement requests. The SMS 2003 Toolkit 2 can be downloaded at `http://www.microsoft.com/ smserver/downloads/2003/tools/toolkit.mspx`. Keep in mind that initially you should view execmgr.log on the client to determine if the issue is related to policy retrieval and evaluation, or something later in the process flow.

After installing SMS 2003 Toolkit 2, the two programs are located under the **Start**➪ **Programs**➪ **SMS 2003 Toolkit 2** program group.

Advanced Client Spy provides information about software distribution execution requests, software distribution history, software distribution cache, and software distribution pending executions. As seen in Figure 15.13, significant detail about the execution request is available with this tool. Advanced Client Spy can be used on a local system or can be used to connect to a remote system, if you have the proper security credentials.

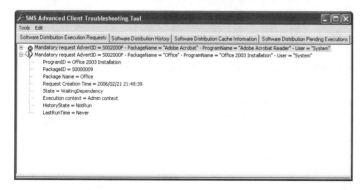

Figure 15.13: Advanced Client Spy.

Policy Spy provides Advanced Client Policy information and allows users to request or evaluate a policy. Local or remote systems can be accessed. The tool does not offer the ability to view execution requests (see Figure 15.14).

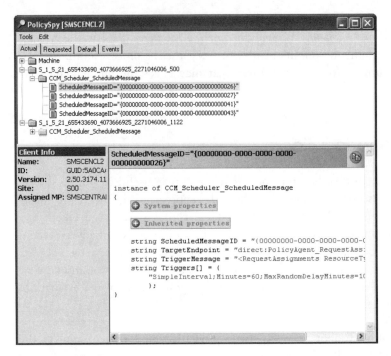

Figure 15.14: Policy Spy.

Summary

Because of the complexity of SMS, troubleshooting problems tend to be overwhelming. In this chapter, you learned that the SMS Advanced Client Software Distribution Agent component is actually several sub-processes that are each comprised of certain client components. You also learned how each of these components is designed to function.

One way to determine if a component is working properly is to compare the way it is functioning to the way it is supposed to function. The actual functioning of a software distribution process can be determined by reading the log files and viewing status messages for the components that comprise that process. The "Client Process" section in Chapter 1 documents the way the Advanced Client is supposed to function.

Another way to determine if client components are functioning properly is to monitor the result of the software distribution process, which should include advertised programs that are successfully installed on targeted clients.

Part V

Extras

Software Distribution Examples

The ability to centrally distribute software to workstations and servers is very valuable to mid-sized and large organizations. Understanding how to distribute common software installation technologies is the key to a successful software distribution approach. Installation programs can be categorized according to technology. This appendix focuses on customizing and distributing packages based on the most commonly used installation package technology, Windows Installer. Other packaging technologies are considered former industry standards, but administrators still need to know about them to deliver programs. SMS administrators commonly need to distribute scripts or simple programs to automate certain maintenance tasks. This appendix explains how to customize Windows Installer packages for distribution with SMS. Finally, there are examples of deploying installation programs that use various technologies such as Windows Installer, EXE programs, and scripts. When you are finished reading this chapter, you will understand how to distribute applications that use each of these installation technologies.

The discussion in this appendix is limited to Windows operating systems that are supported by the SMS Advanced Client, including Windows 2000, Windows XP, and Windows Server 2003 and later editions.

Windows Installer

Today there is only one installation standard: Windows Installer (MSI). Most packaging programs cater to Windows Installer and most commercial software vendors develop their products to install using Windows Installer technology. The very small percentage of vendors that are still releasing software that is not compatible with Windows Installer use a variety of old technologies created prior to any accepted standardized approaches. Typically, these vendors are planning to use Windows Installer for the next version of the program, or possibly the program is heading for end-of-life with no plan of a new version release. The Microsoft Internet Explorer 6.0 SP1 installation is an example of this situation. Many times, there are basic in-house scripts that are developed to perform some simple maintenance routines. These programs are typically written in Visual Basic Scripting Edition, Batch Scripting, or SMS Installer formats. The following sections will help you develop an understanding of how to deploy three software installation types. You can apply this knowledge to help you to deploy other products that use the same technologies.

Microsoft Office 2003

Like most other software packages on the market today, Microsoft Office 2003 utilizes Windows Installer technology as an installation method. The "Command Line Customization" and "Advanced Customization" sections in Chapter 8 provide information on preparing to deploy MSI packages. Be sure to keep the Windows Installer service up to date by applying updates as they become available, as detailed in Chapter 8. Beyond its being an MSI distribution, you must consider a few other issues when deploying Office 2003. Because of the many installation options available with this product, you must plan its distribution carefully. Many organizations treat a Microsoft Office upgrade like a formal project because it affects so many machines and users. Prior to the planning phase, be sure to visit www.microsoft.com/office/ork, to find updates and tools. If you are responsible for managing Office 2003 after it is installed, return to this Web site regularly. Also from this site, download the Microsoft Office 2003 Editions Resource Kit Toolbox. The following tools are included:

- **CMW FILE VIEWER** — Allows you to view files that were created with the Custom Maintenance Wizard.

- **CUSTOM INSTALLATION WIZARD (CIW)** — Lets you create Transform files for Office XP products.

- **CUSTOM MAINTENANCE WIZARD (CMW)** — Allows you to customize Office XP installations after the initial deployment. A .CMW file is created by the wizard and can be applied to the workstation from the command line.

- **CUSTOMIZABLE ALERTS** — Contains the Errormsg.xls workbook, which consists of lists of error messages for Office 2003 applications.

- **INTERNATIONAL INFORMATION** — Contains updated reference files with information about international versions of Office 2003.

- **MST FILE VIEWER** — Opens .MST files created by the Custom Installation Wizard. Administrators can view changes that will affect Office installations prior to deploying the Transform file.

- **OFFICE INFORMATION** — Contains a variety of support files, such as the product file list, comprehensive registry key list, and security certificates.

- **OPS FILE VIEWER** — Opens Office profile settings files.

- **PACKAGE DEFINITION FILES** — These are files that can be imported into SMS to streamline the package creation process. Check the following Web site to determine if an updated package definition file is available: `http://www.microsoft.com/Office/ORK/2003/tools/BoxA18.htm`.

  - Office11.SMS creates packages for all Microsoft Office 2003 product suites.

  - MUI11.SMS creates packages for Multilingual User Interface Packs.

- **PROFILE WIZARD** — Creates a default user profile. Options can be preset so that users don't need to customize their settings.

- **REMOVAL WIZARD** — Provides a more detailed level of control for the removal of previous Office installations than is offered by the Office XP installation or CIW.

Office 2003 Minimum System Requirements

Microsoft has supplied a list of minimum hardware and software requirements for installing Office 2003, as shown in Table A.1.

Component	Minimum
Processor	233MHz
Operating Systems	Windows 2000 SP3 or later
Memory	128 MB
Hard Drive Space	400 MB

Table A.1: Office 2003 Minimum System Requirements.

Getting Started with Office 2003 Professional

Let's look at how to deploy Office 2003 Professional edition. The main setup file is SETUPPRO. EXE. Like some other recently released software products, EXE programs can actually call Msiexec.exe from the local system. These setup programs are actually Windows Installer technologies, even though they do not use the .MSI extension. Because it is such a large application, Office 2003 comes with multiple MSI packages. Administrators can use the setup program and SETUPPRO.ini to customize Office 2003 installations.

Here are some guidelines for distributing this application:

1. **Determine the source management features provided by MSI, Office 2003 and SMS 2003 that will be utilized**. Some of these features include:

   - **INSTALL ON DEMAND** — Allows some programs or program features to be installed after they are first requested by the user. For example, program icons may be available on the computer. The first time the icons are clicked by the user, they install the program. When Install on Demand is utilized, the program contains pointers to the network location containing the program or component. This network location is known as a *resilient source*.

   - **SELF HEALING** — This is when a program feature or component determines that it has broken or corrupt files and then returns to its original installation source (or a *resilient source*) to re-copy the necessary files.

   - **RESILIENT SOURCES** — These are locations on the network, possibly multiple locations, designed to serve as sources where program installation files can be obtained for the purpose of Install on Demand or self healing. Administrative installation points are one example of resilient sources. During the installation process, Transform files can be used to provide the computer with a list of resilient sources.

   - **ADMINISTRATIVE INSTALLATION POINT** — This is a location on the network where the files necessary to perform the installation are decompressed from the installation CD. This can be on an SMS distribution point or any network share. The application will attempt to use files from the administrative installation point in the future if they are needed to run self healing or Install on Demand operations.

   - **WINDOWS INSTALLER SOURCE LOCATION MANAGER** — Product Source Update Management is a component of SMS 2003 that allows client computers to dynamically update their Windows Installer network locations, also referred to as source locations. This feature can even be used for MSI applications that you distribute through other methods. See Chapter 8 for more details about this topic.

   - **OFFICE 2003 LOCAL INSTALLATION POINT** — This is a special feature offered by Office 2003. During the installation, a hidden share is created that allows the source files for the installation to be cached locally. These files can remain indefinitely, providing local access for Windows Installer-related product features. Space requirements vary, depending on whether a compressed CD image (a copy of the source CD) or an uncompressed administrative installation point is used. A compressed copy requires 400

MB. Using an administrative installation point requires 632 MB. To take full advantage of local installation points, download Office 2003 Setup.exe (Enhanced Version) and the Local Installation Source Tool from `http://www.microsoft.com/office/orkarchive/2003dd1.htm`.

See Chapter 8 for more information about Windows Installer resilient resource management.

2. **Plan the deployment**. Because this is such a large package and will likely be deployed company-wide, pay close attention to detail. Consider issues such as:

- **BANDWIDTH** — If there are sites that are connected by very slow links, it may make sense to use the following approach:

  - Send an administrative installation to the site on CD.

  - Copy the files to a network location at the remote site.

  - Call the Microsoft Office 2003 MSI package from the local network share. Even in the best of situations regarding bandwidth, staggering the installation will be necessary. Target groups of systems based on NETBIOS names, IP addresses, departments, or other delimiters.

  - Use the Courier Sender feature to copy the SMS package to CD, transport it to the remote site, and then import it at the remote site.

  - Use the Package Loader tool (Preloadpkgonsite.exe) included with the SMS 2003 Toolkit. This tool allows you to manually copy packages to child site DPs.

- **DISK SPACE ON DISTRIBUTION POINTS** — As a good rule of thumb, there should be twice the available free space on selected stand-alone distribution points as the size of package source files that you plan to distribute. Similar to any file server, this precaution will allow manipulation of the source files.

- **TIME ZONES** — When starting mandatory distributions manually, be aware of the time in targeted offices in different time zones. Scheduled advertisements are based on the time on the client machine, regardless of the time zone where the target machine resides. For example, if a distribution originates on the east coast of the US, and it is scheduled to begin at 6 p.m., it will begin to run when the target machine registers 6 p.m. (18:00) at the office located in Mannheim, Germany.

- **LENGTH OF TIME FOR EACH INSTALLATION** — Larger installations, such as Office 2003, may need to be run after business hours. Depending on the installation scenario that you choose, the installation time could take over 30 minutes.

- **END-USER SECURITY RIGHTS ON THE LOCAL MACHINE** —The program must be configured to run with administrative rights. On the SMS **Program Properties** sheet, select the **Environment** tab and then select the **Run with run with administrative rights** option.

3. **Develop and test the MSI package**. There are so many possible installation scenarios that an entire chapter could be written on the topic. Fortunately, Microsoft provides some helpful guidance on the subject. Download the document entitled "Using Microsoft SMS 2003 to Distribute Microsoft Office 2003" from `http://www.microsoft.com/ smserver/techinfo/productdoc/default`.mspx. Create the installation point(s). There are several possible options here. If space allows, creating an Office 2003 Local Installation Point is an option. Another option is an administrative point or points on the network.

   Based on the product options that will be configured—and the user interface that will be required—determine the necessary combinations of command line options and Transform files that will be necessary. Because of the many options available for multiple job functions, there is a good chance that multiple transforms will be necessary for any given organization.

   If Transform files are necessary for product customization, use the Custom Installation Wizard to create them and place them with the source files.

4. **Call the setup program from the command line of a test machine**, with any options or transform files necessary to install the desired features and components. See Chapter 8 for available options. If a wrapper script will be used in the distribution, create it and begin using it on the test machine. Continue working with the options and wrapper script until the setup is perfected. The proper command line syntax is:

```
<Path to setup> SETUPPRO.EXE <options> <path toTransforms>=transform
⮑<path and name>.mst <basic UI options>
```

   Here is an example:

```
\\SMSCentral\pkgsource\O2K3\SETUPPRO.EXE
⮑Transforms="\\SMSCentral\ pkgsource\O2K3\mynew.mst /m OffXPIn
```

5. **Create the SMS package and advertisement objects and then target a collection.** The package objects include package, program, and distribution points.

6. **Create and configure the SMS package.** For the most efficient transfer of program files, use a copy of the Office 2003 CD as the source, because the files are compressed. Include any necessary supporting files, such as wrapper scripts or transforms.

7. **Create and configure the SMS program.** Use the command line that you developed during the development and testing phase, with the exception of the path to the setup file. All the required files should now be located in the distribution point share. The Microsoft Office 2003 command line can quickly become long and cluttered. It may make sense to place it in a DOS batch file or other wrapper file to simplify the SMS program command line.

 **NOTE**

Windows Installer-based programs should include the path with the Transform file when the transform is accessed from a network share or DP. The path isn't necessary if the advertisement is configured to download the source files from the distribution point.

---

8. **Create the target collection.** Place only local test machines in the target collection.

9. **Create the advertisement.** Perform this step carefully.

10. **Continue distributing to test systems that have the various operating systems used by your organization installed on them.** Try to pilot the distribution using a good cross-section of your user population.

11. **Follow your organization's standard distribution policy for testing and communicating with end-users.** Then distribute the package.

Office 2003 Package Definition Files

The Office 2003 Resource Kit Toolbox comes with a product package definition file, OFFICE11. SMS, and with a Multilanguage package definition file, MUI11.SMS. Package definition files are an alternative way to create an SMS package and programs. The .SMS files must be imported into SMS. To do this, perform the following steps:

1. Right-click on the **Packages** node. Select the **New⇨ Create Package from Definition** menu option. The **Create Package from Definition Wizard** will launch. Click the **Next** button.

2. The **Create Package from Definition Wizard** dialog box will appear (see Figure A.1).

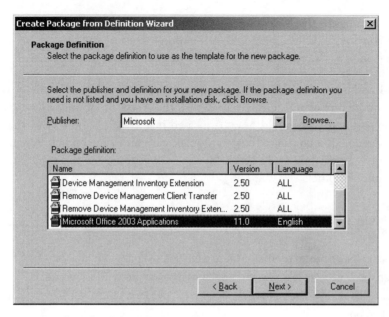

Figure A.1: The Package Definition Wizard.

Click the **Browse** button. Navigate to the location of **OFFICE11.SMS** and select it, and then click the **Open** button. Besides .SMS files, you can also import MSI or PDF packages with this wizard. Notice that you have imported the file into the SMS primary server. The **Create Package from Definition Wizard** dialog box will reappear. Scroll down and select **Microsoft Office 2003 Applications**. Click the **Next** button.

3. A screen will appear, requesting information about source files (see Figure A.2). Click the **Always obtain files from a source directory** radio button. Click the **Next** button.

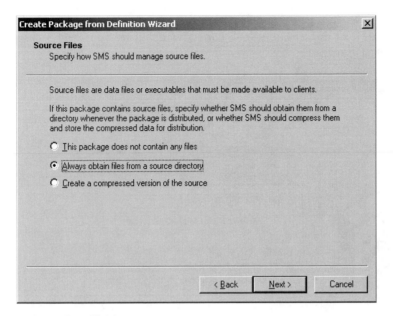

Figure A.2: Source File Information.

4. A screen will appear, requesting information about the source directory (see Figure A.3). Click the **Browse** button and navigate to the CD image (network copy) or the administrative installation point for whichever deployment method you have chosen. Click the **OK** button.

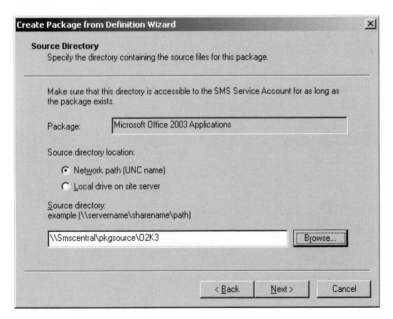

Figure A.3: Source Directory Information.

5. The screen shown in Figure A.4 will appear. Review your selections and then click the **Finish** button if all the selections look correct. You will see your new package appear under the **Packages** tree.

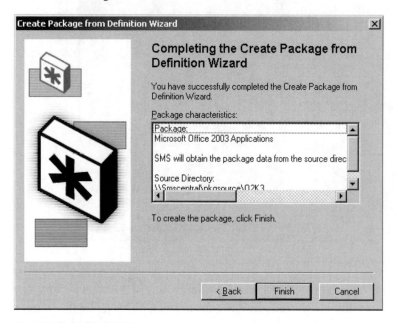

Figure A.4: Review Your Selections.

6. Open the **Programs** tree under your new package (see Figure A.5). Four SMS programs will be available.

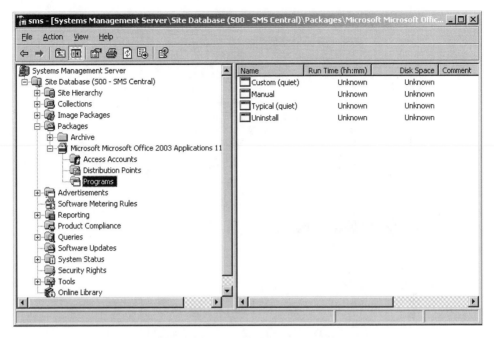

Figure A.5: Viewing the Microsoft Office 2003 Programs Created by Definition File.

7. Select a program that you want to use and view its properties to ensure the configuration suits your rollout plans. The Microsoft Office 2003 command line can quickly become long and cluttered. It may make sense to place it in a DOS batch file or other wrapper file. Then just enter the name of the wrapper file into the **Command line** text box to simplify the SMS program command line.

8. Configure the **Windows Installer** tab (see Figure A.6) to utilize the Windows Installer Source Location Manager. See Chapter 6 for more details about configuring SMS programs.

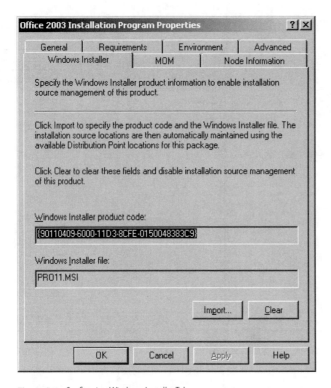

Figure A.6: Configuring Windows Installer Tab.

Uninstalling Office 2003

At some point, you may need to uninstall the program. For example, it could be that some of the testing was not performed properly and the installation conflicts with other applications. It is also possible that when the next version of Office is released, you may want to remove Office 2003 and perform a fresh install of the newer version. To perform a silent uninstall of an MSI-based application, use the following command line syntax:

```
Msiexec /x <packagecode> /quiet
```

In the syntax above, *packagecode* is the Globally Unique Identifier (GUID) given to a Windows Installer application. The GUID for Microsoft Office 2003 is 90110409-6000-11D3-8CFE-0150048383C9. The GUID will exist in the following registry key: **HKEY_LOCAL_MACHINE\Software\Microsoft\Windows\Uninstall**.

To perform a silent uninstall of Microsoft Office 2003, create and distribute an uninstall program with SMS, using this command line syntax:

```
Msiexec /x {90110409-6000-11D3-8CFE-0150048383C9} /quiet
```

Silent uninstalls cannot be cancelled.

To perform a *standard* uninstall of Microsoft Office XP, create and distribute a standard uninstall program with SMS, using this command line syntax:

```
Msiexec /x {90110409-6000-11D3-8CFE-0150048383C9}
```

Answer the questions asked by the Microsoft Office XP Setup wizard. Standard uninstalls can be cancelled.

Internet Explorer (IE)

In the past, Internet Explorer has proven to be a complicated program to distribute. Fortunately, IE 6.0 is more compatible with SMS distribution. Like Microsoft Office, there is an IE-based administration tool. The Internet Explorer Administration Kit (IEAK) can be downloaded from `http://www.microsoft.com/windows/ieak`. If possible, select IE 6.0 SP1 over older versions, because it lets you install with elevated privileges. The application can be installed as though a local administrator were logged on. This is a much needed improvement over earlier versions.

The following tools are included in IEAK 6.0 SP1:

- IEAK Help

- IEAK Profile Manager

- Internet Explorer Customization Wizard

Table A.2 shows the IEAK system requirements.

Component	Minimum	Recommended
Processor	486/66MHz	Pentium III
Operating Systems	Windows XP Windows 2000	Windows XP Windows 2000
Memory	32 MB	128 MB

Table A.2: IEAK Minimum and Recommended System Requirements.

IEAK Help

Before beginning the custom installation process, view the Custom Package Checklist within IEAK Help (see Figure A.7). This printable checklist will help you consider the various IE features and installation options. If you print it out and make selections from the lists and notations, it will be much easier when you begin creating the installation package.

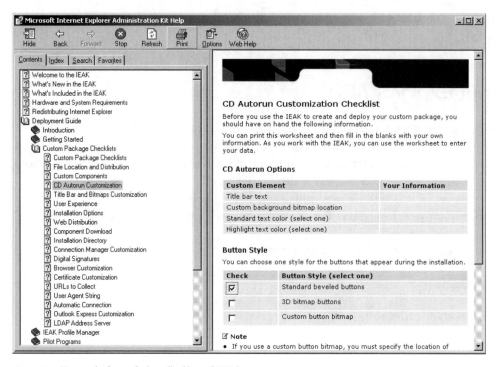

Figure A.7: Viewing the Custom Package Checklist in IEAK Help.

IEAK Profile Manager

Internet Explorer can be automatically detected and configured from a central location. Profile Manager provides the ability to maintain browser settings on user machines, and is used to configure the .INS and .CAB files located at a central point. Profile Manager can also be used to turn on auto-configuration.

Internet Explorer Custom Installation Wizard

Use Internet Explorer 6.0 Custom Installation Wizard to create a custom installation package. This involves progressing through five stages (see Figure A.8):

1. Gather Information

2. Specify setup parameters

3. Customize Setup

4. Customize the Browser

5. Customize Components

Completing all the steps in the Internet Explorer Custom Installation Wizard results in the creation of an installation file named IE6Setup.exe.

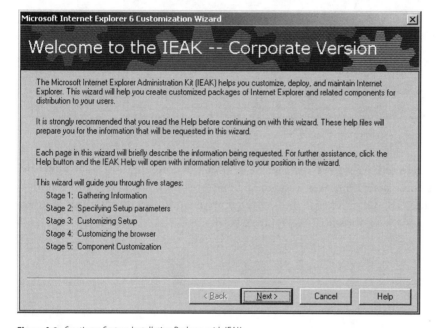

Figure A.8: Creating a Custom Installation Package with IEAK.

The IEAK Installation Process

Previously, low-rights users posed an issue for IE distributions. IEAK 6.0 provides a simple workaround for this issue: on the **User Experience** screen, select the **Enable logon after restart with user-level access** check box (see Figure A.9).

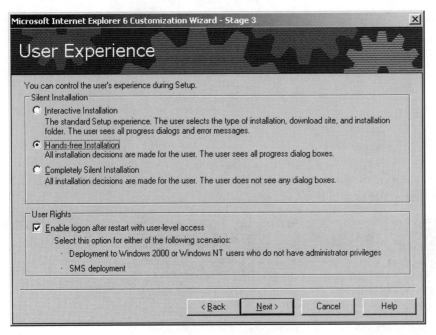

Figure A.9: Using the Workaround for Low-Rights Users Who Install IE 6.0.

When this option is selected, Windows Installer takes over the configuration stage after the reboot. It completes the installation, even though the end-user may not have administrative rights on the machine. IE 6.0 must still be delivered with administrative rights, though. Otherwise, the installation will not start (see Figure A.10).

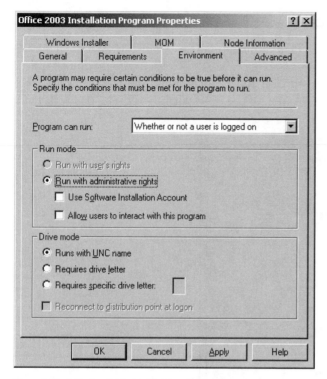

Figure A.10: Delivering IE 6.0 with Administrative Rights.

A list of installation switch options is detailed in Table A.3. For example, to silently install IE and suppress the reboot, use this syntax in the SMS Program Properties command line field:

```
IE6Setup.exe /Q:A /R:N
```

Switch	Action
/Q	Specifies quiet mode. This switch does not suppress prompts when Windows Update Setup is running.
/Q:U	Specifies user-quiet mode, which presents dialog boxes to the user.
/Q:A	Administrator-quiet mode. No dialog boxes appear to the user.
/C:<*path*>	Specifies the path and name of the Setup .INF or .EXE file.
/R:N	Never restarts the computer after installation.
/R:A	Always restarts the computer after installation.
/R:S	Restarts the computer after installation without prompting the user.
/T:<*path*>	Specifies the target folder for extracted files.

Table A.3: IEAK Install Syntax.

Distributing Internet Explorer

This section describes the specific steps required to distribute IE 6.0 with SMS.

1. **Create a custom version of IE6Setup.exe and begin to build the SMS package.** The source folder should be set to the location of the IE installation files (see Figure A.11).

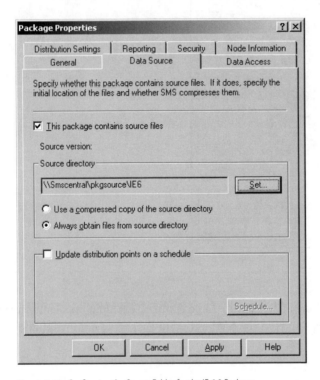

Figure A.11: Configuring the Source Folder for the IE 6.0 Package.

2. **Create and configure the program**. When distributing IE to Windows 2000/XP systems, low-rights users are a concern. Internet Explorer must be installed by a user with administrative rights on the local machine. To do this, select the **Run with administrative rights** option from the **Program Properties** property sheet **Environment** tab (refer back to Figure A.10).

If you are installing IE from a network location other than an SMS distribution point, with no user logged on the machine, or if the logged-on user doesn't have access to the network share, use the **Advanced Clients Network Installation Account**. This account is configured using the **Site Hierarchy**➪ **<site name>**➪ **Site Settings**➪ **Component Configuration**➪ **Software Distribution** node. The program can be configured to use either the **Only when no user is logged on** option or the **Whether or not a user is logged on** option. The account must have access to the network directory where the files are located. The **Use Software Installation Account** option is only applicable for the SMS 2003 Legacy Client, which is not a topic in this book.

3. **Select distribution points.** Consider the time of day and WAN links. The distribution can become quite large.

4. **Create the Collection.** The collection should only contain the resources that you want to target.

5. **Create the advertisement.** Proceed with caution; view all tabs before clicking the **Apply** or **OK** buttons.

Workstation Maintenance Distributions

Simply put, the SMS software distribution feature acts as a delivery vehicle for software installations. Virtually anything that can be executed in a program or script can be delivered by SMS. Tasks that administrators commonly perform include SMS client maintenance, upgrade workstation system components, and simple file or registry modifications. Typical scripting languages include VBScript, SMS Installer, and batch scripting. Files of .VBS, .EXE and .BAT are delivered.

Delivering a VBS Script that Creates an Installation Status MIF File

Formerly, one drawback of using VBS scripts to perform automated maintenance tasks was the fact that custom installation status MIF files would not be created. Installation status MIFs are custom files that are placed on the local system by the program to provide specific information about the success or failure of a program after it runs. The SMS 2003 SDK offers a workaround for this issue in the way of a DLL (Ismif.dll) that needs to be placed on the local machine and registered with the OS. After Ismif.dll is registered, VBS scripts can pass arguments to the DLL and a MIF will be created.

 BONUS

An example script that showcases the use Ismif.dll is available as a free download when you register this book at www.agilitypress.com. For details on downloading bonus materials, see the last page of this book.

When delivering program command files with extensions other than .EXE, the SMS program command line needs to be created differently. When configuring the **Command line** property, as described in the "Creating an SMS Program" section in Chapter 6, click the **Browse** button. The **Open** file dialog box appears. Select the **Files of type** drop-down box at the bottom of the dialog box. Select the **All Files** option (see Figure A.12).

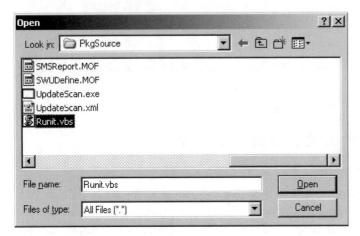

Figure A.12: Selecting VBS Program Files to Distribute.

From the window, select the proper command file from the window. From here, continue to configure the program properties.

 TIP

It is good practice to use the **Browse** button rather than typing the file name on the command line text box. This ensures that the source files path entered in the package properties is accurate, because it is this location that is used from the **Program Properties** sheet.

There are a few additional considerations when distributing VBS scripts. Sometimes VBS scripts are programmed to display error messages. To instruct the wscript engine to run the program and to suppress any error messages, prefix the command line with *wscript.exe //B*. If cscript.exe is used as the default script engine, your end-users will see a blank DOS command window appear for a few seconds. In some environments, automatic execution of VBS scripts is disabled as a security precaution. If this is the case, the OS won't know what to do with the .vbs extension.

Summary

In this appendix, you learned about distributing common software installation technologies with SMS 2003. You learned how to customize and distribute the most commonly used installation package technology, Windows Installer. You were able to see examples of deploying installation programs that use various technologies such as Windows Installer, EXE programs, and scripts. Detailed descriptions of installing Microsoft Office 2003, Internet Explorer, and workstation maintenance programs helped to provide real-life examples to reinforce the information provided in the rest of the book.

BONUS

The following bonus chapters are available as free downloads when you register your book at www.agilitypress.com (see the last page in this book for instructions):

► Clients Actions.zip — This utility extends the SMS Administrator Console to allow the execution of commands remotely on SMS Advanced Clients.

► MakeColl.zip — This script allows SMS administrators to automate the creation of collections with static membership rules.

► IsMifExample.zip — This script showcases the use of IsMif.dll, which provides installation status MIFs when delivering VBS scripts with SMS.

► SMS Process Flow.doc — Provides details about the processing of SMS software distribution components when an SMS package is created and distributed.

► Sample Project Plan.doc — An example of an SMS project plan.

MIF File Example

This is the installation status MIF file for Office 2003 Professional Edition.

```
START COMPONENT
NAME = "WORKSTATION"
  START GROUP
    NAME = "ComponentID"
    ID = 1
    CLASS = "DMTF|ComponentID|1.0"
    START ATTRIBUTE
      NAME = "Manufacturer"
      ID = 1
      ACCESS = READ-ONLY
      STORAGE = SPECIFIC
      TYPE = STRING(64)
      VALUE = "Microsoft Corporation"
    END ATTRIBUTE
    START ATTRIBUTE
      NAME = "Product"
      ID = 2
      ACCESS = READ-ONLY
      STORAGE = SPECIFIC
      TYPE = STRING(64)
      VALUE = "{6102E382-135B-4261-BA67-F6F09B6A6483}"
    END ATTRIBUTE
    START ATTRIBUTE
      NAME = "Version"
      ID = 3
      ACCESS = READ-ONLY
      STORAGE = SPECIFIC
      TYPE = STRING(64)
      VALUE = "Microsoft Office Professional Edition 2003"
    END ATTRIBUTE
    START ATTRIBUTE
```

```
      NAME = "Locale"
      ID = 4
      ACCESS = READ-ONLY
      STORAGE = SPECIFIC
      TYPE = STRING(16)
      VALUE = "Intel;1033"
    END ATTRIBUTE
    START ATTRIBUTE
      NAME = "Serial Number"
      ID = 5
      ACCESS = READ-ONLY
      STORAGE = SPECIFIC
      TYPE - STRING(64)
      VALUE = ""
    END ATTRIBUTE
    START ATTRIBUTE
      NAME = "Installation"
      ID = 6
      ACCESS = READ-ONLY
      STORAGE = SPECIFIC
      TYPE = STRING(64)
      VALUE = "DateTime"
    END ATTRIBUTE
  END GROUP
  START GROUP
    NAME = "InstallStatus"
    ID = 2
    CLASS = "MICROSOFT|JOBSTATUS|1.0"
    START ATTRIBUTE
      NAME = "Status"
      ID = 1
      ACCESS = READ-ONLY
      STORAGE = SPECIFIC
      TYPE = STRING(32)
      VALUE = "Failed"
    END ATTRIBUTE
    START ATTRIBUTE
      NAME = "Description"
      ID = 2
      ACCESS = READ-ONLY
      STORAGE = SPECIFIC
      TYPE = STRING(128)
      VALUE = "Insufficient disk space."
    END ATTRIBUTE
  END GROUP
END COMPONENT
```

Index

Notes

Notes

Notes

Notes

Notes

Notes

Notes

my**IT**forum.com®

Powered by you

myITforum.com offers **FREE** resources for IT professionals worldwide to interact with each other for peer to peer support including direct access to Microsoft product teams.

As the largest systems management community and web site, myITforum.com is the premiere online destination for those responsible for managing their corporation's Microsoft Windows systems, with a special emphasis on Microsoft Operations Manager and Systems Management Server. The centerpiece of myITforum.com is the member forums where IT professionals actively exchange technical tips, share their expertise, and download utilities that help them better administer their Windows environments.

myITforum.com is a significant part of the daily lives of admins worldwide with a newsletter that delivers the day's fresh articles, industry news, site news, links to valuable websites, and useful downloads. IT workers can pursue their daily tasks with the confidence that there is a caring and helpful community to rely on for quick answers to questions and timely information that is on topic.

- Forums
- Downloads
- Email Lists
- User Groups
- Industry News
- Web Blog Services
- Technical Articles

www.myitforum.com

IMPORTANT NOTICE
REGISTER YOUR BOOK

Bonus Materials

Your book refers to valuable material that complements your learning experience. In order to download these materials you will need to register your book at http://www.agilitypress.com.

This bonus material is available after registration (for a description of each item, see page 416):

▶ Bonus Utility: Clients Actions.zip

▶ Bonus Scripts: MakeColl.zip and IsMifExample.zip

▶ Process Flow.doc

▶ Sample Project Plan

Registering your book

To register your book, follow these 7 easy steps:

1. Point your browser to:

   http://www.agilitypress.com.

2. Create an account and login.

3. Click the **My Books** link.

4. Click the **Register New Book** button.

5. Enter the registration number found on the back of the book (see Figure A).

6. Confirm registration and view your new book on the virtual bookshelf.

7. Click the spine of the desired book to view the available downloads and resources for the selected book.

Figure A: Back of your book.